Inside Vogue

My Diary of Vogue's 100th Year

ALEXANDRA SHULMAN

PENGUIN BOOKS

PENGUIN BOOKS

UK | USA | Canada | Ireland | Australia
India | New Zealand | South Africa

Penguin Books is part of the Penguin Random House group of companies
whose addresses can be found at global.penguinrandomhouse.com.

First published by Fig Tree 2016
Published in Penguin Books 2017

001

The permissions that appear on page 325 constitute an extension of this copyright page

Typeset in 10.8/13.28pt Dante MT Std by Jouve (UK), Milton Keynes
Printed in Great Britain by Clays Ltd, St Ives plc

A CIP catalogue record for this book is available from the British Library

ISBN: 978-0-241-97837-5

www.greenpenguin.co.uk

Penguin Random House is committed to a
sustainable future for our business, our readers
and our planet. This book is made from Forest
Stewardship Council® certified paper.

For Sam and David

Author's Note

I kept a diary of *Vogue*'s Centenary year in part because I knew it would be worth remembering in detail, but also because writing a story has always helped me during times of tension and anxiety, both of which I anticipated heading my way. I wrote almost all of the entries first thing in the morning or when I got home from the office. Over these nine months, so much has changed both in my world at *Vogue* and in the world outside, but what I have written is my immediate impression of the day's events at the time – for better or worse.

There is a lot of detail about the workings of the magazine here. Were I writing a personal Dear Diary I might not have included this – the system of department-store adjacencies, the process of fashion shoots, the sometimes tedious business of office meetings – but I have put these details in to make the story more comprehensible and to give an insight into how a magazine like *Vogue* functions. Mainly, this is the story of one woman's life during an extraordinary year.

Alexandra Shulman
July 2016

2015

SEPTEMBER

1 September

Three nights ago, in a restaurant by the sea, just off a coastal road in Puglia, some children at the long family tables next to ours were playing with their pencil cases, lining up the coloured felt tips in order. Today, back in London, it is like the first day of term, and I wish I had a new box of coloured pens that I could bring in to work with me, and which were shiny and neat and full of promise. Though of what, I couldn't say.

The first of September was my father's birthday. If he were still alive he would be 102 today. Instead his ashes were shot into the sky eleven years ago in a rocket my brother, Jason, made from *Evening Standards*, the newspaper where my father worked for over forty years. He loved being a journalist, having a soapbox and a public voice, whether that be theatre criticism or politics or anything, really – just so long as he was heard. I don't feel that way about editing *Vogue*. It's *Vogue*'s voice, not mine. Although I do, of course, have a choice in what that voice says. After three weeks on holiday I feel disengaged, and not sure I have anything to say on any subject relevant to the magazine. It will take a few days to re-immerse.

This morning the streets are wet, and through the night I could hear the drip of water from the broken drainpipe outside our bedroom window. I put on a striped shirt from Zara that I bought before the holiday. It's refreshing to wear something new – ammunition for the day ahead. I never usually wear shirts, but a shirt feels as if it has a clarity of purpose, which will be helpful. Even so, it's strange: a costume rather than the holiday clothes of the past days. Before leaving for the office I go to Gail's bakery down the road and buy croissants and a Chelsea bun for my son, Sam, whose flight home from New York is scheduled to arrive at ten thirty this morning. He's been away for nine weeks. I'm so excited to see him. Tonight I'll roast a chicken for us. I won't relax until I get the text saying he's landed.

7 September

I've returned to work with five large projects to achieve: a Centenary issue, a big party to celebrate our 100 years, the 2016 Vogue Festival, the filming of a BBC2 documentary about the magazine, and the successful installation of an exhibition at the National Portrait Gallery. When I consider them all, I want to go back on holiday. This morning is the press launch for the *Vogue* 100 – A Century of Style exhibition. The young and relatively new director of the National Portrait Gallery, Nicholas Cullinan, arrives, a little upset that he has just nicked the fabric of his very smart, slim, tailored blue suit. Richard Macer and Charlotte Rodriguez have now started filming the documentary and Charlotte holds a huge boom above the conversations, which is not entirely relaxing. I know I have to get used to them since I agreed to the film but at this early stage their presence is extremely unnerving.

The fashion entrepreneur Leon Max is sponsoring the show, and he and his pale-skinned, long-haired Ukrainian wife, Yana, are there, fresh from cruising round Italy. Leon says he's suffering from vertigo after spending so long on the boat, and he's concerned because in November he has a huge shoot at Easton Neston, his estate in Northamptonshire. He leans back as if to aim his gun to demonstrate how it's making him feel sick with dizziness. I recommend some eye exercises I was once taught that are meant to train the brain, eye and ear to minimize dizziness, but I can see he isn't listening. Leon left Russia when he was seventeen and has made a fortune. Now his company is not only a fashion line called Max Studio but he manufactures for many enormous stores in the States. I once asked him how he made his money. 'I made some good investments early on,' was his laconic reply. He has a broad Slavic face, and you have to earn your smiles.

Just before we go into the auditorium Nicholas takes me aside and tells me that he has met with the Duchess of Cambridge's team, who have said they're considering agreeing to my request for a cover shoot for the Centenary issue. This is amazing news and I'm completely surprised. I had written to the duchess to put forward this idea but hadn't yet heard anything from her office and had thought it wasn't going to happen.

The question of what might be on the Centenary cover had been bothering me intermittently for at least a year. What could encapsulate a century? I didn't want to put a single model on (and not Kate Moss, as we so often have for these commemorative issues) and had been leaning towards the conceptual or typographic treatment we have also tried previously, such as a plain silver for the Millennium, which sold incredibly well. But the Duchess of Cambridge would unquestionably be the best bet. Of course her photo has been on the cover of many magazines, but she has never been shot for a magazine before, and with *Vogue*'s history of royal portraiture, she would be part of a continuum. I was trying to think of a twist that might appeal to her and remembered, literally as I wrote, that she is Patron of the National Portrait Gallery.

Nicholas says it sounds as if they're keen to work with a young photographer for whom this would be a big opportunity. As he says it, I know this could be difficult to cast. *Vogue* needs someone who will take a sure-fire hit image, and the younger photographers are simply not as experienced at – or as interested in – delivering cover gold as the tried-and-tested, like Mario Testino and Patrick Demarchelier. But, still, this is terrific. It would be such a coup for this special issue. I have his words buzzing in my head as we continue with the press conference.

We all troop into the Ondaatje auditorium for a sound check and sit on the stage, crammed round a small table that wobbles in a worrying way. 'A nice piece of Ikea,' Nicholas observes, and the mics are tested. When the audience arrive, I can see a disproportionate number of Condé Nast faces, even though they didn't need to come out this morning to learn about the *Vogue* exhibition, but I'm glad they're here – they're filling seats. I realize that nowadays far fewer people attend any launch like this in person, especially when they can get the basics by email. It's another depressing side of twenty-first-century journalism.

The exhibition has been four years in the making, and it's important that it's a success. This means attracting a lot of visitors and critical acclaim. It's been expensive to mount, as the artistic director, Patrick Kinmonth, the curator, Robin Muir, and I are keen that it's memorable. In my mind this means having more complex staging than simply pictures on the wall, and I'm excited by Patrick's designs, which take the visitor through the decades. Nicholas and I speak one after the other, and both thank Leon for his generosity.

Leon says he's delighted to sponsor the exhibition because he loves and collects portraiture. Then Robin, also the informal photographic historian of the magazine, gives an inspiring talk about the exhibition's content, and describes the treasure hunt that has taken place to compile it. He adds that, after thirty years spent in the *Vogue* archive, he still finds something new and interesting every time he delves into it.

We are asked the usual questions about lack of racial diversity in the show, which must be based on supposition: at this point no one in the audience could know whether or not that is the case. Even though it is. However, given that it is meant to be representative of

the magazine's 100 years, and that for more than eighty relatively
few black or Asian figures featured in British arts, fashion and what
you might term high society, it would be difficult to represent
many. I realize I've made the point a little weakly, and Robin says,
more pertinently, that in the sixties we were the first fashion magazine to feature a black model, Donyale Luna, on the cover. I resolve
to get some figures on racial diversity in the UK, so I have a better
sense of what I'm talking about.

After the launch some of us go across the road to the Orange Street
boardroom for Thermos coffee and an update on the show. We see
the cover of the catalogue wrapped around a dummy of the book
and it looks pretty splendid. A vermilion-haired Linda Evangelista
in a Versace showgirl gown from a Patrick Demarchelier shoot in
the eighties. We're all a bit de-mob happy that the launch is over

and seemed to go well, and I spend some of the meeting on my iPhone under the table trying to find out the address of a tailor I know who can mend Nicholas's suit.

8 September

Last night I co-hosted a dinner with Amanda Wakeley to celebrate her twenty-five years in business. I sat next to her partner, Hugh Morrison, who is one of those good-looking, sorter-outer men, a kind of Sebastian Coe type. On my other side I had Charles Dunstone, of Carphone Warehouse, who was easy to talk to – two children and 'one on the way'. He had lost a stone on the 5.2 Diet before his summer holiday. He said he thought men found it worked better for them because they were 'binary', and it was easier for them not to eat one day, then eat what they want the next, rather than cut out this and that in a system that involved complicated food groups. It may be true – although over the years I've known many men who have lost huge amounts of weight on a variety of diets. More often than not, though, once they're past fifty, I tend to think they looked better before the weight loss – which makes some appear anxious and diminished, and the skin of the face hangs in sad folds.

The dinner was at the private Harry's Bar in Mayfair, and the room looked very pretty with three big tables. But it went on for hours. Amanda had done all the organization and her team had shown me the menu last week. I saw there were four courses, and asked if we could lose the risotto Amanda had planned. They had agreed, but after an hour of antipasto 'sharing' plates, the risotto arrived anyway. In my opinion, nobody needs four courses. Charles agreed it wasn't necessary, but then we decided not to stress about it. 'Don't sweat the risotto' is to be my new motto. I'm trying.

9 September

Meet Stella McCartney for coffee at Clarke's restaurant in Notting Hill before I go to the office. We've been meaning to have a catch-up for months but time has slipped past and it must be more than a year since we just chatted. It's one of the things I should spend more time doing – just meeting up with designers to hear their plans and tell them ours. Stella is wearing a camel coat and jeans and looks great. I'm really impressed by how hard she works, especially as she has four children. She's not a distant mother, delegating childcare to staff, and she's very controlling of every aspect of her brand. She tells me how competitive getting your children into the top private schools has become because now you're competing with the many Chinese parents who want a British education for their children, whom they push relentlessly. She thinks she may need to bring in a tutor. I remember that she was sent to the local state school in the countryside. Education is so different now.

Before I leave, she asks if we would be interested in featuring the mastectomy bra she has designed after talking to Angelina Jolie about how hard it is to find anything nice to wear in that department.

10 September

We have no hot water at home and I can't get someone out to fix the boiler till tomorrow. This is making me bad-tempered, and even less receptive than I might be to having a camera following me around, now that Richard and Charlotte are well into the swing of the filming. We have completely run out of expensive low-fat pellets for our cat, Coco, so I have to dash to the vet and collect the order. Despite her diet we are always being told poor Coco is overweight. The vet is next to the local school, and as I park the car, the parents are dropping their kids off. I'm wearing a blue lace skirt, blue Christopher Kane tank top, and a pair of white leather Manolo Blahnik high heels. The adults on the school run are almost all in trainers, jeans and parkas so I look as if I'm from another planet as I run along the cobblestones into the vet's. I know that wearing trainers and jeans doesn't mean your life is easier, or less complicated, but at the moment that's how it feels to me.

Sam left at 7 a.m. for a final week's holiday with friends in Italy before university starts. We've spent scarcely any time at home together, and now he's off again. When he gets back I'll be in New York for the collections. At least he's old enough to look after himself. When he was a child, the prospect of four weeks of shows and travel was terrifying. I absolutely hated leaving him with his nanny, always crying in the car on the way to the airport.

14 September

The garden at home never looks lovelier than when I'm about to get on a plane. Yesterday morning the figs had finally ripened enough to eat, and the sun was shining on the new autumn colours that are peeping through all the dusty green.

As I left the house on my way to Heathrow, I felt incredibly sick, and as I waited for the flight I was feeling so bad that I nearly cancelled the trip. I've hated flying since I was nineteen, and the degree of my terror waxes and wanes. A few years ago I had a very successful course of hypnotherapy. I still don't know how it worked, but at some point, high above the Sea of Okhotsk on the way to Tokyo, I looked down on a sunrise without fear, and almost with pleasure. For a year or so I've been much better, and can sleep in the days leading up to a flight and no longer interpret every minor event as a signal that I shouldn't board a plane. But during the summer it got worse again, after a particularly turbulent flight to Ibiza. Last week I had a top-up session and now I can't work out whether the stomach upset is because I have to fly across the Atlantic or if something's actually the matter. I try to work on the former assumption, and hope that once I'm back on land, the affliction, whatever it is, will disappear. Anyway, cancelling wasn't an option since the BBC had already arrived in New York to film me at the shows. In the end, once we were in the air, I crashed out, slept for three hours and woke up with only half the journey left, and a much-improved stomach.

Once we've landed, I'm always excited to look out of the window at the tarmac. If you believe you're bound not to survive a flight, arriving intact is hugely pleasing. Diane von Fürstenberg was my first show and I went there straight from the airport. At the end, in true showman style, she appeared, fiery-maned and running down the catwalk with her still-incredible legs on display, shaking hands and locking eyes with the audience, reminding me of Bill Clinton. I had forgotten what a multicultural crowd the NY fashion scene is. Hundreds of American Asian kids chattering, and the number of black faces nearly equalling the white. All week there was a Greek chorus of 'Awesome' or 'Totally cool' from the crowds queuing to get in and out of shows.

New York collections are often a commercial version of what Europe provided for the previous season. It's what America does so well: the designers turn someone else's idea into something that makes money. Even on the first day I could see the huge Céline influence in the longer lengths, the silhouette, the heavy clumpy shoes that everyone loves. When Phoebe Philo arrived at Céline in 2008 she seemed to tap straight into a style vein that so many women relate to. Not exactly mannish but devoid of classic sexy clichés or ostentatious glamour. Instead it has a stealth chic and utility to it, even though she has moved on from the plain black trousers and white shirts she began with. Here it is her fringing and longer asymmetric length of last season that the designers have looked to rather than the A-line, short, fitted styles from Paris – Nicolas Ghesquière at Louis Vuitton, or Raf Simons at Dior. Unsurprisingly, the American designers hate the notion of copycatting, even more than their stereotype as successful 'sportswear designers'. However, commercially they've had the last word, and over the past forty years the American market has been the primary powerhouse of the industry – giant malls, massive department-store chains, numerous large cities.

It's changing now, though: China and other Far Eastern countries are becoming the leading players. Nowhere is it clearer that we are in the last days of the American Empire than in the fashion industry. Fabrics and designs are being tailored to the requirements of the Eastern market. The big brands are spending fortunes expanding there, and although many Middle Eastern women are hidden behind burqas, their wardrobes contain some of the most ravishing Western fashion.

I woke this morning at five thirty, which is A plus in jet-lag terms. It's lovely here in the Lowell Hotel, where they all say, 'Welcome back, Miss Shulman,' when I arrive. I've been staying here throughout almost my entire tenure at *Vogue*, although it's unfashionably uptown, and most of the shows and appointments are down around Soho and Tribeca. But the rooms are cosy, and I've been given an upgrade, which includes a pretty sitting room, with deep armchairs and a fireplace, on the fifteenth floor. It has one of those astounding Manhattan views over the Legoland blocks, with airconditioning units and water tanks on their pin-like tripods.

16 September

It's practically impossible to provide a logical rationale for the existence of fashion shows today. Originally, they enabled relevant press and buyers to see what a designer was producing. The former would report on what would eventually be available, and the buyers ordered clothes that reached their store five or six months later.

Now across the four main fashion cities – New York, London, Paris and Milan – there are, at a conservative estimate, more than three hundred shows (on the formal schedule, which doesn't take into account the hundreds of off-schedule shows and presentations), and that number again of showroom appointments. The audiences are huge, seated in feudal order with those each fashion house deems the most important in the front row, and stretching back sometimes two or three rows, often more. Viewing a show is no longer the preserve of the fortunate. Many can be watched via live streaming or, more often, Instagram or Snapchat, posted by the audience or the company. And much of what you see may never reach the stores since the big spend from the buyers has taken place in advance from more basic 'commercial' collections.

The show enables a designer to present their vision in its purest form. The looks are put together in the way their creator wants, worn by models they choose, accessorized by a set or music designed to enhance what we see, in a location that adds to the atmosphere. And more than that, this glorious circus is about the buzz and collective opinion-forming that happens when you've amassed a band of interested parties in one place. It's about the excitement that develops when these people see something they admire and want to acquire for their fashion shoot, their front cover, their store or even for themselves. The incalculable impetus that occurs around the shows is why my presence is vital. To be absent is to miss the game in which I'm a player, even though at times it seems I spend a lot of days sitting on a bench, waiting for a fifteen-minute show to begin, then sitting again, waiting for a traffic jam to ease.

Another wonderful day in New York. The temperature is in the eighties but it's not humid and the sky is sparkling. The traffic is another matter. It took me an hour and a half to get downtown this morning with my anxiety about missing the Michael Kors show slowly building. I had Richard Macer filming me in the car, which provided a diversion, but increased the worry. In the end I got out and walked the last four blocks, and ran in – the last person there – only to discover there had been some drama backstage and the show was delayed another half an hour. The whisper went round that one of the models had passed out. I sat next to Mario Testino, who was fanning himself with the programme and greeting all and sundry, including one of Michael's backers, Silas Chou, who looked at the small camera dangling from Mario's wrist and barked, 'Take one. Me and my wife.' He ran off down the front row to get her and the couple presented themselves for a snap, which Mario, the photographer for the Michael Kors campaign, obligingly took.

Pepe, my Chilean driver, has been brilliant at ignoring my traffic-induced stress and we've had some good chats about the upcoming presidential nominations, when I haven't had my nose down sending emails. 'Trump is unelectable,' he says of Donald T, who is currently riding high in the popular imagination, but, he adds, 'He's saying what no one else will about immigration. I'm an immigrant but first thing I did when I came here was go to school to learn English. To learn the rules of the country. Now you got illegals doing things illegal and then demanding things from the country.' Not that he had much time for Hillary either, when I brought up her name. Neither did Kevin Mancuso, who arrived to do my hair this morning. Kevin says Hillary acts 'too entitled'. The thought of Trump in charge of the States and Corbyn of the UK strikes me suddenly as an extraordinary, but now perfectly likely, possibility.

I don't normally have someone come to the hotel to give me a blow-dry. Often I don't even go to a hair salon, as blow-dries are one of my least favourite activities, although I know they are considered by many a luxury. It's so boring to sit there with someone tugging when I don't even like the effect of smooth hair. But even I realize that after a long flight, and with a camera crew in attendance, a blow-dry is a good idea. Kevin manages to make me look much more American, with glossy locks in tame waves rather than my trademark bedhead. In general, though, I have made the decision, which no doubt I will regret, not to be prepped for filming every day. The thought of having my hair and make-up done daily for me seems unbearable.

The film crew have had their first taste of a fashion week, and my team and I have had our first taste of walking around with a microphone pack hung on our waistbands. I seem to have been filmed for hours looking out of the car window at a traffic jam, which I don't imagine will make thrilling television. More interesting for the film crew was my meeting with a suntanned, and tiny, Victoria Beckham in her huge showroom, wearing a crushed-silk long skirt and top, and lots of shimmering eye make-up. They had been asked to get there an hour early to set up and get the lighting right, which struck us all as unnecessary, but Victoria appeared to be completely at ease with them, in a way she wouldn't have been a couple of years back. She talked through the collection very professionally, and was quick with her responses to any questions they asked. It had had very good reviews and was accomplished and wearable, if, like so many of the others, a bit overly Céline-referenced.

Just before we left, I discovered about six of her team crammed into a small space behind a heavy black curtain, hidden from the cameras, all laughing at their confinement. It wasn't clear to us why they couldn't be on show. Brand Beckham is extraordinary. The family are all brilliant at what they do, and each of them reflects back their success to increase the total power of the whole unit – even Harper, with her pigtails and tiny-tot style.

18 September

Land back at Heathrow to a barrage of emails, which I check while waiting at the carousel for my luggage: who should interview Karlie Kloss for the December cover story now that her agent has repeatedly cancelled her interview time and we no longer have our journalist in New York?; news that tonight we're expecting the wonderful combination of Secretary of State John Kerry and Donatella Versace at Winfield House for the London Fashion Week party I'm hosting with the ambassador and his wife, Matthew and Brooke Barzun; my agent Eugenie sending me the slightly disappointing sales figures for my novel *The Parrots*. Luckily, that's followed by a fan email from someone who's just read it.

Back home I can see that in the four days I've been away, autumn has claimed the garden. The yew hedge is speckled with red berries and the vines outside the kitchen are heavy with clusters of grapes that I have no time to pick and turn into a delicious jelly or jam.

Every year I feel guilty that they go to waste, as do the morello cherries in June, which end up as bird food, staining the paving slabs with black juice and littering them with the stones. It's such a different view from the window compared to yesterday morning's: lime trees and fading climbing roses, washing lines and slate-tiled roofs. I feel a moment of hankering for the monumental New York skyscape, and certainly the clarity of light, as here torrential rain and bleak grey is forecast for the day. I hope that the rain will have cleared by 6 p.m., as the garden at Winfield House is one of the delights of the place, along with the *joie de vivre* of Matthew and Brooke.

19 September

Last night was heavenly, and I went to bed a happy person. I arrived at the neo-Palladian Winfield House in Regent's Park fifteen minutes before kick-off, to be prevented from entering by the massive security detail outside the gates. It's always intense there but it was heightened because of John Kerry's stay. It was some time before my argument that I was *hosting* the party there got me anywhere. But eventually I was led past the kids' skateboard slope that the Barzuns had erected outside the front door and into the house.

The usual gathering of photographers, communications directors, assistants and caterers (and on this occasion DJs) greeted me. Often at these professional parties the room appears full before a single guest has arrived and I spend some time being photographed pointlessly alone before anyone else photo-worthy arrives. Sacha Forbes, who helps me organize all of the *Vogue* parties, came up and whispered that Donatella had now cancelled.

One of the first guests was Alexa Chung, who had just filmed a series on the future of fashion, which has been a success on the new *Vogue* YouTube channel. In the videos, she has to interview different people in the fashion business, from designers to academics and students. It's meant to be entertaining, and slightly educational, and it succeeds at both. She's light and clever. When I introduced her to Brooke, Alexa said she was pleased to see Jack Daniel's being served, and Brooke told her that the bourbon was her family's business.

This is the second time we have given this party jointly with the Barzuns and the second time J. Crew have sponsored it to help with the costs. Ambassadorial entertaining appears in the main to be paid for by somebody else, just like ours at *Vogue*. Brooke was loyally dressed in a J. Crew black jumpsuit, which looked terrific. She is a lithe, very attractive woman with fantastic social warmth and the ability to make everyone feel she's interested in them.

I very much liked their predecessors at the embassy, Marjorie and Louis Susman. The Susmans were of a different generation, in approach most especially Louis, a big man, who was prone to

remaining more of a silent elder statesman when confronted with some of Marjorie's social enthusiasms. In contrast, Matthew wanders around in an open-neck shirt with a drink in his hand, chatting to all and sundry. Different styles, although both couples have an interest in, and own, some terrific art.

Victoria Beckham arrived to the usual accompaniment of flashbulbs, but in terms of celeb power she was upstaged a few minutes later by John Kerry. I imagine he could have slipped in through a back door and headed to bed, or at least for a private drink upstairs, but he gamely confronted a heaving room of partying guests. Victoria was introduced to him almost immediately, and stayed talking to him for so long I thought he might never meet anyone else, but he hung out at the party for well over the half-hour I had been told he might be there. He's so tall that eye contact is almost impossible if you're my height, and although he bends down, he tends to stare into the room rather than look at the person he's talking to. In a noisy room, ear contact is not that easy either. He said the next day he was going, as a guest of Arsenal's American owners, to the Arsenal–Chelsea game, his first British football match. The social temperature of the room soared when news of his being there spread; he was the real stardust that transformed the party. I loved seeing him chatting to Boy George, and standing, propped against the doorway to the garden, as he watched Lion Babe, Vanessa Williams's lion-maned daughter, Jillian, perform a few tracks.

Later I found Victoria on the terrace with her shoes kicked off. I asked her what she had talked to Kerry about. 'He said he'd seen me at the UN,' she answered, referring to a speech she had delivered earlier in the year, 'and he said, "We gotta talk about Syria."' Her look showed she found that suggestion as surprising as I did. Certainly it demonstrates that even global politics can't escape the lure of the celebrity. That evening, news was breaking of America and Russia entering talks together on exactly that subject.

★

Now I have an hour and a half till Robert Spensley arrives. He has been employed to drive me around London Fashion Week. It's a beautiful day and I want to go for a quick run in the park opposite. As I do my usual circuit, I see the little kids (almost all boys) playing Saturday-morning football, surrounded by fathers. It seems so recent that Sam was one of them, standing there in his too-large QPR shirt. Then I was the new generation of mums in the park – now I'm the old guard on the block.

21 September

Louis Vuitton has come to town with its touring exhibition. It has been installed in a disused office block on the Strand and you weave through rooms of various LV trunks, and bags, and clothes, with technologically amazing video installations. The fact that Louis Vuitton wanted to be part of London Fashion Week is a mark of how highly it's regarded as the cool ticket.

The dinner after the opening was at Robin Birley's club, 5 Hertford Street. Invited for 9.30 p.m., I made the error (by now I should know better) of arriving at 9.35 to find the place almost empty. Dasha Abramovich arrived and politely asked me about my novel, which features a young Russian woman married to a very successful older Russian man. I couldn't quite ask her if she'd read it. Then she turned to my boss, Jonathan Newhouse, to see how he was finding things 'in our motherland'. He knows a certain amount about Russia, from launching *Vogue* there in 1998, then *Vogue* Ukraine in 2013. He takes the view that Putin is leading in the long-running cat-and-mouse game that is US/Russia politics, and reminds Dasha of the Khrushchev/Kennedy stand-off in 1961. She is incredibly attractive: a large-eyed, broad-faced woman with all the confidence of being married to one of the most famously wealthy men in the world.

After about forty minutes the place suddenly filled with beautiful models, and LV honchos. Lily Donaldson, towering in a cloud of white fur, Alexa in a short striped shirt dress – she was manning the decks for the night – and Nicolas Ghesquière, who as always was looking very friendly and relaxed despite being a tightly controlled designer. I was seated between the CEO, Michael Burke, and Jonathan at a long table, like the top table at a wedding. Young things were wedged onto the extending arms, paying a token visit to the dinner table with little interest in eating – Cara Delevingne with her girlfriend, St Vincent, and her sister Poppy (impossibly blonde with an equally blond husband). It was like musical chairs as various people arrived, uninvited, and were squashed in. But since everyone kept squeezing out for cigarette breaks there was normally enough space at any one time.

23 September

There was a huge fashion-press contingent on the 9.25 a.m. BA flight to Milan, all yawning from the dinner Victoria Beckham had given in her shop on the last night of London Fashion Week. I sat with Simon Fuller, her business partner and manager, who had moved to LA for his American wife, who is about to give birth to twins. He said he'd prefer to live in London but it doesn't really make much difference which city he's based in. He shuttles back and forth. I wish Victoria would show in London rather than New York. After all, she is meant to be a British designer and she's had a huge amount of support.

We're staying, for the first time, in the Palazzo Parigi Hotel in Milan. I used to love hotels but now I realize they're extraordinarily unrelaxing places. The transience of their occupancy infects the space so that I always feel I should be going somewhere, even on the rare occasion when I can settle down to room service and a book or a movie.

My room has a rooftop view of the city, and a balcony. Curiously it's very hard to get a beautiful view of Milan whether high up or on the ground. From the ground there is no vista – the buildings are right up against you – and there are no distant horizons. Even up here, the shapes are ugly, with a lot of modern intruders of no great style cropping up among the old streets. But there was a fantastic rainbow just now, following the torrential rain that poured down from the moment we landed.

Most people had arrived to see the Gucci show. Everyone made their way through a sopping wet industrial estate to a warehouse, via a slow crawl of cars through the city. There, a cream carpet printed with snakes was interspersed with screens of vintage-style wallpaper. Gucci is the first of the big Milan shows and the room was filled with stylists, photographers, editors and retailers, chatting as they waited, as if most of us hadn't seen each other yesterday.

The show had an entirely different feel from the past decades of high-gloss Gucci, which were held in a sleek dark room with dramatic lighting. The glam-geek aesthetic that Alessandro Michele introduced last year, when he was catapulted into the role of creative director only weeks before the show, had matured, and it was clearer to see what he was doing. There were so many bags, and belts, and pieces of jewellery, like glamorous old treasures rather than an 'It' bag conveyor-belt. The clothes were wildly expensive thrift-shop style, with fur trims and jewelled details in golds and emeralds and nerdy ochres and mustards.

24 September

Despite the rain and chill, last night's dinner, in honour of Alessandro, was held in a large tent in a garden. Robert Triefus, from Gucci, told me that when they had done the first walk-through in June his worry was that it would be too humid inside the tent, not that it would be sopping. Even yesterday morning they'd had no idea it would be so wet.

Two long tables and one long menu – four courses recited in detail by the chef, one of Italy's finest we were told – each course from a different part of the country. An ambitious plan to have such a foodie meal for the fashion industry. The area between Milan and Rome was represented by something I read as 'osso buco', but which materialized as a small pool of deep red jus with some crispy risotto rice floating in it.

I was introduced to a smiling man with dark-rimmed spectacles, whose name I didn't catch. It was some time until I realized he was Federico Marchetti, who heads up the newly merged Net-a-Porter and Yoox business. Everything I had read about him made me envisage him as a sterile businessman, but he appeared nothing of the sort. He is humorous and talkative, with a young English wife.

Since the merger he spends two days a week in London and was looking for a good hotel to stay in, west of the city. His offices are at the Westfield Centre in Shepherd's Bush. I was really interested to meet him, since Condé Nast have just entered the realm of e-commerce with the launch of Style.com next year. He said that if he had known what he knows now about the business, he wasn't sure he would have started.

Alexa was on my left at dinner since the person designated to sit between us didn't show, and on her other side François-Henri Pinault, our host, spent almost 100 per cent of the meal talking to American *Vogue*'s Anna Wintour, on his other side. Good for me, as I got Alexa. Across the way was Dakota Johnson, who, Alexa said, was going out with her best male friend, and giving him a tough time. Even so the two girls were texting each other throughout the meal.

We have Dakota lined up for the February cover so I was pleased to see how appealing she looked, with a natural, slightly tomboyish face, and shaggy bobbed hair. When you see people in the flesh they so often look completely different from when they're on-screen – she looked better. It's always difficult to judge who is right for a particular cover. Dakota's fame comes primarily from the film *Fifty Shades of Grey*. Her new film, *A Bigger Splash*, which will be out when she's on the cover of *Vogue*, is a much smaller deal.

On my other side was Hamish Bowles of US *Vogue*, in a terracotta floral Gucci suit. His job is like that of a not-so-secret agent, infiltrating the worlds of the fashionable and wealthy to bring back stories for the magazine, and he's Anna's walker at various fashion events. I'm not sure Hamish has ever asked me a question about myself, but if you stick to his subjects he's a master in charm. He told me he has more than four thousand pieces in his vintage clothing collection, spread all over storage units in the US. To manage and organize a collection of that size is really a career in itself, let alone travelling the world being a professionally charming weapon.

Woke up this morning to brilliant sunshine – hurrah – and I'm about to head off to a day of shows after sending David and Sam a reminder about putting out the correct rubbish bins for collection. Our local Brent Council has now instigated a system of unbelievable complexity with four bins and different collections. One is a tiny green thing into which food waste is meant to go. When I complained that there was no way we could fit our weekly food waste into this container I was told they would send round somebody to teach me how to use my food more efficiently. For example, the operator suggested, instead of throwing out old cheese, had I thought about making a quiche? Really?

I have a paper street map with me but I still find the one-way traffic system in Milan mystifying. Because I'm always in a car I have no sense of place in this city so this time I'm determined to walk more and get a feel of how it all connects. Having a car and a driver is meant to be empowering, but often it is the opposite and becomes infantilizing, making you unable to manage without.

26 September

My trip to Milan has been dominated by a heavy cold, which makes me feel slow, sluggish, and certainly an unappealing proposition to be close to, with all the sniffing and sneezing. There are others in the same boat and we pool remedies – Lemsip, ibuprofen, oscillococcinum. None makes the slightest difference. I put some high heels on and my driver Massimo's face lights up when we meet. He says, 'You look glamour today,' and he stands exaggeratedly upright to indicate my increased height. I take this as a compliment. Would others find it intrusively sexist? So often now I realize that the way men behaved when I was younger would be regarded as intolerable now, the general flirting, touching and teasing. We found it amusing, sometimes flattering and at worst tiresome. Nowadays the offenders would be facing an HR inquisition.

The city feels more lively than usual and I've been able to squeeze in a visit to the Fondazione Prada where Miuccia Prada and her husband, Patrizio Bertelli, have created a huge art compound for the city. Then Massimo drove me out to the suburbs to find the Hangar-Bicocca, an enormous Pirelli-funded arts space situated next to industrial units and railway lines. Sam had emailed earlier to tell me about five new Kiefer paintings that had been added to the already monumental installation *The Seven Heavenly Palaces* in the huge hangar. Although I don't begin to understand Kiefer's work, I'm always overwhelmed by admiration for it. Those pictures were staggering and, in the dark, echoing space alongside the original towers, extremely powerful. I always try to include some non-fashion-related activity in my trips. In New York, I got to see the new Whitney Museum and the Picasso sculptures at the Museum of Modern Art. You have to get out of the bubble, let your mind register something different and escape the cabin fever. Four weeks of travelling around with the same people can drive

everyone crazy, and occasionally it all gets a bit *Lord of the Flies*. Okay, an exaggeration, but it's certainly claustrophobic.

Milan is a strange city with wonderful things that are almost impossible to find. I have lunch with Carlo Capasa, who is now in charge of the Camera della Moda – they organize the fashion week here. An attractive man, and a successful businessman, as well as co-owner of the label Camera Nazionale, he is trying to make the city more appealing for foreign visitors during the shows.

This is good, but the most helpful thing would be to remove a day from the Milan schedule and give it to London, or at the very least allow us a day to travel there. However, he said it's impossible for him to convince the houses to change anything about the schedule. As it stands, an important brand shows every day, meaning that if we leave early, we'll offend one or other of them. Clearly it makes more sense to have two or three on each day but they won't agree to share days because they feel it will jeopardize the amount of press coverage and general attention each will get. Gucci wouldn't share with Prada, I suppose, or Dolce & Gabbana with Armani. And each wants hours of preparation with the models, too, which makes it hard to have two huge shows. The rivalry is very Italian – Montague versus Capulet.

Other cities don't seem to have this problem. The top designers will share days with each other – if slightly grudgingly. And nowadays press coverage is different. No longer is it all about a column in the next day's newspaper. Important reviews are online within the hour, and it's perfectly possible for everybody to have equal billing online. The old hierarchies of print, such as number of pages, size of headline and position of the story, are irrelevant.

The conversation about the length of the schedule, and which city has which days, has been going on since I arrived at *Vogue* in 1992 and, no doubt, well before then. There is never any shift, just more meetings.

28 September

It's strange to be back, and then to be going away again immediately. Golden autumn – and I woke up to a screen of gold leaves outside the bedroom window painted by the sun. Last night was a blood moon. We went into the garden to look at it when I got home – and there it was, around 10 p.m., hanging a brilliant red. In another life I would have set the alarm to see the eclipse around three in the morning but I needed the sleep. I arrived back to discover feathers all over the kitchen floor, presumably the debris from a bird-killing spree by Coco. It was unclear who had left them there for so long but evidence pointed to Sam, who has been alone in the house, ignoring them for some time. David cooked me scrambled eggs and I collapsed into bed, leaving the unpacking until the morning.

I have come back from the shows convinced that we need to work out how we can use print and digital better, to try to find a way through this new world where every day a new app or technological device seems to demand a new response. Given how quickly everything moves, I'm not sure we need to do *everything* just because it's there. Perhaps it would be worth waiting to see how things pan out for others, rather than jump on the driftwood because it's something to cling to.

The December issue is on the wall in the art room, and it looks good. I love the party section, but then I would as it was my idea. There are great little pieces that really capture the magic of a special party. The process of the magazine coming together is a kind of alchemy, which is hard to pin down. I make a plan of what I think it will contain but in the end it has its own life. Some stories don't work as planned, some need more space, and others don't look quite how I'd imagined and I change the mix. A great deal of what we publish is expensive to create so I'm limited in what I can ditch completely, especially fashion shoots. Often I'm surprised by the result, which is one of the things I most enjoy about editing. It's why I hate to plan too far in advance or not leave room for things to change. Although it would seem to make sense to have a collection of stories that can be slotted in at any time, the reality is that if they hang around too long unused my enthusiasm to publish them goes stale. I'm always complaining that we don't have any 'stock' or non-date-tied features, and somebody will invariably tell me it's because I go off them.

OCTOBER

3 October

The first couple of days in Paris were, as always, a hive of specula-tion. It was as if three weeks of shows had amassed into a bonfire of rumours, and by the last week it's ready to burn. My online team tell me that everyone is saying this will be Raf Simons's last show for Dior. I don't take this too seriously as so often everyone has it on good authority that one designer or another's collection is going to be their last, or that another is definitely about to be made a creative director of some big brand, or that a magazine's editor is shortly to be fired, or that a major label's clothes are all burned if they don't sell. The longer we all sit on the little benches, trying not to hunch, being yelled at to 'uncross our legs' by the photographer pack at the end of the catwalk, avoiding eye contact with certain people, the more we need to entertain ourselves in this way.

I left on Wednesday, on a very early Eurostar, as one of the advance guard to Paris. The team divides up for the shows so I will be there with only one, maybe two others at the beginning. The business lounge was already full when I arrived, even though I thought I'd got there with way too much time to spare. At five o'clock in the morn-ing every moment you can sleep is not to be wasted. When I got to the Gare du Nord, I rushed across to the Jardin des Tuileries for John Galliano's Margiela show, which had a good turnout. I thought it was the first time he had managed to weave together his own romantic and historical aesthetic with that of the original house.

The next day I met with Sidney Toledano, CEO of Dior. I wanted to see him as I hadn't for years, not since he'd installed Raf Simons to replace John. The meeting room was on the fourth floor of the avenue Montaigne building with Dior-grey walls and leather chairs and, as he demonstrated to me, a view from the narrow balcony over to Les Invalides. It was a perfect morning – blue sky and the grey-white of the elegant Parisian avenues. He was accompanied by Olivier Bialobos who has been at Dior for ever and never appears to age, with his cashmere scarf wrapped around his neck. He did not, it must be said, appear any more pleased to see me than he had at any other time I've met him.

Sidney had a copy of the magazine marked up with colour-coded transparent stickers for every page that featured Dior, every page that credited other houses and various other criteria. Someone had been through the issue with a yellow highlighter marking up every mention of the house. According to their calculations, he was concerned that Dior seemed to be less in favour than the previous year. Not having seen these calculations until now, I was unable to explain to him why that might be so, although you only need a big story on a particular designer one month to skew the picture, as with McQueen for the opening of the exhibition at the V&A. Anyway, luckily we were able to move on and I had an interesting hour talking with him about the business, and also about the number of fashion-industry leaders who, like him, had originally come from Casablanca, such as Joseph Ettedgui.

Yesterday I had a day back in the office. The November issue arrived on my desk and the cover of the new Bond girl, Léa Seydoux, looked more vibrant than I had thought it might. It is pretty, with a textured pink background, with Léa in a flesh-coloured Dolce & Gabbana dress with a large scarlet rose. However, she does seem very stern.

Thank heavens: it looks like we've almost got our Harrods sponsorship contract sorted out for the *Vogue* Festival, and I saw a virtual visual of how the marquee I want to erect will look next to the Albert Memorial. Today is Saturday, and I went for a run in

Kensington Gardens to have a look at the proposed place – it was an incentive to keep moving. I like the idea of being so close to the road through the park, so that people passing by will see the marquee and, I hope, some branding for *Vogue*.

4 October

Back in Paris, and a dinner hosted by Hermès and Apple to celebrate their collaboration on the Apple watch. I sat next to a man previously from Adobe who had been working on the technology of the watch for three years. He was called Kevin and said he only allows his small children half an hour a night on iPads or other devices. But he was passionate about the watch and what it could achieve. It's certainly made more beautiful by a lovely leather Hermès strap but I'm still not quite clear what I'll use the one they have kindly given me for. Apple, though, are so enthusiastic it seems churlish to bang on about that. Fashion and technology are involved in a mating game. Each wants what the other has and, increasingly, fashion businesses are hiring people with tech expertise, and vice versa.

8 October

London. Daylight is only just arriving outside and I'm waiting for the park to open so I can run. Four weeks of shows takes a huge toll on my shape – too many long, late meals, very little exercise, and the lure of very good bread on every table in Milan and Paris. I have gained seven pounds and I'm not happy about it.

There is a sense of peace now that I've completed the show marathon and I'm both daunted and excited by the next stage of work. So much to do.

Yesterday I think I secured my first festival speaker: Grace

Coddington. I want to pair her with Lucinda Chambers, our fashion director, who used to be her assistant back in the seventies and early eighties. I think two generations of *Vogue* fashion directors, who also used to work together, will be a huge sell. I nabbed Grace in the reception of the Shangri-La Hotel in Paris to invite her, and then we found ourselves in the same carriage of the Eurostar last night. Between the Shangri-La and the train she had already spoken to Lucinda about it and what pictures they might use, which I regard as positive. Next year she's launching a perfume with Dover Street Market, and her autobiography is set to be made into a film. She had thought that Saoirse Ronan would be her first choice to play the young her, but then wondered if, in fact, Ronan might already be too old. Grace has an extraordinary face – Elizabethan in its whiteness and austerity, surrounded by her trademark flame hair.

13 October

To Kensington Palace to meet the Duchess of Cambridge's team. I'm so keen not to be late that we arrive thirty minutes early and I sit in the car outside Wholefoods waiting. I have been briefed about ID documents to bring with me but, nonetheless, when I present my passport to John, who is sitting in a chilly hut by the police barrier, he smiles at me and says, 'I know what this is.' I look blankly at him and he shows me the passport, which has Sam's face, not mine, staring out of it. At least I'm not trying to board a plane, and he just says it happens all the time. I had grabbed the passport that morning in a rush to get out and not bothered to check.

Nicholas Cullinan and Pim Baxter, from the National Portrait Gallery, and I meet with Rebecca Deacon, the duchess's private secretary, and Jason Knauf, the royal couple's communications secretary, to discuss the possibility of a *Vogue* cover shoot. We all put our cards out – I say I need a cover that will help sell the magazine, that people will admire and won't be too dour, and they say they want something that makes sense in terms of her role at the gallery.

I have brought samples of work from about ten British photographers, ranging from high fashion to portraiture, that my creative director, Jaime Perlman, has put together under oath of silence. Some of the reference pictures are not ideal, such as the designer Jonathan Anderson wearing a straitjacket, by Tim Walker, and as I look at them through their eyes, I can see it's hard to imagine how this will translate to working with her. Their instincts are that the duchess will like the younger, less-established fashion photographers but they want to leave it with Nicholas Cullinan and me to make a smaller edit for a return visit.

19 October

I'm going crazy trying to get everything in order for our holiday to India. There's never a good time to take a holiday but this seems particularly bad in terms of the millions of decisions that have to be made.

We are still waiting for the contract to be signed by Harrods. They are worried we will be branding areas with other names that will contravene their role as sole sponsor. Even a flyer with a taxi company would be a problem. We're trying to reassure them this isn't going to happen but discussions seem to be stuck. Without that confirmation I'm concerned about paying for the early production expenses that are now overdue.

Fortunately my January cover shoot of Gigi Hadid has come in and there are four great options. I had been very involved in the clothes for this shoot so I'm delighted that they all seem to have worked well. We research some of our covers with prospective buyers and, in the case of this one, the picture that both the fashion editor and photographer preferred has rated higher than the ones I liked. So, with an editor's prerogative, I've asked for another round of research. The comments in favour of the one I like least are that she looks more sophisticated and *Vogue*, whereas I prefer the looser, more relaxed look with a bare navel, white jeans and a Bella Freud sweater. In many ways, of course, such a clear idea of brand *Vogue* is a great problem to have. In others, it makes it hard to move things on at all.

Today we had another meeting at the National Portrait Gallery about next year's exhibition. There is still a decision to be made about who will be working on the technical side of the video and other moving imagery that is now part of what *Vogue* creates. I said it seemed very late to be making this decision but Sarah Tinsley, the head of exhibitions, sharply replied, 'It isn't late in our terms. If it were December it would be late. We're where I would want us to be at the moment.'

There is to be an audio guide in which Patrick Kinmonth, Robin Muir and I will feature with a photographer, who is yet to be agreed on – an almost impossible decision to make. For some reason the two first choices for narrator are Tom Hiddleston and Anna Friel. I'm sure both would be good, but I wonder what the criteria were for those suggestions since the two actors seem quite different.

We discussed the signage, and what I know now is called 'interpretation', which, to a layman, means the information that helps you understand what you are looking at. There is a huge snobbery about interpretation in some galleries, where it is felt that it dumbs down an exhibition. I was pleased to hear that neither the team at the gallery nor Patrick seems to share that view. Another show that's on at the moment was discussed, and we all agreed that we didn't want to handle it in the same way, using an app: 'A step too far, too soon, too wrong,' Patrick snappily put it. Then there was the question of what images will be turned into postcards. There is a picture of Kate Moss by Mert and Marcus for which they can't get rights clearance so they were thinking of one from the famous Corinne Day shoot of 1993. Their suggestion shows her in a white vest, lying back with her arms above her head. I don't love it because she looks dead. Patrick thought it looks 'a bit roll-on'. I suggested they use the famous picture where she's framed by a string of fairy lights. Hopefully, they can make this happen. If not, we all agreed that there's one of her wrapped in a duvet that is stronger than the first choice.

23 October

Jodhpur – under the Mehrangarh Fort. Leaving London was hell, in the way pre-holiday departures always are. To make things more complicated, I tried to get a room at home repainted in the colour of my office – a shade of pink of which I'm very proud – but it went horribly wrong and turned out Germolene. I now have no idea what it will look like when we get back. Already I want everything to be the colours I can see here: bright, vibrant and strong. My homes have always suffered from endless choices made on the run. I can't imagine what a life would be like when you could have the time to mull things over. Maybe that would make decisions even harder.

Audrey Tom, my long-suffering yoga teacher, has suggested I try to practise a bit more resignation and acceptance, so I decide to try here in India. I'm not sure I can alter my character in two weeks, or whether those characteristics – resignation and acceptance – are compatible with editing *Vogue*. But having resigned myself to a long flight, I was surprised that it was fine, and we arrived at midnight in Mumbai.

The next morning we flew here and arrived at the Raas Hotel, which is pretty close to heaven. A huge, comfortable room with a view towards the incredible fort that looks as if it has been carved from the hillside where it towers over the city. Yesterday we walked around the market trying not to buy things, then watched a giant papier-mâché Ravana, the evil god, being prepared for incineration. Young men painted and adorned him and little boys did a kind of sword dance around him. After an hour or so he seemed no nearer his doom so we wandered back to the hotel for dinner.

26 October

Birds circle above the fort. In the morning they appear large – pale with a zigzagging pattern on their wings – but now, at dusk, they're smaller. I had meant to bring binoculars with me but forgot, which I regret. Last night we went to the opening of the Rajasthan International Folk Festival in the fort. We were shown to a pair of striped circular chairs in the front of the audience next to David's friend the Maharajah of Jodhpur – from here called Bapji – who was positioned in the front row. Bapji was David's contemporary at Oxford and has large eyes that at first appear mournful, but then you realize it's just their shape, and what lies behind them is unclear.

Today I don't really feel as if I'm here. I can see the people and hear the constant beeping of horns, and the call to prayer that comes from the mosque next to the hotel, but it doesn't feel real. We went to the temples of Osian this morning, driving in a comfortable, white air-conditioned car. At the large temple there was a long, long queue of people, which never got shorter, waiting to go in and give offerings. Now the lights on the terrace, where the restaurant is, are on, and the fort is about to be illuminated. I sit here on our own private terrace looking across at it. I haven't worried about the office for a second. I'm so lucky to have such a brilliant team, which allows me this total escape. Or am I being hubristic?

NOVEMBER

1 November

It's hard to believe it's November. In Mumbai it's in the high thirties and felt very humid when we were sprawled by the glamorous pool at the Taj Hotel for our last morning, or in the wicker chairs on the terrace for our last lunch. At breakfast I'd read the *Observer* profile of Germaine Greer, who had been banned from speaking at Cardiff University because of her views on transgender. What makes a woman a woman? Overall I agree with her, and was about to ask

David how many transgender people he thought there were in the UK when we both simultaneously whispered that the woman sitting across from us, marking up a book, looked a bit like Germaine. She was alone and immersed in her reading, in a loose white top and black leggings. We agreed in the end that she wasn't Germaine – in fact, she didn't really look like her at all. There's something about travelling, and especially big hotels, that makes you inclined to think you recognize people – it's possibly a way to make unusual territory more familiar. But the moment reminded me of the time I had met her when I was twenty-six, and my boyfriend at that time was one of her young courtiers. He had taken me to dinner in the flat of her friend the writer Gita Mehta, and I can only remember the torture of having to play Trivial Pursuit with them – two renowned brilliant, opinionated older women.

After lunch we went to the Mumbai Literature Festival to hear a discussion on the relations between China and India. Now I organize the *Vogue* Festival, I'm interested in the mechanics of festivals – how they're put together and paid for. As the discussion finished and we rose to leave, there was an announcement that the final address would be given at 8.30 p.m. by the guest of honour, none other than Germaine Greer. So the woman who kind of looked like GG, but not really, *was* her. I wished I'd approached her at lunch, but since she was obviously prepping for tonight she probably wouldn't have welcomed the intrusion.

I'm starting mentally to re-enter work. I've been blessed with hardly any emails from the team, bar one from my publishing director, Stephen Quinn, telling me that our November sales have been good. I'm so lucky to work with a colleague who would only email me on holiday with pleasant news. Someone else, though, emailed to ask which politicians and royal family members would be attending our Centenary gala. As if I knew! I decided to put that to the back of my mind, it being the kind of question that stresses me.

I've returned to an England that is now covered with rust-coloured and golden leaves. The clocks have changed, and it's dark in the afternoon. One of the things that surprised me about India was how early the light was lost – by 5.30 p.m. in Udaipur it was sunset, and only fractionally later in Mumbai. I associate heat and holidays with long, warm dusk.

Re-entry to work was difficult because of the many meetings – every day, one after the other, like a marching band. By Friday of the first week back, I was beginning to feel I'd achieved something, but those first couple of days were terrifying: just a lot of questions and a jet-lagged brain that was finding it hard to come up with the answers. The new-season fashion shoots are now half commissioned. All the editors have submitted the ideas they want to shoot and Jaime, my creative director, and I have been through them trying to make a balance of photography and fashion information. As usual, it has been difficult marrying the photographers to the ideas and the issues, and at the moment we don't have one of the most influential trends of this season – the sort of nerdy chic Gucci-trunk-in-the-attic, being shot for the International Collections issue in March. Now so much of the relevance of the print magazine is that the pictures be wonderful and interesting, rather than necessarily conveying big trends – perhaps it matters less than it used to.

David is having a horrible time. One of his closest friends was diagnosed with advanced cancer yesterday, almost out of the blue, and another is very ill. It makes my worries about work seem so unimportant and confusing. It's not possible to operate on a daily basis by appreciating every moment of life, or by letting everything drift past you, because that way I would never have the impetus to achieve anything. But it does show yesterday's failure to make a list of subjects for Tim Walker to photograph for the Centenary issue in a different light. How much does it matter? It depends how you cut the cake.

We seem to be over-budget for 2015, despite my trying to claw back money in the December and January issues. When it comes to fashion shoots, money is like water in a bucket with a hole: it trickles away. If it doesn't go on the studio set, it's the location scout or the air fares, or the hotels, or the number of assistants. The current problem is how to send my fashion editor, Kate Phelan, and Alasdair McLellan to the States to shoot their prairie-style story. I'm going to suggest they try Spain, or somewhere nearer home – they may not have the Wyeth clapboard there but they would have the light at a fraction of the cost.

The BBC team are in the office most days. They seem to be a little frustrated in their attempts to find some narrative trails, which include dealing with problems. I tell them there are many problems spinning around in the ether, but they just aren't that interesting or filmic. In the meeting where we looked at all the visuals for the February issue, they thought they'd found one when our managing editor, Frances Bentley, told me that there wasn't enough budget to shoot a cover for the Westfield-sponsored supplement in March.

'You sounded annoyed about that. Were you?' asked Richard hopefully, from behind his camera.

'Yes, it was annoying.'

'Why?'

'Because it's annoying not to have enough money to do what we need to do.'

'And why don't you?'

I explained that it was to do with the dull logistics of moving from a catwalk, picture-based supplement to a supplement where extra expenses are incurred with the need to photograph the merchandise. I sensed his disappointment and boredom.

They're planning to go to New York soon to film Patrick Demarchelier and Lucinda shooting a fashion story. At least there will be a real-life model there, something that seems a bit *Voguey* rather than endless meetings around a table talking about expenses, which appear to be taking up all my time now. I had promised myself and the others that we were not responsible for providing entertaining fodder for the documentary. Yet, oddly, I *do* feel responsible when I know they aren't getting what they want. The journalist in me sympathizes with their need for a story and Richard's need to probe. But the others just think his questions are simple and weird.

10 November

At dinner last night David asked whether I knew that he liked endives.

'Endives?'

'Yes, endives. You had them in the salad the other night. Are there any in this one?' He poked around fruitlessly at the endive-free plate. It reminded me of the newly married butler, Carson, finding fault with his poor wife's cooking at their marital dining table in *Downton Abbey*. Binge-watching television series is my new switch-off – I watched almost all of the last *Downton* series on the return flight from India.

Breakfast yesterday with Nicholas Coleridge, who runs the UK company, at George. We both ordered mashed avocado with chilli flakes and lime, and poached eggs – no toast. What have we come to? Are we simply fashion-lifestyle victims? Nicholas had a scribbled list of issues to talk to me about, which included the idea of an African *Vogue* supplement, and who I was planning to invite to the Centenary dinner. George Osborne? Ed Vaizey? I answered that I was planning to ask Jeremy Corbyn, and I'd see if Emily Sheffield, my deputy editor, could exert some influence on her brother-in-law David Cameron. There's only room for three hundred guests and, given the number of big beasts in fashion, it's going to be tricky to get the right balance for the guest list.

As the new chairman of the V&A, Nick had spent his first week firefighting a news story about the museum's rejection of Baroness Thatcher's clothes, which they were offered many years ago. He has a great sense of humour, and instead of looking stressed, he regaled me with tales of the chain of curators, punctuated with lots of laughter. He says the structure is pretty well identical to that of a magazine. One day he'll publish a brilliant memoir. His combination of a great memory, marvellous mimicry, and no real compunction to be entirely factually accurate will be invaluable when he does.

11 November

Armistice Day. Last night David and I were invited to the launch of Tania Compton's book *Great English Gardens*. In the new issue of the magazine we have a story on Claudia and Jonathan Rothermere's garden, created by Claudia at their Wiltshire house, Ferne Park. Jonathan inherited Associated Newspapers, which publishes the *Daily Mail*, from his father and the pair famously avoid publicity. However, Claudia is a trustee of the Garden Museum, one of those little-known London treasures, and the book is in support of the museum, of which Tania Compton and my sister Nicky are also trustees, and she has agreed to an interview. So the wheels of connection turned and Nicky interviewed Claudia, who is very pretty and steely blonde, for us. She was very cautious about what could and could not be written. Nobody is less keen on freedom of information about their own doings than proprietors and editors of media groups.

The party was held in the big glass atrium at the headquarters of Associated Newspapers, on what looked like the directors' floor, with the mandatory smattering of wooden furniture and paintings outside the lift marking it out from the journalists' floors. Claudia was recruiting speakers like Simon Sebag Montefiore for the Chalke Valley History Festival she helps organize.

'And this time you must stay with us at Ferne,' she offered Sebag.

He replied that he wasn't very good at staying with people as he got restless. I said I thought people divided into natural guests and hosts.

'Well, don't you agree that for Jews it's all about the bathrooms?' he suggested. 'You're sort of Jewish?'

And, yes, I sort of am. And it's also true that there's little I enjoy more than a really comfortable bathroom.

'What do you want in the bathroom?' Claudia asked him.

Sebag answered, 'A bidet.'

Jasper Conran, whose garden also features in the book, was huddled with the *Mail* columnist Sarah Vine, looking at pictures on their phones of her husband, Michael Gove, in ceremonial garb at what I imagined to be some parliamentary occasion. He introduced us and I said of course I knew Sarah because she was always writing unpleasant pieces about *Vogue* in the *Daily Mail*.

'But I was nice about *you* in the last one,' Sarah replied. It's true, she was, but that observation aside, the thrust of the article was 2,000 words of vitriol about the clothes in our big September issue. I had been on holiday at the time and had found a text on my phone asking if I'd like to write a reply to her article for *The Times*. Then I discovered a flood of emails from the office on the subject, which meant trying to find the piece to read. It had briefly pierced my holiday bubble. She said she, too, had been away when the *Mail* had called her and said 'the editor' wanted her to write a piece on how dreadful the fashion in *Vogue* was.

'I'm amazed that Paul Dacre looks at *Vogue* and has any opinion on the fashion,' I said, wondering whether he'd been looking at it over breakfast or in the bath like many of our readers.

'Well, that's what they said, and since I hadn't seen it I had to go into Frome and buy a copy before I could write the piece,' she answered, trying to remove an element of personal responsibility for the diatribe and also making it clear she didn't buy the magazine for herself. At least it boosted our West Country circulation by one.

My main priority right now is finalizing our March issue. My desk is covered with A3 sheets of paper showing photocopies of the exact catwalk looks all the fashion editors want to shoot. Once again it amazes me that they all pick exactly the same look from the designers. There might be seventy-nine outfits in the Louis Vuitton show but they all make the same one or two choices and are competitive about who gets them. And that extends outside our office. How often do we call in something only to hear that American *Vogue* has asked for it as well? All the fashion magazines are using the same samples to photograph, so the same dress or jacket or shirt travels constantly around the world, each trip leaving it more ragged.

My features team have put together a list of ideas for the next few months, and are suggesting that we run a story around a collection of Rolling Stones costumes that are going to be exhibited at the Saatchi Gallery. I'm wary of photographing old clothes as still lifes or on mannequins, as they can look dreary, but I still haven't got Kate Moss, a contributing fashion editor, doing a story for March. This sounds like something she'd be interested in, if we could mix up the old Stones costumes with some contemporary fashion, and either shoot them on her or on other models. Better still, Mick Jagger and Keith Richards are going to be in a studio during the days we're hoping to do this story, so fingers crossed that the lure of Kate and *Vogue* might get one or other of them in front of the camera too. Kate Phelan, who will work with Kate M on the shoot, remembers how she was once introduced to Jagger by L'Wren Scott and was surprised to see him sitting in front of the TV watching cricket with a cup of tea on a tray – not so rock and roll.

Kate Moss came on board styling shoots a couple of years ago. Photographers love to work with her and she's done some really good stories. They're always the same vibe – her own – rock-and-roll sexy, so this idea could work. When she comes in and looks at the rails she picks up the clothes and sometimes tries them on. Then rags turn to stardust. She just knows how to make clothes work – how to move her body in them and how to twist them, hoick them, drape them so that they look their very best. Time-keeping is not her strong suit and sometimes I wait days for her to get to any proposed meeting. But whenever I see her I'm always charmed. Luckily Kate P, who is her *Vogue* nanny-cum-collaborator, is a mild, patient and saintly character and she doesn't seem to mind the prevarications.

13 *November*

I woke up to a beautiful morning, with a carpet of gold leaves outside. It's crazy to be fifty-eight and still excited about a birthday, but I am. I got a happy-birthday text from Sam to say he had just landed from New York, where he had gone for a week, which was the best present.

Back at Kensington Palace with our edit of photographers, I suggest that Josh Olins would be our first choice. Josh makes women look very beautiful but also human. His work has a gloss to it, and I thought that as a personality he would be someone the duchess would like and someone I would be able to work with on this as I'm going to have to be closely involved. I also put the case for Mario Testino but I can see that would lead to inevitable comparisons with the pictures of Diana, Princess of Wales, on the cover – although Mario didn't shoot her for British *Vogue*. That was Patrick Demarchelier. Rebecca, the duchess's private secretary, listens to Nicholas's and my thoughts and will now present the ideas to HRH.

17 November

My birthday was entirely lovely and I felt very spoilt. Mum, Sam, my brother, Jason, David and I went to the Italian restaurant Locanda Locatelli for dinner, which was a real treat. As we got into the car to drive home, Sam, as usual, was checking his phone and announced, 'Something's happened in Paris.' It was about 11.30 p.m. and the information was still chaotic and unclear, but news of the massacre at the Bataclan concert hall, an attack on restaurants and an incident at the Stade de France was coming through. We got home, switched on the TV and spent two hours watching the chilling reports. Life turns on a dime. One minute I was stuffing in pappardelle, the next hearing of slaughter in Paris.

David and I spent Saturday night at the Lamb Inn, East Sussex, as part of my birthday celebration, and for a large part of the time we lay in our room watching the news on the small television, which only got worse and worse with growing numbers of casualties. The next day we went for a walk in the water meadows and tried out the present my brother had given me: a strange contraption that looked like a leather S&M gizmo but is called a Murmurizer and is meant to summon clouds of starlings if you wave it around. It replicates their call, apparently. The promised starlings didn't emerge, but it seemed to encourage birds to fly into the air from the fields, and the cows all looked up.

This morning I was meeting the duchess. I went into the kitchen to make some coffee and decant the chicken stock I had made last night into the freezer. As I scrubbed at the recalcitrant corners of the chicken's roasting tray, it occurred to me that when I don't have this job I will have to spend more time scrubbing tins clean. Washing-up is part of the domestic life I often think I crave more of, but as I battled with the burned chicken fat, I had to admit that it has very little to recommend it as an activity.

At the palace we met in a different room, decorated as always in traditional English style, shades of muted green and dark wood. Fame is fascinating – rooms containing famous people are utterly unlike those that don't. I could see the duchess ahead as I walked in – it's always a surprise how tall she is. She's wearing a polo neck and blue skirt with black tights and long boots, and that swingy, shiny hair. When she sits on the sofa she somehow manages to make herself less present physically, which encourages ease in her presence. That's in complete contrast with her husband's mother,

Diana, Princess of Wales, who did the opposite – she *made* people look at her in the way she walked, the way she sat.

It was a huge relief when the duchess said she liked 'the first' photographer, which was Josh. She was keen to know what kind of a narrative, if any, we wanted the photographs to show. Was it to be the personal side of her life or the work? What kind of location did we have in mind? She speaks quietly and clearly and has a wonderful smile that breaks the ice immediately. At this stage she seemed keen that the pictures reflect her pleasure in the outdoors: 'Don't laugh, but I love building bonfires. Is there something we could do there?' We spoke about a log cabin as a location in the grounds, the possibility of a small beach nearby. But the shoot is scheduled for January so light and weather will be difficult.

We spent an hour there and agreed that it would be good to shoot her in informal clothes – checked shirts, jeans, Breton stripes. But I think we should also get something like McQueen options in as well. Now I must let Josh know this news. I'm absolutely sure he'll have no idea what I'm about to tell him.

18 November

Mission accomplished. Telling Josh he'd been chosen for this was like giving a child the huge shiny toy they wanted for Christmas. It was lovely to hear his delight, swiftly followed by what I imagine was a stunned silence, so I gabbled away, filling it with detail. Last night I dreamed we'd been unable to keep it secret – I do hope it won't become a repetitive dream for the next six months.

I draft a letter today for all the people we want to include in our Hall of Fame shoot for the Centenary issue by Tim Walker. Now I need to personalize each one since the list is as diverse as Apple designer Jony Ive, Gaia theorist James Lovelock, Bryan Ferry and

Michael Clark. Some of the decisions as to whom we want to include are predicated on whether or not Tim is likely to make a good image of them. He is a photographer who is at his best with people he admires or sees a picture in.

Looking through the choices of portraits that will be shown at the *Vogue* 100 show, it's clear that a person's ability to be photographed is a relevant factor in their fame. It's much more difficult for low-key 'normal-looking' people to become famous than people who create a recognizable trademark look. In the fashion industry there are so many people who have done the latter: Karl Lagerfeld with his ponytail and high collars; Anna Wintour with her bob and sunglasses; Suzy Menkes with her quiff. It's a way of making a statement about yourself and ensuring that you stand out. But it's not fashion alone. Think of David Hockney and his glasses, Churchill with his girth and cigar, Boris Johnson with that blond schoolboy thatch. Even the Queen has created a style that marks her out – single-colour outfits in a simple but graphic shape.

On Friday I've agreed to be interviewed about an upcoming parliamentary inquiry on body image. I must be crazy. It will just descend into the usual complaints about models being too thin and looking unhealthy. But I feel it's important to try to open up a more helpful line of questioning. Weighing models for their BMI is clearly insane, as if they were heifers or Tamworth pigs. I'm not even sure that it would ever be legal to legislate against employment on the basis of weight. But it's certainly true that the fashion industry is often blinkered when it comes to using very thin girls to model, and I don't mind admitting that. What will be hard to explain is why, if I feel that way, I can't wave a magic wand in my capacity as editor of *Vogue* and change it. How long have they got?

Mayfair has turned into Tinsel Town. The Christmas decorations are up: toy soldiers on the roof of the Claridge's ballroom; white reindeer outside Richard Caring's 34. It all looks incredibly pretty, and utterly unlike anywhere else in London, a gilded world of money and privilege. The weather has changed, and today is chilly. This morning I was eating breakfast in the kitchen when I heard rattling, then detected a very odd smell. At first I thought I hadn't switched the gas on the hob off, but that was not the case. Then I saw that one of the rubbish bins under the counter was on fire, and thick smoke was pouring out as the black bag melted. When it cooled down I tried to find out what had happened, but it remains a complete mystery. There was nothing in it but two Diet Coke cans, one empty catfood pouch and paper instructions for printer ink. Spontaneous combustion. Most weird.

The fire held me up so I was late for the ITN news crew who were already in my office to tape their film in advance of the inquiry. I defended *Vogue*'s choices of models and tried to explain that measuring BMI seemed the wrong route to progress as it's not necessarily a marker of health, and can easily be fudged. I also made the point that being a model is a career choice. As I said this, I realized that such an observation is unlikely to gain much agreement, but it's true that few people are forced into modelling. So do I feel responsible for them?

'Yes, on our shoots, of course.'

'Who is responsible for the young girls who are pressurized to be thinner than is healthy by agencies or designers? Where does the buck stop?'

I said I didn't know: another mistake. It is rare to hear an interviewee say they don't have an answer. Professionals and public figures are trained to avoid that, and usually provide another answer to an entirely different question. In the case of models' weight, it's a tangle, hard to see the beginning and the end. It would help if questioners didn't start from the premise that anyone they speak to is culpable. A more even-handed approach might make more people speak out. But asking Victoria Beckham to participate in a cross-party inquiry is clearly ludicrous, since the press coverage would end up being only about her. No wonder she hasn't answered their request.

23 November

The first frost has covered the roofs on the other side of the garden, and the sky is fleshy pink towards the east. It's hard to force myself out to run but at least the park looks beautiful in this light. It's projected to be clear and bright and cold today, which is lucky as we are shooting Edie and Olympia Campbell on location for the March issue. I listen to Radio 4's *Today* as I run: Brussels still in lockdown because of a rumoured terrorist attack, Ed Miliband discussing climate change. He makes the point that climate change is a difficult subject in politics because politics is all about short-termism – the next five years – whereas climate change is going to affect generations ahead. So the fact that he's now out on the fringes politically makes it easier for him to get engaged. That's true about so many fields. The people who are at the centre, making the decisions, are almost always balancing some immediate achievement they have in mind with the long-term good.

Tonight it's the British Fashion Awards and last night we were at the *Evening Standard* Theatre Awards. The *Standard* has a Milton Shulman award for best director and Mum has attended religiously for decades, originally with him when there was a jolly luncheon at the Savoy, and later on her own at the rather more circumspect and formal event it has become. David and I are dropped at the red carpet where a towering Nicole Kidman is parading with her shorter husband, then behind her, Ruth Wilson. I'm addicted to *The Affair*, which she stars in, and I have a moment of total fandom – I can't believe it's really her. I keep wanting to go up and gush, but there's never a good moment.

David and I sit with the Alexander McQueen V&A team, who are collecting a special award for the Savage Beauty exhibition. Sam Gainsbury, who is the designer of the show, is next to me. She's worrying that four of them are all planning to give the same speech. The creative director, Sarah Burton, is on a different table and comes up looking harassed, with a scrap of paper containing her speech. Sam says it's too long and I suggest they go off to the loo and edit it together.

Although there are a large number of awards, the ceremony is not too long. Vanessa Redgrave wins the Evgeny Lebedev award. Introduced by her tearful daughter, Joely Richardson, and a bearded Ralph Fiennes, she takes the stage and speaks in her slow, quavering, mesmerizing voice about the family of the theatre. I notice she doesn't touch Joely or register any pleasure at the emotional tribute her daughter has just given her. Nicole Kidman wins the Natasha Richardson award, reinforcing the relevance of that particular Redgrave family.

Over dinner Sam Gainsbury asks whether it's true that Victoria Beckham has won Designer of the Year at tonight's British Fashion Awards. I hadn't heard that – but I have no pre-knowledge of winners. I suppose it probably is true as I know Victoria is attending and she generally doesn't turn up if she hasn't won something, even though nominees are not meant to know in advance. I doubt that Nicole Kidman would have been there last night had she not known in advance she was winning.

24 November

Well, I was wrong. Totally. Victoria and David were both at the British Fashion Awards but it was Jonathan Anderson who won Designer of the Year. So I feel mean-spirited in the last entry. The awards were held at the Coliseum, which looked very pretty and glittering in candlelight. There was a good turnout of fashion-world celebrities; Jourdan Dunn being presented with the Model of the Year award by her pal Olivier Rousteing, and Anna Wintour presenting Karl Lagerfeld with his Lifetime Achievement award, and us with the fascinating fact that Karl had built a tennis court in his house at Biarritz expressly so that she, as a tennis fan, 'could feel myself'. Some people put flowers in a guest's bedroom, others build tennis courts. We had invited Erdem and his boyfriend Philip Joseph to our table, and Alexa Chung, who, it turned out, was presenting Erdem with his Establishment award. It appears that I was the only person who didn't know who had won what in advance. Anyway, it made the evening more fun, with an element of suspense. Jack Whitehall was a brilliantly funny MC, which also helped. Two nights of awards in a row is quite enough.

Christopher Bailey was hosting a Burberry table with Mario Testino, Rosie Huntington-Whiteley, and Naomi Campbell in a short black wig. Christopher's husband, Simon, told me they are expecting a second daughter in a couple of days. I'm trying to think of a good baby present – sending clothes is a bit coals-to-Newcastle.

25 November

Today is insane. First, Alexa interviewed me for a special edition of the future of fashion *Vogue* video series about different jobs on the magazine and what they involve. Normally this would have been fine but this week I'm in panic mode, trying to find a new organizer for the festival, who can deal with the daily nuts and bolts. The person who was meant to be my wing-man resigned the other day, and Serena Hood, who is currently doing the work, is about to go on well-earned maternity leave. What with interviews for that, maternity-leave cover for the features editor, and finding a new junior member of the fashion team, all the cracks in my day are now filled with interviews. I am often tempted to delegate interviews to other people but ultimately finding the right people to work with is one of the most important aspects of the job. I like to know why they want to work at this magazine in particular. People often say they want to work at *Vogue* but I'm keen to know what they think that means. In general I simply hire people I take an immediate liking to – who have energy and conviction. And that's worked pretty well over the years both at work and when I was looking for nannies at home. No disasters in either place.

Lunch with photographer's agent Giovanni Testino, Mario's brother, who was half an hour late because of terrible traffic. We talked about how photographers are now being asked to film video footage on shoots, and also the often more vexing question for them of not being asked, and a different crew shooting video of a personality. There wasn't enough time to get into this satisfactorily as I had to dash to an editing suite off Carnaby Street to see early rushes of *The Crown*, the huge Netflix series Peter Morgan is writing. It was brilliant. Utterly compelling and watchable in a *Downton*-like way except it's all real: Eileen Atkins as an ancient Queen Mary on the day of her son's abdication, our Queen (Claire Foy) at Treetops on the day she acceded to the throne; a marvellous Churchill played by John Lithgow, and an oddly delicate-looking and tall Prince Philip as a besotted young husband, played by Matt Smith. Fiona Golfar, *Vogue*'s editor-at-large, brought us this story months back and is trying to organize a fashion shoot with the cast before they all disperse. You realize what an extraordinary story even the smallest slice of the monarchy contains, how many dramas and large personalities there are within the family.

Philip Green calls to talk about my request for him to be filmed for the documentary. He says, 'Of course, honey. What do you want me to do?' Then he starts lambasting the food at the fashion awards – 'What planet are they on?' Always one of his favourite phrases – followed by a vivid description of how he had to get the Dorchester restaurant to stay open for him when he got back. 'I never had a morsel of food. Every single person I spoke to was saying, "Did you eat? Did you eat?"' Actually, Philip never likes other people's food and even less their wine. He always asks if he can order his own when he comes to one of my *Vogue* dinners.

26 November

The big clock in the kitchen has broken. I bought it at a shop at the Pompidou Centre during Paris Fashion Week shortly after we moved here in 2007, and I never knew until now how many times a day I look at it. A small part that connects the hands to the giant knitted face fell off, as it turns out, into Coco's food bowl and somebody binned it. Last night I went through the whole rubbish bin by hand looking for a minuscule metal pellet.

Full moon last night. I'm not at all folklore susceptible but I do know that full moons disturb my sleep. Unusually, though, I slept well and turned up for a *Vogue* team away-day excited by the prospect. We spent seven hours at the Belgraves Hotel in, unsurprisingly, Belgravia – twenty-one of us at a long table. I had wanted the different arms of the magazine to tell us what they each do, with the goal of finding out if we're focusing on the most efficient activities in areas such as video, website, print, and digital devices. It was interesting. Social media is vastly important, not only as a way of communicating information but crucially, for us, as a way of letting people know what content we have. A story on the website is useless if nobody bothers to tweet it or link it to Facebook. As one who doesn't use either of these platforms regularly, it's hard for me to relate to it, even if I understand it.

We started at 9.30 a.m. and by 4 p.m. my brain was bursting with information. It's hopeless when this kind of gathering turns into a competition – you waste too much time with one person disputing another's facts, but today everyone was really collaborative and engaged. Best of all, I came away with a list of really good ideas to publish in our Centenary issue.

Ideas are the hard part; the execution of them is not such a problem. Many may be time-consuming, but they're not difficult. I love the idea of a *Vogue* cost-of-living comparison through the century – the cost of a lipstick, a photo shoot, a bar of soap, a haircut – and the suggestion of asking people what they would put in a time capsule to be discovered in another hundred years' time.

Tim has decided he now wants to shoot only people working in fashion and the arts for his portfolio so it has meant rearranging the list and rewriting the letters I had drafted to the original names. I take his point that it will give the end result more consistency, although I'm sad there'll be people we can't include whom I would like to commemorate. Perhaps I'll find another place for them.

Mert and Marcus, our planned photographers for the Stones/Kate Moss shoot, have pulled out, which is infuriating, so at the moment we're in danger of not having either the fashion story or a cover for April. Sometimes it amazes me that people can be so unreliable in this business and feel so little responsibility, but those two don't often work with us so I guess we're not at the top of their list. Certainly they're no longer near the top of mine.

It's the weekend now and I'm not going to fret about it – Monday is another day. But it'll be hard to make this work. We have the clothes only until Christmas and we have just four possible dates with Kate until then, after which she's signed off till late January. It doesn't look like we'll get either Mick or Keith to be photographed for this either. Finding a great photographer at two weeks' notice at this time of year is a hard call.

This morning I finished reading *Jumpin' Jack Flash*, Keiron Pim's biography of David Litvinoff. He was one of those characters who swam between crims, toffs, rock and roll and the art world of the sixties and seventies, and I can't decide now whether I would have found him compelling or just irritating, if I'd met him. Certainly, he was one of those extreme characters – a clever, self-obsessed exhibitionist. He was Jewish, and some chapters relate to his relationships in the music world, which made me realize that none of our big music names are Jewish: the Stones, the Beatles, Led Zeppelin, Cilla Black, Adele, Oasis . . . there's not a Jewish name among them. When I made this point at dinner the other day, somebody reminded me that Amy Winehouse was an exception. In the book it's clear that there was a kind of anti-Semitism among the crowd Litvinoff hung with. Not so much discriminatory, but more an awareness that being a Jew set him apart.

29 November

It's Sunday today. Mizzle and dank. Last night David and I went to see *Steve Jobs*, which I thought confusing and contrived. I was interested to see Kate Winslet's portrayal of Joanna Hoffman, the head of marketing, as I remember how at the Hermès/Apple launch, various members of the Apple team had obviously thought it was not an entirely accurate portrayal. I wonder if she was made a more, or less, sympathetic character in the film.

When we left, I thought of how Burberry, who have invested a lot of money and effort in the digital arena, are similar to Apple, and, of course, their last CEO, Angela Ahrendts, left to join Apple. How the brand message is so vital to what they do. How the brand name is used again and again in any presentation or advertising, and how careful these large successful companies are about sticking to the message and hammering the brand home. In 1964 Marshall McLuhan published *Understanding Media*, in which he wrote, 'The medium is the message,' but nowadays I think the message itself is the powering medium. It's more important than any methods of transmission now that there are so many.

This morning I've been battling with our doorbell, or lack thereof. We haven't had one for over a year now and I'm finally tired of it. But I'm at a loss to work out what kind to get and where to find it. I don't want an intercom system, which sounds just like the telephone and is often ignored by everyone in the house as they think someone else will pick it up. This sort of thing defeats me: I usually give up and decide to deal with it another day.

As I type, a Google alert pings through on the email. I click: '*Vogue*'s Alexandra Shulman says size zero models DON'T give girls eating disorders.' Well, that's not news, I think, and click on the link to see a hideous picture of myself looking smug above a piece that is related to the release of my interview on ITN. It seems to come from the *New Zealand Herald*. I'd forgotten that was all coming out tomorrow.

I decide not to look at another link related to it. In a minute David and I are going to see the Peter Lanyon exhibition at the Courtauld and a show on Empire art at the Tate, which is what I would rather be thinking about. No doubt there'll be time for it tomorrow. I hope I'm not going to regret giving that interview, in which I clearly stated that legislating around BMI is unworkable and a bad idea anyway. I leave the doorbell unsolved.

DECEMBER

1 December

The ITN interview was transmitted. I couldn't bear to watch it as I hate to see myself on TV but I was sent a transcript. Of course, the nuance of everything I'd said was lost. It makes you realize why politicians are always so maddening and don't answer questions with any balance when they're interviewed. There is no way that anything other than a blunt opinion, on one side or the other, will be reported. There is no interest in a 'Well, you might say that in this circumstance or that in another . . .' Anyway, it won't even be a fish-and-chips-paper-tomorrow situation, since the probability of bombing Syria in less than forty-eight hours will knock anything else off the news agenda. I don't even know if the proposed parliamentary inquiry has been held.

Thank heavens we've got Craig McDean to shoot the Kate Moss/ Stones story. He'll be excellent, and it's close to a miracle that he can do it at such short notice.

6 December

The parliamentary inquiry was held and, as far as I can tell, the resolution was to do something but no one knew what. I gather that even the head of the inquiry, Caroline Nokes, agreed that legislation on BMI was unworkable. My own comments seemed to rate about 40:60 in the approval stakes, more saying that I was part of the evil conspiracy of fashion than those who thought I'd talked sense. I got a heart-breaking letter from a woman saying that her twelve-year-old daughter had just come out of a 'mental hospital' for eating disorders, and how unhelpful my view was that thin models should be allowed on the catwalk.

We had the annual judging of the *Vogue*/British Fashion Council Designer Fund. From floor twenty-five of the Shard, London looks very brown. The Thames is a thick brown slug, and streets of low brown and grey buildings stretch out for ever, struggling to be seen amid the city of cranes and towering skyscrapers poking up among them. We were in a vast, empty office with glass walls on every side and thousands of lights for the video that the BFC uses for promotional purposes. Everything has to be filmed now. Each move and breath we take. It's exasperating. But I'm in no position to object, as I'm spending a large amount of my time persuading people to agree to be filmed for the *Vogue* documentary.

I had asked Victoria Beckham months back if she would be the honorary judge, and she arrived in a pile of white, eight-ply cashmere, joining the rest of us, Lisa Armstrong of the *Daily Telegraph*, Topshop's Mary Homer, Ian Lewis, now of Harrys shoes, Caroline Rush of the BFC, Sarah Manley representing Burberry, Susanne Tide-Frater who works as a freelance consultant and also with Victoria, Mrs Burstein, the beloved founder of Browns boutique, and Samantha Cameron. When I thanked Samantha for coming on an early morning, the day after the Syrian vote, she said she had been in the House for it, one of the few occasions she had been there. Her husband must have been pleased by his majority. I have no idea which way I would have voted, but certainly Hilary Benn's speech in support of extending the bombing would have been likely to convince me. It wasn't so much what he said as that he would have been preternaturally inclined (I assume) against it.

We had five contenders in front of us. The main presentation is an exhaustive study of their business – financial timelines and projections, staffing, retail opportunities, etc. It's a good exercise for them but no doubt puts off some people from applying. This year it was a hard decision as the five were at so many different stages. Victoria, silent at the start, quickly turned into the chief inquisitor for each contender. Anybody who doubts that she knows much about her own business is entirely wrong.

In the end, the choice of winner this year was between Mother of Pearl, a middle-market but high-design company, and Sophia Webster, who has built a very successful and quickly growing shoe line. In the end we chose Sophia who, along with her husband, Barry, is a real force, and awarded Mother of Pearl a highly commended position. It's always sad that there can be only one winner as all of them had put a lot of work into their submission and care so much about what they're doing.

Took the BBC crew over to Philip Green's offices so they could film a meeting with one of London's big fashion figures. He was in great form, presenting his black lacquered Tina Green-designed office suite, with its wide terrace and view down Oxford Street. In his boardroom, he has a sword on a plinth to commemorate his knighthood although I couldn't read the inscription clearly enough to see who had given it to him. I asked him how business was going and he replied, 'Well, what do you think?' Once again, it was 'the wrong kind of weather'. Although it was the first week of December it was mild enough for bare legs and no coat. That kind of climate doesn't sell winter fashion.

I've heard the 'wrong kind of weather' story so often, particularly from the high street, that it makes me think perhaps someone should refigure what the weather is likely to be doing. Perhaps fewer coats are going to sell nowadays. Perhaps coats for really cold weather should be sold in January rather than November. I suggested something along these lines but Philip was having none of it. Customers want new things all the time – autumn clothes are over now. But what happens when it's suddenly cold and that's when you want to buy a heavy coat? 'Go online,' was his answer.

The issue of when to sell what is a big subject now, and there are such divided opinions. The department stores selling expensive fashion seem convinced that their shoppers want to buy ahead and therefore drive the sale dates earlier to clear space for new stock. If you talk to some of the small boutiques they don't want to go on sale so early and would rather be able to stock on a buy-now-wear-now basis. In general, the whole industry is geared to the notion of supplying clothes before they're needed, a situation that is mainly driven by the US market. Of course, they have a much greater range of climate than we do. Online sales, though, have changed the picture. If you're an online boutique, you have to be able to support, say, the Australian market with lightweight clothes in our winter, and vice versa.

Wednesday morning, but it feels like Friday. Why do days have different personalities? Last night was the office Christmas party. Sacha Forbes, my irreplaceable right hand on *Vogue* events, had organized it at Mark's Club in Mayfair, which looked wonderfully festive, with a garlanded staircase and glimmering glasses of cocktails and champagne. I had left all the arrangements to her and, although I'd helped with the guest list of contributors and people we work with regularly, I'd forgotten who was coming. It's more fun that way. I never know with our Christmas party if it's more enjoyable for people to have an evening like that, where the emphasis is less on the *Vogue* staff, or when it's just us and maybe our partners. I think I prefer the latter as it gives me an opportunity to find out more about the people I work with every day. Last night I spent most of the time at the door greeting people.

I hope when I get to the office the Stones/Kate Moss pictures will be in. It sounded as if it was quite difficult to get everything done in time as Kate didn't arrive until midday. Also, they haven't shot a cover with any contemporary clothes – in every version she's wearing Stones memorabilia. I'm not sure whether I can make that work. I guess if the picture is good enough, it'll be fine, but in general people like to see real clothes on the cover, not archive costume. The documentary team were happy with what they shot, though.

Sad news yesterday of the closing of Jonathan Saunders's label. I like Jonathan but his business has been constantly up and down since he launched. We put one of his dresses on the cover of *Vogue* after his first show – the only time I've ever done this. He was rescued last year by Eiesha Pasricha, who invested in the label, but clearly something has gone wrong. It's so hard to make these independent labels work financially. At least four collections a year, fulfilling orders from stores who often don't pay on time, maintaining a global connection – the practicalities are massive even if the creative strength is there. And so many designers are rotten at business, and need someone they can trust to manage the business and the money. So often that doesn't work out.

Things to achieve in the next ten days:

Approach everyone we want to photograph for Tim Walker's Hall of Fame in *Vogue* 100
Plot the whole Centenary issue of the magazine
Fill the April issue
Approach the leading festival speakers
Start work on the festival programme
Write introduction to the *Vogue Shoes* book
Write March issue editor's letter
Map out May issue
Get the Mario Testino story for June outlined
Plan our digital fashion-show coverage for next season
Buy another twenty Christmas gifts
Organize food for Christmas lunch
Deliver gifts to my family

15 December

I slept appallingly last night – work-anxiety dreams where I didn't know what season's clothes we were meant to be shooting. Woke at 3 a.m., then skated on consciousness for the next four hours, drifting in and out. I imagine it was because I was worried about the meeting today at Kensington Palace to introduce Josh and Lucinda to everyone. My natural pessimism is definitely taking pole position over this and I worry at every step that the whole thing is going to implode.

*

Josh arrives in the office looking very smart in tweed suit and a tie. In a patronizing, quasi-maternal way, I had thought of calling in advance to tell him a tie might be good and then had forgotten to do so. He has great manners, something I always notice in men – less so in women. He, Lucinda and I meet briefly in my office to work out what we need to ask. Can we take a producer with us? What about catering? Is there a room for the wardrobe, hair and make-up? Might she be photographed with her dog? Josh's father is very ill and he has just been with him in the hospital, so this shoot is one of those examples where something terrible is happening simultaneously with something wonderful.

We arrive early and wait once more in the little check-in cabin at the gate until we're walked in to meet HRH. She is again charming, friendly and easy to talk to, although she is capable of dropping a curtain on a subject and not elaborating. We discuss the shoot location and whether there will be heaters, can we bring in a sofa or armchair, and if we photograph her with a bonfire, where that might be.

When we talk about clothes it's hard to get a clear steer. Having agreed that it would be very downplayed and natural, the duchess then says, 'But I want to do what's good for you.' We agree Lucinda will bring a selection of different things and she can see how she feels on the day.

When we leave, Josh and Lucinda both say how beautiful she is. 'She's like a real princess, isn't she?' says Lucinda. I'm hugely relieved that they've both come away such fans since it wasn't a given. She's very much not a 'fashion' person and her personal taste is mainstream and classic. As we walk to the car that will take us back to the office Josh starts to talk about whether we can put her into 'high-waisted Céline trousers'. Lucinda and I say it's not going to be about the high-waisted-Céline kind of thing.

17 December

It's so mild that it's impossible to grasp that Christmas is now in a week's time. I hanker for frost on the roofs and the proverbial nip in the air, but yesterday was as mild as May. It makes global warming seem much more of a reality. Driving home from work the other day I heard a news item about polar bears becoming more active as they had to walk further and faster to get their food. It's a bit like working in print journalism. Now, like the bears, we have to be lighter on our feet, and do a great deal more to make the same amount of revenue.

To that end, I've commissioned an article for our online site about what's happening to the traditional fashion-show schedule. The US fashion body, the Council of Fashion Designers of America, is looking at different options that might include small appointments at the traditional show time for press and buyers, then a big show where clothes can be bought, aimed at customers, or consumers, as they're called. Whether that's a good idea or not is hard to say, but it's certainly a good idea to look at what the whole industry is doing currently. I've been saying for years that the system is utterly inept, and quite insane – more of a networking opportunity than a way to sell clothes.

A shake-up would certainly change what we can put in the magazine and how we organize it – dramatically. At the moment, we're shooting all our spring fashion to run in issues from February, published in January. The reason why magazines are published in the month before the month on their cover is lost in the fog of history, but it had its roots in everyone wanting to be first on the newsstand. I learned the other day that in Korea they're more like six weeks earlier. The clothes we feature will be in the stores somewhere around February. But by our May issue (published in April) many will be unavailable – sold out or returned to make way for new stock. It sounds confusing and it is.

When I left work last night, I felt for the first time that the Centenary issue might actually come together and be really good. I'm grateful to the people I work with for their persistence in making things come together, and their commitment to creating something exceptional. Almost everything in that issue is complicated in some way, and it needs to demonstrate that *Vogue* is simply a better magazine than most – daunting, but exciting.

Sam and I went shopping at lunchtime for some clothes for his Christmas present. I no longer feel confident that I can get the fit right for him if he's not here. He wanted a vintage sheepskin coat and some boots. The coat was easy and we found one quickly at Rokit in Covent Garden, but the boots were trickier. I tried to explain that if you have a very specific vision in your mind of what you want it's always hard to find. He said I was much better at shopping than him because he couldn't really *see* anything when he was presented with it. When it comes to buying something for myself, for a specific purpose, I can often spend hours and come back with nothing. I've learned it's best to buy clothes when you find something you really like, even if you have no reason to wear it, rather than have to get something for a job interview or a party next week and inevitably fail or run amok.

22 December

No matter what day of the week Christmas falls on, the last few days before are hopeless for achieving anything at work. Offices are only half full, both ours and everyone else's, so the day is filled with small frustrations. I'm always there till the bitter end as people leak away. It's annoying, not being able to chase up those I want photographed for the Centenary issue, or to finalize the details of some upcoming fashion shoots.

One of our freelance fashion editors, Joe McKenna, comes in today to look at the clothes he has called in for Sheridan Smith, who is getting rave reviews as Fanny Brice in *Funny Girl*. There are five huge rails of predominantly black dresses and a few white shirts. A lot of the black dresses have come from William Vintage, as vintage clothes fit women of real proportions, unlike samples. Joe says most of what he wants isn't there, even though he appears to have every black dress in London. Size, of course, is the problem as we're asking to borrow stock and the shops want to hang on to what they have in the hope of selling it around Christmas and New Year. Sheridan is only five foot two and a size ten, which is pocket Venus proportions, but sample sizes are based on size eight or six and the girls are often at least five foot nine.

He also says that the shoot he's planning with Jamie Hawkesworth for the next issue is not coming together. Yesterday I was told that they'd decided to shoot in a London studio – financial music to my ears since Plan A had been to travel to Louisiana – but now apparently Jamie wants to postpone because he can't find a girl (a.k.a. a model).

Joe says, 'Don't explode – just listen to this, and give me an answer tomorrow. How about a transgender model?'

I don't explode. In fact, it could be interesting. I guess it depends on what she looks like, or is it what *he* looks like? I know it theoretically doesn't need to be either of these but I'm not brilliant on the new nomenclature. But any indecision at this stage is not a happy state of affairs. Losing at least two weeks' work over Christmas means it'll be hard to get everything in on time.

The Craig McDean pictures have arrived. The story is really wonderful. Loosely inspired by the famous photographs taken at the Villa Nellcôte when the Stones were recording *Exile on Main Street*, Kate looks beautiful, and louche, and really rather extraordinary in Jagger's old catsuits and velvet jackets. The cover picture is, I think, very appealing, but it's a risk. She's wearing the original red-tongue studded T-shirt, now copied on a million market stalls, under a leather jacket. I'm not sure that it would work on anyone else, but the combination of her and that T-shirt (which we can also show was worn by Jagger) strikes me as pretty irresistible.

I dropped in earlier to see Bella Freud's new store in Chiltern Street. I had suggested Bella write the piece to go with the pictures because she's a friend of Kate's, and knows the Stones a bit because her husband, the writer James Fox, worked with Keith Richards on his memoir. I also thought she would have a feeling for the glam androgyny of the Stones costumes.

Flora Fraser's Christmas party last night was great fun. I talked to Lu Guthrie, who is a friend and does all the calligraphy for *Vogue*'s invitations. I've known her since the eighties and she was reminiscing about her affair, at that time, with one of London's leading designers, who then worked with her in a boutique. She had him two nights a week, and another boyfriend another two nights of the week, and at weekends he went back to his long-term girlfriend.

26 December

The lead-up to Christmas went with all the momentum of a crescendo: presents to be bought, commissions to be made, letters to be written, meals to be planned. And then, today, that point has been reached, Christmas is over, and there is the somewhat bleak feeling of nothing to reach for. It was a full moon on Christmas Day and I woke up at 1.30 a.m. with white light falling on the floor, overriding the yellow of the streetlights. I was wide awake and unable to sleep, worrying about whether it was the right time to creep up the stairs to Sam with his stocking – as if, aged twenty, he cares whether he can see me or not. And when I wasn't worrying about that, I was worrying about whether I'd be able to make the Centenary issue of the magazine good enough, even though, only a couple of days ago, I was surfing the wave of confidence.

Christmas Day, when it dawned properly, was lovely: friends, family, incredibly good wine, a massive meal, which I cooked, with David doing the peeling, on Christmas Eve, and my friend Jane Wellesley, acting as my sous-chef for the last hour. Sam was sick and stayed in bed all day.

2016

JANUARY

3 January

Back to work tomorrow. I'm absolutely terrified of what I need to achieve in the next six months or so because so much of it is out of my control. I want everything that we do to be really extraordinary and have the very best people included in it. I want *Vogue* 100 at the National Portrait Gallery to be regarded as a benchmark in the history of magazine photographic exhibitions, my festival to be clever and lucrative, the gala dinner to be gossip-worthy and glamorous, the Centenary issue to be exceptional, and the BBC documentary to make *Vogue* look intriguing, rather than foolish.

After ten days' break, I woke up this morning and went to the farmers' market in the pouring rain. I stewed some apples with cinnamon, put on a stock to simmer, and wondered whether it would be possible to have (and if I would enjoy having) a life of just reading all the books I've now got piled up on the big table in the bedroom, and do very little work. I could run every day, make vegetable soups, let my hair go grey and . . . And then what? Would I be content? David, who had just woken up, said that for thousands of years philosophers have pondered this same question.

4 January

The boiler has another fault so my first day back at work starts with no hot water or heating – again. Richard Macer and Charlotte Rodriguez come in to update me on the documentary. They have started editing, and are looking at how they will divide the material into two programmes. The last thing I wanted was this film to include a great deal of footage of me, but they make it clear that from now on, because of so much being about the 100th year, they want to be tracking it through me, and what I'm trying to do.

An immediate priority is the April issue, which is crashing around my ears. Jamie Hawkesworth and Joe McKenna still haven't agreed on a model and it's hard to work out how this can be. It has taken since October not to agree either that or a location. Joe showed me a picture Jamie had sent him of a boy who looked like a youthful Patti Smith, wearing a white utility-style dress, standing by a brick wall. When I said I wasn't keen on the shoot looking like that, he was exasperated and said I wasn't listening to him: the picture wasn't about the clothes but the kind of image Jamie is interested in. I'm not sure what aspect of this I'm meant to find relevant – is it the mop-haired boy in a dress? Is it the brick wall? He said he asked a casting agent to get in touch with agencies in the Netherlands for some transgender model options. I couldn't help thinking it would be so much easier to use a pretty girl we already know of. But I can also see how transgender could add an interesting element. So we continue with no resolution.

Another shoot's dates have moved so it looks like we won't have those pictures in time either. So far, all we have is Kate Moss in an old catsuit of Mick Jagger's, which is a great story but can't carry a whole issue.

Luckily, late in the afternoon, the catalogue for the National Portrait Gallery exhibition arrives, with the silver-foil box of postcards that will be on sale. The catalogue is truly rich and glamorous and I feel a very real sense of achievement as I look through it. Not that I have done very much in its creation, but it makes the whole Centenary programme start to seem real.

The Christmas sales results for the high street are coming out. Next is down, John Lewis is up, but those are headlines and probably don't tell the true story. Predictably, the weather is heralded as a reason for Next doing less well than expected. Clearly the trend now must be for clothes that are multi-seasonal, rather than catering to either extreme. From my point of view, good retail results are helpful. *Vogue* is easier to run when business is good.

Patrick Demarchelier calls. Although he has lived in New York for decades his accent is impenetrably French, and he talks incredibly fast. I manage to glean that he was in St Bart's for Christmas and is now in Los Angeles. He says a few sentences, which I don't really understand. Then, 'If you want me to do something FANTAS-TEEC, I come to Europe. Okay, big kiss.' He signs off. If he really wants you to know the point he is making, his accent tends to diminish a little. I like Patrick. He does what we ask him to do without making a huge song and dance about it, and he always tries his best to fit dates in. He is one of the few photographers who work regularly for the magazine who was a big part of it when I arrived in 1992. Then he decamped, along with my predecessor Liz Tilberis, to *Harper's Bazaar* for a big contract. Like all of them, he returned eventually.

This afternoon we had the last meeting at the National Portrait Gallery before the exhibition opens. It was extraordinary to be sitting there, around their big boardroom table, with only weeks to go until this – this *thing* we've been talking about for so long – will finally happen. There have been so many meetings, starting three years ago, and it's been even longer in the planning. There is an exhilarated feel to the gathering – everyone is excited, and all the pieces of the jigsaw are fitting together. The first catalogues are in, the merchandise for the shop will soon be there, the illuminated three-sided pillars or 'Toblerones' of *Vogue* covers are to be colour co-ordinated, and there is an endless programme of dinners, late-night openings and press launches.

The hang of the photographs is starting on the twenty-fifth. I ask Robin Muir to make me a crib list of top points about the show that might be interesting. We talk about which photographers could be interviewed for press purposes, and I urge their PR team to check names with me. I don't want anyone going rogue on us, as Michael Dugher, the ousted shadow culture minister, did last night on the radio, having been fired in Jeremy Corbyn's reshuffle. Understandably he was aggrieved and keen to speak out, but the communications people at Labour looked as if they had lost control. Hopefully, most of the photographers represented would be interesting and generally nice about the magazine, but I know that David Bailey, for instance, makes no bones about how much he hates fashion magazines now. Which reminds me that I must call him and make a date. It's been too long since I've had my dose of Bailey verbal abuse. For the first five years I was at *Vogue* he called me Rebecca.

10 January

In the late morning I force myself out for a run. The sun has made a rare appearance and I plan a reward of an afternoon spent reading Patti Smith's *M Train*. The last time I ran in this spot (a patch of land locally known as Dog Poo Park) I was assaulted. At least I think that's how it would now qualify, albeit in a pretty minor way. It was a morning just after Christmas Day and a sturdy man in a woollen hat and track pants smiled at me as I passed, then started to jog alongside me in jovial fashion. I thought it was just post-Christmas bonhomie and laughed with him, but after a minute or so I felt uncomfortable with his company and ran ahead. When I stopped at the park gate to open it, I heard him just behind me.

'Hello.' I turned around and he stepped forward. I thought perhaps he was lonely and just wanted somebody to relate to him, even if only momentarily.

'Twice. Twice.' He waved at the park to indicate another circuit.

'No. Once only,' I replied.

He moved closer to me and leaned forward to kiss my cheek, saying, 'Happy Christmas,' in an accent I couldn't identify.

'Happy Christmas.' I didn't wish to be hostile but was now definitely wanting to get away.

Then he clutched me in a bear hug and kissed me again. This time I became fearful and melodramatically wondered if he might have a knife. I pulled away sharply but he yanked me back and lunged at my breasts with his hands, then jumped away with a grin as I bolted through the gate.

At the time I just wanted to get out of the park, but a few minutes later, as I continued my run along the pavements, I began to feel upset and questioned myself. Why hadn't I shouted at him to get away? Why wasn't I furious with him, rather than feeling furious now with myself for not reacting? What if I'd been a teenage girl alone in the park? What if he had become violent?

Then this New Year there were the reported attacks on women in Cologne, and their descriptions of being groped and grabbed reminded me of it again. Today I looked around warily but there was no sign of him among the usual dog-walkers. That's wrong: I don't want consideration of his presence to become a part of whether I run there or not.

A bleak day. Turned on the radio when I woke and they were playing 'Space Oddity'. It seemed curious and I assumed it was a link into a story about Major Tim Peake and the space station. But David Bowie had died. It made me cry a little, and then I wanted to write a tribute for our website, for myself as much as anyone else. That's my privilege as editor. It's a strangely effective balm, writing about things that affect you. One of the greatest pluses of being a journalist.

We won't run a story on him in the magazine and that's a huge change. This is the first time I've felt that it didn't make sense any more to publish a tribute in print that, with our deadlines, couldn't appear for another six weeks. So many people learned the news on waking up to Instagram posts of him – old pictures, album covers. The first major Instagram death. Would he have liked that?

All day people ask for my comments on him as a fashion leader but I don't want to provide them. It feels more personal than that. He gave me and so many of my contemporaries a thrilling vision of an unusual way to be. The older among us in the office feel bereft; the younger – even by a decade – are not affected in the same way. It's probably similar to how I felt when I heard John Lennon had been killed, or Elvis had died. It was news but it was somebody else's news.

At any rate the whole day has been depressing, and I was weeping again listening to the radio as I drove back from work.

12 January

At yoga yesterday Audrey, my teacher, told me Mercury has entered retrograde. I have no idea what that means except it's something people say when things go wrong. She said all her clients had problems. I doubt that Bowie dying had much to do with the movement of Mercury but perhaps, on closer thought, it did, with 'Starman' and 'Space Oddity', and things planetary being of interest to him. Anyway, last night the boiler broke again.

Today is a better day although reading the newspaper coverage of Bowie started more tears. I arrived ten minutes early for a lunch in Kensington with Federico Marchetti of Yoox/Net-a-Porter, which we had mooted back in September when we met at the Gucci dinner in Milan. To kill time I thought I'd look in at Marks & Spencer across from the restaurant and see what they had on the floor since I'll be going to their headquarters tomorrow. They've had poor press following the announcement of their CEO Marc Bolland's resignation at the same time as the release of pretty unremarkable womenswear sales figures. I watched women shopping, mainly but not exclusively over fifty, short, size fourteen plus, almost all wearing padded jackets and black trousers. I can't believe they relate much to the high-fashion pieces highlighted at the elaborate press events that target us.

There was a navy parka pulled out on display, which would have been great, except for a strange black fake-fur collar that removed the chic of the rest of the jacket. The cashmere, which felt lovely, was toxic shades of pink, blue and green, as opposed to more flattering ones. A white cardigan with a black trim could have been really smart but had strange gathered shoulders, and all the trousers are hung horizontally in a way that makes them look particularly big-bottomed and unattractive. M&S should be the very best place to go for basics for everyone. In some areas it still is. Their underwear is fantastic. But, of course, it's always easy to criticize what other people do. From the outside, solutions appear obvious and mistakes incomprehensible. People outside my business can never understand why the magazine features impossibly beautiful, thin models and clothes relatively few can afford. Or why we don't photograph the clothes on women of more diverse ages.

Lunch with Federico, who is great company and very funny, was extremely enjoyable. The Yoox/Net-a-Porter business employs thousands of people and he has offices around the world, although he splits the majority of his time between London and Milan. He has now found a hotel he likes in London – primarily because it has a good pool where he can swim each morning. If you move around as much as he does, it's small points, such as being able to do your exercise, that become huge determinants in whether the travel is tolerable. We talked about art, which he collects, he said, in a small way. 'On paper I am a very rich man but in reality, now, I am not.' Before lunch I had googled him. He shares a name with an Italian footballer, who plays for Lazio, and the Yoox/Net-a-Porter merger meant that the company was valued on the market at around £4 billion.

He told me he used to date Armani's niece Roberta, so he and Giorgio know each other well, but it's always hard to find something for the designer's birthday. He has everything and he's not particularly interested in cultivating new interests. Federico's most successful present to him was a cat, and the cat Armani currently has is the offspring of that gift and he adores it. The story reminded me of going to the designer's apartment in Milan several years back: it was so immaculate and minimal that you felt even breathing might stain it, but there, in the middle of the floor, was a brightly coloured rubber mouse. That makes sense now.

Lunch during the week is either a real treat or a total waste of time. This was definitely the former and I felt buoyed up after it.

I have only four weeks to finalize the line-up for the festival – eighteen talks and only two so far set up to any degree. Like so much of my job, it's a jigsaw puzzle and you can only work out if one piece is in the correct position when you can see the next-door pieces, which makes it incredibly hard to fix. But I've done this four times before, so I know it can be done. At least, that's what I keep telling myself.

Over the weekend I finished reading *M Train* in one go. It was like drinking the perfect cup of coffee. Dark, slightly bitter and delicious. I envy that life of words and photographs and music, although she often sounds sad. She packs the same things on every trip she takes – the same socks, T-shirts, Ethiopian cross, Moleskine graph-paper notebook, dungarees and black jacket. If only I could do the same. The shows are coming up and I will soon be packing for them again. The contents of my suitcase will be very different from hers.

14 January

Snow is forecast in the next few days. I love snow childishly – watching it fall and hoping it will stay on the ground, the glistening cover when it does, the hush of the city on a snow-covered early morning and even, I suspect, the possibility of a snow-day, although I don't remember the last time snow prevented my going to the office. Last February I was in New York during the blizzards and that felt very different. There was no appreciation of the placid beauty of a whiteout there when I was far from home and worried about whether my flight back would be able to leave.

Yesterday we had the Condé Nast outing to Marks & Spencer for lunch. I was the only editor there – the rest of our group was from the publishing side, with Nicholas Coleridge. The huge, relatively new building has all the ingredients of modern corporate interiors. There were colourful lidded bins for clothes recycling, a counter with tea on tap, coffee-tables spread with in-house magazines and an impressive glass lift that swooshed us way above the grimy urban spread of Paddington Basin. In the upstairs lobby there are portraits of the company's CEOs and chairmen over the decades, including a curious one of Lord Sieff in the sixties – half factual, half symbolic, with four or five carriage clocks floating above his desk, an almost mythical stream outside a window (perhaps he was an angler) and a small dreamlike woman in the distance (his wife?).

Marc Bolland appeared with a winter suntan and slicked-back hair. Despite the news of his upcoming departure, he still demonstrates the standard habits of corporate power: the quick stride flanked by a flotilla of colleagues, the mandatory keeping us waiting for about ten minutes. Once we were all seated in their dining room – a really wonderful Lowry marketplace scene on one wall, a Monet on the other – he updated us on their new initiatives.

In business we're all relentlessly upbeat and you would never imagine that those sales figures must have been difficult to deal with only a few days ago. Patrick Bousquet-Chavanne, who masterminds their marketing, was proud to tell us of a new plan to use an established designer or figure to produce small stand-alone collections. The first is with Alexa Chung, who has worked on a range inspired by the archives, which they are going to show at London Fashion Week. Alexa always does good work and I'm sure she will for them. I already knew about this as we had been asked to run the first story on it, but the only aspect that seemed right to me for *Vogue* was to have Alexa write about it and she wouldn't. It probably required too much time and effort on her part. The food at lunch was like a sixties abstract painting – scallops and chicken on splashes of bright green and orange sauce.

15 January

Our boiler is causing more stress than the whole of *Vogue* 100. The temperature outside has dropped for the first time this winter and we have no heat at home. Actually, correction: we have heat very occasionally when the boiler, having provided the barest minimum recently, suddenly wakes up and the hot water and radiators are baking, usually just before we go to bed. There are twelve people coming to dinner tomorrow night and I'm wondering whether to email them and tell them to bring sweaters. Such is my line of thinking as I rush to the butcher this morning to get the meat for that meal.

By the time I get to the office, after the boiler and the butcher divert, Jane How, one of our contributing fashion editors, is here to show me the rail of clothes she wants to shoot with the photographer Harley Weir. She works on a couple of stories a season for us and I feel bad as I walk in because I have to tell her she can't shoot two brands I know she'll want to include. We've covered them so much already and it's important to keep a balance. While we're free to photograph what we want, sometimes the wind blows every stylist in one direction, and the many brands who are not working in that direction are put out at their exclusion. In some ways the fashion industry expects to be treated as I was at childhood speech days, when almost everybody was given a prize so that they didn't leave unhappy.

*

Hurrah, it's bright sunshine for the second day of Joe McKenna's shoot, which was at one point to use models whose gender was visually ambivalent. After a huge casting of boys who looked like girls, and boys who have transitioned, and girls who looked like boys, Jamie Hawkesworth, the photographer, and Joe have fallen for a girl who looks like a girl and want to photograph only her. That means some of the pictures they shot yesterday of the now redundant boys may not be handed over to me. Since they're working outside, in Hyde Park, I hope this good weather means they can shoot enough to make up the numbers. I'm disappointed as I'd liked the idea of that curious mix of models, which would have been a good way to address the question of gender fluidity in fashion without making a big meal of it.

On another note, we're still trying to get Rihanna confirmed for the cover of the May issue. She and Manolo Blahnik have worked on a shoe collaboration, which is why she's keen to be featured, but every aspect of the organization is like pulling teeth. We still don't know if we're getting an interview with her. Her 'people' want all the pictures to be in black and white, and there is a specific pair of thigh-high denim boots they want featured on the cover – which may well be hard to achieve as our covers in general are crops. And we don't get told what clothes to put on them.

Yesterday I learned that neither Christopher Bailey nor Nicolas Ghesquière can speak at the festival: the dates are impossible for their schedules. I'm starting to really worry about getting a strong enough line-up. Normally the festival is in April. I wonder if late May is a bad time for the designers. But when is a good time? Everyone's diaries are booked up months ahead. Mine included. It's horrible knowing where you're going to be every day for the next four, five, six months. But in fashion, where so many people travel so much of the time, that's the reality.

Hazel McIntyre from HR comes up with a spreadsheet of my staff's annual salaries. I stare at it with a flashback of familiarity, which at first I can't identify. Then I realize it reminds me of the book of logarithm tables we had at school for maths. What on earth did we ever do afterwards with that information? I don't even recall what it was for. I'm sure Sam never had one of those books. The spreadsheet is meant to help me see how much I'm spending on salaries as we progress through the year but I find it impenetrable. I also find it depressing how little some of our most junior staff are earning. It's so hard for them all.

16 January

There is dire news for the stock market and David appears at the kitchen door to say that we will all be going to Hell in a handcart as he waves a newspaper. I mainly ignore his gloomy predictions, which only encourages him to return an hour later as I'm finalizing my marinade to read out huge chunks of the *Financial Times* about redundancies in the media. This is not what I want to hear and, momentarily, I wonder whether the whole Centenary programme will be a bit of a fiddling-while-Rome-burns exercise. Then I return to chopping cauliflower for dinner tonight.

18 January

I hate the days when I don't manage to strike anything off my to-do list and today has been one of those. Richard at Timebased Events said that the marquee we are building to house the *Vogue* Festival in the park has been pushed further away from the road than we had originally thought, because of 'leaf drip'. They have devised a kind of tunnel entry so we still have an entrance near the road. His team suggested a living wall of green at this entrance but Anna Cryer, who is organizing the nuts and bolts of the festival, and I both said we didn't see the point of bringing a living wall to a park, which is just one huge living wall anyway. In late May the trees will be in full leaf and the grass will be a brilliant colour. Richard was, as always, very gracious in our rejection of his plan, as he also was when I didn't like the general look his team have suggested. It was too stark and minimal, and didn't have the elegance I want this year. He said they'd suggest something different to us soon.

In the meantime the boiler at home is still broken and the new plumber we'd set our hopes on failed to turn up yesterday as arranged. Added to that, the fridge has stopped producing ice. Mercury in retrograde indeed. Audrey is about to arrive for my yoga and I must ask her when Mercury is planning to move on.

Audrey says it must be moving on soon . . . she thinks. Meanwhile she finishes the session telling me to imagine my face as a warm beam of sun. By the time I reach the office, any vestiges of sunbeam have disappeared as I'm late and have to walk straight into a meeting with Bay Garnett that's being filmed. Bay is presenting the pictures of her shoot, which mixes vintage clothes with new, and is clearly a bit nervous about whether I'll like them. I think it makes the point well, that the difference between some vintage and some contemporary fashion is almost indiscernible. The pieces look good together. Anyway, if the stock market plummets, as the worst predictions say, we may all be joining Bay in her thrifting excursions.

The afternoon was crowded with decisions to be made without allowing me any time to consider. The Joe McKenna and Jamie Hawkesworth shoot arrived with only one picture of the beautiful boy, Maarten, I had been keen on and the rest of the shoot on the girl they had added only the day before.

It's frustrating when I think I'm getting one thing and it turns into something else. The pictures do have a real point of view and strength but I still think they would have been stronger had they stuck to the original gender-bending idea. I asked if there were any others of the boys we could include. Jamie said he'd take a look.

Most importantly, the shoot we're planning in two days with Rihanna in Paris is wildly over-budget and, for reasons I can't discover, nobody understands how it became so expensive so late. Too late to cancel and too late to do much about it. I look at Kate Phelan's rail of clothes in the fashion cupboard – souped-up rhinestone cowboy with studded leather, and sequinned Tom Ford mini-dresses, Marc Jacobs denim and sparkling Lanvin. Will it look too blingy and stereotypical for a black woman?

Lucinda and I go through the clothes for the shoot with the Duchess of Cambridge that are on rails in the fashion room. There are white shirts and striped sweaters, denim in every shape imaginable (including many pieces I can't imagine the duchess wearing – like a pair of tight dungarees), a sea-green chiffon dress, especially designed by Jenny Packham (sworn to secrecy), a ruffled white creation by Erdem and a deep blue gown by Westwood. We can't tell anyone why we're calling in the clothes, which makes it tricky for Katie Franklin, Lucinda's assistant.

The duchess has made it clear she doesn't want to be dressed as a fashion plate so there are dozens of trench coats, simple sweaters and blazers, but it would be ideal if she could be persuaded into one gown. I'm pleased that we've pulled in so many clothes – three huge rails. Lucinda generally likes to do a very tight edit and have a precise idea of exactly what will be worn in each shot, but on this occasion it's impossible to do that. The priority is not what we want, but what the subject wants.

I've seen pictures of the props that are being taken – checked blankets, sofas, trugs, richly patterned carpets. I ruled out a croquet set, which struck me as too clichéd, but a few gardening props are fine. It's always helpful for photographic subjects to have something to do with their hands. The setting is a huge field and a barn. It looks very flat (as you would expect in Norfolk, where it is taking place).

Like the rest of the crew, I'll be there the night before in a nearby inn. I can't believe it's next week. So close and yet, until it's done, so nerve-rackingly far away. Once we have the pictures it'll be a massive relief.

Jaime Perlman, my creative director, comes in to tell me that she thinks the best plan to get the pictures immediately is for Josh Olins to hand me a hard drive of the shoot before I return to London, but she's not sure he'll want to do this. The key thing is to avoid them being sent by email with attendant lack of security. I'm suddenly worried that I haven't been stern enough about how very important it is that I see the pictures as soon as possible, and tell her she must insist that we get the drive before he flies back to New York. I dread being the person in charge of a magazine that manages to publish pictures that everybody hates of the nation's sweetheart. I'm terrified of a lack of control and wish I could take the photos myself.

19 January

It's pitch black outside the kitchen windows. I've been awake since five and my dreams seemed to interweave metallic gold and green thread with the photo shoot tomorrow and some nameless people all trying to uncover what was going on. I weigh myself and have gained three pounds in anxiety. Others lose weight when they become stressed and I gain it, hoarding water like a camel in preparation for a long trek across a desert.

I've packed three pairs of socks, some waterproof boots and a thermal vest. The radio has just announced it's minus seven in southern England and the temperature is falling. It's hardly a glamorous wardrobe for a day with a future queen but I can only stick so far to *il faut souffrir pour être belle*. The less *souffrir* going on the better, I feel.

I should tell Sam I'll be away tonight. It'll be the first time I've ever lied to him about where I am. Last night before he went to bed he said he was getting a cold, and almost certainly I'll hear a wan voice on the phone hoping for hot lemon and honey and my attention rather than absence. But at least he's an adult now and not the small person I was having to leave so often in the early years. Thank heavens for all those wonderful nannies who made it possible.

I'm going to take a late-afternoon train to King's Lynn and hope that en route I'll work out a programme of activities for the festival so that we can crack on and get some organized. The days are now starting to speed together, after a slow start to the year, and I'm aware of the time shrinking to get everything done for the Centenary issue and, more pressingly, the festival and gala dinner.

Sam emails me, not to say he has a cold but that he's got great marks in two essays. That's the best instant stress-breaker. Once again, motherhood has helped me regain balance. Sam's existence has constantly put into perspective any problems at work. He doesn't even *ask* where I'm going, so my prepared lie is redundant.

Mandy Tucker, HRH's hair stylist, Sally Branka, the make-up artist, and the rest of us are picked up at the station by Gawain Rainey, the on-set producer and general fixer, and driven to a pub near the location. Mandy is wonderfully chatty and we compare observations about Norfolk and how far it is from London, and Gawain points out one of the gates to Sandringham. It's too dark to see much. He says the duchess has seen the clothes and is happy, which is a huge relief. It's odd to be away from home and the office with something so important happening. There is a huge degree of unreality. My room has silver-and-maroon-flocked print wallpaper and a very smart faux-bamboo-looking shower and bathroom. It is stiflingly hot and the windows are tricky to open. All the crew are here and we have dinner together at a long table, talking about everything other than what we're doing the next day.

20 January

We left the hotel early this morning to reach the set, the fields hung with a silvery mist and the sense of bright light somewhere above, but not yet making an appearance. There are very few cars on the road as we drive through calm, pretty Norfolk villages.

We arrive at a building and outhouses, in the midst of fields. They might once have been a couple of farmhands' cottages, two up, two down, but now they're one space and unlived-in. The production team arrived the day before with Josh and Lucinda to set everything up and scout around for locations. Inside it's toasty warm with blazing, wood-burning stoves, rails of clothes lining the walls, a huge wooden table pushed to one side for a make-up station, and a lovely small room with another stove designated as the duchess's dressing room. I want to remember every detail of this day, which I'm so aware will be one of the most exceptional of my life, and I peer into every corner – the prop flowers in a steel bucket in one of the loos, the front doors painted a fashionable duck-egg blue and the walls painted white.

I know it's important that Josh feels confident and hope I'm not projecting my own stress on him. I want him to feel totally supported, not scrutinized, so I keep to myself the areas I'm concerned about – that we get pictures of her smiling (photographers notoriously prefer not and think a smile looks cheap), that we don't spend too long on each shot so that she gets tired and bored, and that we know we've shot a cover relatively early so that we're not trying to do this later when, again, she may be tired and bored.

We've already agreed that we'll keep the cover loose, rather than having a formal pose, but sometimes enforced informality creates its own problems and insecurities. We drink coffee and chat until the small team the duchess has with her arrives, and finally our subject herself, her hair in big rollers and her lovely bright, inclusive smile, is walking through the door behind Mandy Tucker, who is wheeling a small case of hair products. The duchess looks really pretty and attractive, in a parka, skinny jeans and boots, and greets everybody in an easy way, having met Josh and Lucinda and several others the previous day.

Lucinda and I have been through the clothes again and decided that, ideally, we'll try to shoot the cover in a checked Burberry shirt. I know the duchess wants to look real, not as if she's in a *Vogue* construct, and the shirt with its gold buttons and strong colour seems a good option to me. There is the rail of gala gowns,

Westwood, Erdem, Jenny Packham, that Lucinda has brought in case the duchess feels prepared to go that route, but I'm sure that for the cover she will want something more everyday.

We agree that for the first shot, which is often tricky as nobody's warmed up, we'll suggest a blue-and-white-striped dress and a leather apron. It's more costume than real clothes and I'm not sure she'll buy into that, but she gamely puts on what is suggested. Digital photography means that it's possible now to see the pictures as they're shot, and while Josh is shooting her and a vase of flowers in the little dressing room, I can see the pictures coming up on a small screen shaded by a black fabric. She is laughing, completely naturally, and it looks as if sun is shining onto the painted walls. At that moment I know it's going to be okay.

On shoots there is always a cast of thousands but we'd kept this to a minimum, keen to ensure there wasn't a crowd watching and increasing the tension. I've been wildly impressed with everyone we've brought up and how calm and focused and quiet they are – Katie, Lucinda's assistant, patiently putting tape on the bottom of boots to protect them, Sally silently watching, waiting to adjust the make-up, if necessary, Max the prop guy lacing some of the bare branches in the field with blossom (not that you ever see that in the pictures). He had driven up a whole household of blankets, rugs, trugs and tables. Everyone just gets on with their jobs rather than abandoning them for a piece of the action.

There is not much time between shots as everyone is keen to get as much done as quickly as possible but there is still a lot of chat. I've grown to like and respect Rebecca, the duchess's secretary, and Jason, the couple's communications secretary, who are acute, funny and have been unexpectedly nice to work with. They're going to India and Bhutan at the end of the week on a recce for the Cambridges' trip in April. Jason tells me about the work Her Royal Highness has been doing with women in prisons, and we also discuss the state of the American presidential race (he is American), and the EU issue. As I write, I realize that by the time this book is published we'll be on the verge of knowing who the next President of the United States is, which, since Trump has just added Sarah Palin to his team, has the potential to be terrifying.

The duchess is unassuming, gentle and phenomenally polite. We keep asking her if she is all right about doing another picture or wearing a certain piece of clothing, or indeed being made to stand in the freezing cold, and she only replies that she's happy if we are. Of us all, she is the only one never to check her smartphone. Does she read Twitter? Is she on Instagram? I wonder but don't ask. She has the narrowest of waists and, despite two children, there is no bulk at all to her torso. She is also devoid of vanity, scarcely checking herself in the mirror once dressed and never fussing about how she looks. It is quite extraordinary.

We race through the shots. I'd hoped we might get a cover and three for inside, but by the end of the day I think we have seven. Josh feels rushed and I know he would have liked to spend longer on each one but I also know that photographers often feel they haven't quite got the shot. He's obviously unhappy about the first picture with the flowers, but it's one of my favourites and I keep banging on about how lovely it is. By three o'clock Rebecca clearly thinks we should start winding up, but the duchess surprises us all by volunteering to do one more outside because the light is so beautiful. We choose a striped red T-shirt and a pair of navy trousers for the picture hanging over a gate, and in some ways she seems her most relaxed for this one.

Before leaving she makes a point of saying goodbye to everyone, including the assistants, and adds that she hopes we've got what we need.

Everyone is packing up and Josh, Lucinda and I look through some of the shots on the computer. There are so many wonderful pictures, and part of me wants to stick a pin into one from each section and just go with it, rather than worrying about every hand pose, every stray hair. Once you look at pictures with the eye of a surgeon you can so easily miss the overall effect and make the wrong choices.

The landscape here is unbelievably beautiful – with a sky that changes constantly from silver, to blue, to a grey-pink and long sharp shadows. As we're about to leave, a huge white barn owl flies low over us. I resolve to start looking at property sites in the area to see if I can find somewhere to rent. This is a very common reaction of mine to leaving London, and rarely goes much further.

I cannot believe that I'm now on a train home after a day that went more flawlessly than I could ever have imagined. The King's Lynn–King's Cross service is more like a tube carriage than first-class rail, and there's no room in the small space for Sally's two huge cases of equipment, which have to stay in the corridor.

Meet Sam for pasta at the Italian restaurant Essenza in Notting Hill. He thinks I've been interviewing Victoria Beckham, which I am, in fact, doing tomorrow, and asks how it went. I say it was good and that I'm covered with mud because she was doing a photo shoot in a field. Of course I'm fizzing with excitement about the day and can't bear being unable to tell him or anyone else. I think of Josh sitting in the hotel alone, poring over the hundreds of images, and hope he doesn't start over-editing. If you look at something for too long, the way you see it changes, just as when you repeat the same word over and over again, it ceases to make sense. I won't really relax till I have that hard drive in my hand.

21 January

I don't understand Battersea. To me it's a kind of black hole in the city where nothing actually happens and you're never quite sure when you're getting there or leaving. Victoria Beckham's offices are in a warehouse complex here without a name on the downstairs bell or indeed anywhere until you're inside, where a small reception area greets you with a scented candle and a vase of white flowers still tied in their string.

I'm here to interview Victoria for a book being put together by Tania Fares, who is a friend of mine and has raised a lot of money for the British Fashion Council, and journalist Sarah Mower, who works with the BFC. I knew when Tania asked me if I'd interview Victoria that I was going to be snowed under and had tried to avoid being sucked in, but Tania is very persuasive and has helped me in various ways, so I agreed. At that stage it was a dot in the far distance that might, if I was lucky, never become reality.

But it did and Natalie Lewis, Victoria's representative on earth (part Rottweiler, part security blanket), greets me, saying she is sorry Victoria is late but she had the four school runs this morning and an issue to do with casting her show. We sit in Victoria's office, which has a huge wooden trestle-legged table painted in a glossy taupe, more scented candles and another vase of flowers still tied with their string. Natalie had spent Christmas on safari and tells me terrifying stories of their small plane and heat-engendered turbulence. People always tell me scary flying stories, or perhaps I always eagerly ask about them.

Victoria arrives in a pair of Azzedine Alaïa boots with at least eight-inch spike heels and a towering platform, which would certainly have marked her out on all those school runs. She looks very pretty, with her hair back in a long ponytail, cropped wool trousers and a mannish short coat in the same fabric. We chat generally before the interview and I tell her we're going to the greyhound racing at the Wimbledon track with some friends that evening. 'David used to work at Walthamstow,' she says. 'He cleared up the beer bottles at the end of the night.' And, deadpan, 'He's posh, my husband.'

She's become impressively articulate on the subject of her business, describing the design process and how she works with various people on the team. Outside her office, there is a desk area with three assistants ('I don't like to call them assistants') and standing next to one there is a magnum of 1964 Château Latour-Rothschild, which, Victoria said, a woman gave her in the park, wrapped in a tea-towel, during a tea party of Harper's. 'She just said she had been meaning to give me this for moving to London.' Victoria didn't appear to find this particularly odd.

We walk down the galvanized-steel outside staircase to the ground-floor atelier and I keep expecting her heels to get stuck in the grid. Downstairs a large room is filled with men and women, sewing machines, industrial steamers and irons, moodboards and rolls of fabric. 'This is part of the commercial collection that the ladies and gentlemen are working on at the moment,' she says, as she shows me the waffle-knit checked jumper one of the ladies is placing over a stockman, the fabric-covered torso used for fitting clothes. While nobody appears fazed by her appearance there, neither is there great familiarity. I've noticed that is the case with most designers and their ateliers. There is definitely a boss-and-worker structure, although perhaps a visitor to my office would sense the same thing.

When I ask her about her daily routine, she says she does a work-out every morning – 'That's the only time when people don't bother me' – and on Sunday night the family's schedules go up on the fridge: 'So everyone knows exactly what everyone's doing.' She was meant to be going to her fellow Spice Girl Emma Bunton's birthday party the next night but had cancelled to stay at home with Romeo, who is sitting a school exam. 'I was looking forward to it. Having a few tequilas with my friends. But the kids come first,' she says.

She is one of the most driven women I know, and I'm always impressed by the amount she achieves. It's not only about the business but the way she manages to hand out just enough of herself to make you interested and empathetic without ever really feeling you know much at all. So you always want more.

Jaime arrives with the hard drive, which she collected from Josh at King's Cross, and we look at the pictures in my office. It's her first sight of them. I hope she likes them. I think she does. I'm unable to look at them calmly and keep asking her to pull up another, zoom in, zoom out, racing through. I can't remember whether Josh has sent everything I thought we had or not. He has done a selection of each one as a basic start to look at, which we put on a memory stick to move between computers.

During the afternoon I make another attempt to lock down the festival. On my wall I have a timeline pinned up, which shows me exactly how close I am to needing the programme finalized, and as yet still only the same two speakers are firm. Emily Sheffield, Anna Cryer and I meet for a brainstorm and agree that Emily will try to put together a panel of models through the generations, which could be fascinating for our Centenary year. Can we try to get Jerry Hall, Marie Helvin, Twiggy and, say, an eighties girl, like Yasmin Le Bon, as well as a contemporary model talking about the changes and their experiences? We all agree that a fashion *University Challenge*-style quiz would be good, and I think there would be an audience to hear the *Vogue* 100 curator, Robin Muir, talking about the treasures of the *Vogue* archive, the physical space that houses the archive and how the work is kept. The archive has a near-legendary resonance but few are prepared for how small and crowded the library actually is.

By late afternoon everyone is feeling nervous about whether the Rihanna shoot will happen when we learn she still hasn't arrived on set for the shoot she's doing today because she'd been in the recording studio overnight and until ten this morning. Emily, who is doing the interview, and Jaime are meant to be on the dawn Eurostar tomorrow but Rosie Vogel, who does all the bookings and fixing for our fashion shoots, decides to let them have an hour or so more in bed, since we all agree that the likelihood of the designated call time of 10 a.m. working out is most unlikely.

I head to Kensington Palace with the memory stick to see Rebecca and Jason. It's nerve-racking to show them but they seem pleased, although they need to be reassured that it doesn't look too much like a fashion shoot. The next stage will be for the duchess to view them.

23 January

By all accounts the Rihanna shoot did take place but that is about as much as I know. She even appeared by 2 p.m., which the assembled crew felt was way better than expected.

Serendipitously I get a text from a friend saying that a cottage may be available for rent soon on an estate where he rents. It's not Norfolk but it is East Anglia, and it's right on an estuary with the huge skies I love. I'm immediately excited and start planning how we would get there and calculating how I might afford it. This year is so busy that it's ridiculous to think I'll have enough free time to make the most of it, but on the other hand, it would be a fantastic diversion from the work and stress. I also feel that with the timing it might be fated. Perhaps Mercury has finally shifted out of retrograde.

24 January

Sam seems a bit low this morning, and at the very last minute before I leave, I ask if he'd like to come to Paris with me for a couple of nights while I'm at the couture shows. He would, so I call the hotel to ask them to split the bed into twins and we race to St Pancras to buy him a ticket on my train. In the queue for Passport Control I see a mewling baby in a stroller, which reminds me of the first time I brought my son to the shows with me. He was six months old and our nanny, Hayley, came as well. It was lovely to have him there to get back to in the evening and wake with in the mornings. And I suppose I still feel the same, although this time he's coming more to cheer him up than me.

Packing at this time of year is a nightmare. It's far too cold and bleak to contemplate anything spring-like but all my winter clothes appear dull and old. Yesterday I attempted a hit-and-grab on some shops in the hope of finding something with the magic that new clothes can offer to take with me to Paris, but I couldn't find anything bar another grey cashmere jumper of which I have several. Still, it's better than nothing.

25 January

This is my first trip since the Bataclan attacks in November and Paris appears empty. The drive from the Gare du Nord was fast, through dark and ghostly streets until we reached the Champs-Élysées where there was some life. Of course, Sunday night is often quiet in this city and perhaps I was projecting an expectation after the terrorist carnage, but when I arrived at the place Vendôme for the Versace show the impression was enhanced. The majestic square was also dark and empty (particularly since the huge Hôtel Ritz that now anchors it is still closed for refurb) but for one corner where a huddle of paparazzi and press were waiting with a few onlookers, watching for who was entering. Curiously, there seemed to be more press than usual from the UK and more than I had expected from the US. They are famously averse to travelling anywhere that might be considered remotely risky and there was a massive snowstorm on the east coast the previous night that had halted many flights. There were no 'celebs' that I could see, and the usual razzmatazz outside was much dimmed.

Sarah Harris, *Vogue*'s fashion features director, is already seated when I arrive. She will be writing the show reports, which she does quickly and professionally with authority, but also a light touch. They can easily sound so pretentious. Sarah has become a favourite of the street-style paparazzi with her long silver hair and extremely thought-out but minimal style, which includes a lot of denim, grey, navy and white. Her taste is the opposite to the Versace on the catwalk but in its own way as precious and precise. She is also the calmest member of my team, registering only lukewarm on the temperature gauge no matter what the drama.

'So. They think Sarah Burton's got it, right? Apparently it's going to be announced after the show,' she tells me. She's referring to the post of artistic director at Dior, the French fashion house.

'Really? That seems unlikely to me,' I reply. 'She's heavily pregnant, and would she want to leave London?' Sarah shrugs and turns her attention to her iPhone to make notes on the show.

The girls were the usual high-voltage Versace fare – impeccable glamazons in body-hugging outfits, the fabrics slashed to reveal skin, and crystal mesh in white, cobalt, orange and black. Red-carpet gowns and mini-dresses, with the occasional trouser, like the black suit Gigi Hadid wore to open the show. Versace is a brand that sticks to its guns – in their case unashamedly whizz-bang sexiness. It's a good policy in an industry where there is so much competition. At least half the battle of winning the customer must be making sure they know what they're getting when they hear your name. Nobody wants Versace to do midi-skirts and frump shoes. When Donatella comes on at the end to take her bow she has shorter hair, a kind of long bob, which suits her.

Afterwards I meet Sam for a pizza across the road from the hotel.

He says he'd always thought that if you were good-looking and intelligent (which he is), girls would like you. Wasn't that the case? He is feeling bruised by some girl's lack of interest and, of course, as his mother, I'm torn between saying that anybody in their right mind would adore him (*ergo*, there must be something wrong with her) or what an odd notion that is for him to believe. I know that at his age I was constantly being rejected and misreading the level of someone's interest in me and, frankly, that went on for another decade or so.

I suggest he buys a *Pariscope* and finds out everything that's on in the city, including some of the movies in the more art-house cinemas. He says he's already checked out all the museum shows. I know he can get all this information online for free, but I love the thick little booklet, which you can carry in your pocket and have all the details on a page instead of endless scrolling back and forth on a screen.

26 January

This morning I get up and try to creep quietly around since Sam is sleeping but there's a huge amount of phone calls and doorbells ringing. I'm utterly baffled by the new phone in the room. The old one had little buttons with names – restaurant, room service, housekeeping – and you simply pressed them. The new cordless phone has no such buttons and I spend ten minutes trying to find out what number to call to order coffee, unable even to ring Reception or the operator without knowing the necessary numbers. Finally I find a tiny laminated sheet of such information by my bed.

It's easy to forget how beautiful Paris can look in the sunshine when all the gold that tops the many monuments is sparkling, and the low-rise centre, undisturbed by tower blocks and skyscrapers, allows huge expanses of blue sky.

*

I arrive at the Schiaparelli show behind Carla Bruni, who is posing by a step-and-repeat board (love that term!) with the house's official muse-cheerleader, Farida Khelfa. I first heard the phrase for the ubiquitous logo board when we worked with the Ralph Lauren company to launch their Wimbledon wardrobes in 2005. It was also the first time I heard the phrase 'comfort zone' – as in 'We don't want David [Lauren] to be out of his comfort zone,' when he was co-hosting a dinner with me.

Bruni is joking about the photographers needing to Photoshop her but she looks pretty good in leather jeans, ankle boots and a tiny black jacket. Seated next to her is Diego Della Valle, who owns Tod's, a huge leatherwear business his grandfather started as a local shoemaker in the twenties, and who bought Schiaparelli four years ago. He wears his usual thin black scarf, bead bracelets and the little red-and-green button of the Cavaliere, which is like an Italian knighthood and can be bestowed on entrepreneurs. The turnout is very *bon ton*: Daphne Guinness, like a bird of prey with her raven-and-white beehive, seated at the other end of the row from me, and Sabine Getty, the jeweller, one of the younger generation of couture clients.

In the afternoon I nearly miss the Dior show as I get immersed in trying to write up the Victoria Beckham piece, so I ask Jean-Claude, my driver, to high-tail it and we race across the Seine to the Rodin Museum, where the Dior team have constructed a vast box in the gardens for the show. This time the set is mirrored, reflecting the swirls of catwalks that Raf Simons used the season before. Most people agree that the design team at Dior have put together a lovely collection. It's a little softer than those Raf oversaw, the silhouettes less extreme, but there are still the same ideas of proportion and the almost Victorian coats with the techno dresses, the encrusted embroidery, tunic shapes and, this season, an asymmetric neckline that slips off-kilter to one side.

On the way out Bianca Jagger stops me. We have been in touch about a fundraising party next week in honour of our mutual friend the *Sunday Times* foreign correspondent Marie Colvin, who was killed in Homs three years ago. As I type those words I think how horrified Marie would be to see what has happened now in Syria, and how Assad, whom she hated and who in the end took her life, is to some extent back in the bosom of our foreign policy. I think of her in her short dresses with long bare arms and legs, talking, talking. The party is to raise funds for an initiative to help young women working in this field in the Middle East. Bianca says how much she liked what the Dior team had done at the show and then is stopped by a camera crew to give an interview.

At the end of the day I go to the Chanel studio on rue Cambon, where Karl Lagerfeld is doing final fittings for his show. Much to my surprise, Chanel have agreed that Richard Macer can film the meeting. I meet the PR, Jo Allison, in the entrance hall and find Richard there, too, exhausted: the Eurostar he took at five thirty yesterday afternoon didn't arrive until four o'clock this morning. For no apparent reason it was halted some way out of Paris (thankfully not in the tunnel). The lights went off and they must have been there for nine hours. He seemed pretty sanguine about it. I was once stuck in the tunnel for a very long time when I was travelling with Mario Testino. He talks so much that he was a great person to be stuck with, but I was unnerved when he kept making the sign of the cross as the hours passed, and there was still no movement and the water ran out.

When we reach the upstairs studio we meet Laurence Delamare, Karl's right hand at Chanel, who indicates that things are fraught and late, and now is not a good time for cameras. I go in to find Karl surrounded by other journalists with the Italian model Maria Carla in front of him in a long embroidered white dress and styled with eye-liner and a sweeping low bun. On the desk in front of him is a book of Picasso sculptures that have inspired the hair and make-up – such a powerful face carved from stone. Eventually the room thins out and I'm able to talk to him about how British *Vogue* is 100 years old.

'But we don't look back, we look forward,' he says, and mentions that French *Vogue* is ninety-five. Amanda Harlech is, as always, beside him and is pointing out that this is an ecological collection with splinters of wood stitched into the dresses and ties of string and twine. Karl says that last time the collection was all about techno, this time eco, 'but in fashion you have to exploit the moment'. This is something that he is extremely proficient at. Being the creative director of a fashion house is about so much more than designing the clothes and Karl is a *Meister* of messaging – utterly at home with the idea of the power of the image.

He controls the room from the big desk, like a benevolent Bond villain, if such a thing can be imagined. Everyone there responds instantly to his slightest request or comment but in a respectful rather than fearful manner. The girls always seem very fond of him as he examines each in her outfit from behind those famous dark glasses.

Richard has been allowed in and, to my mind, is poking his camera much too close to Karl.

'Mr Lagerfeld,' Richard says, too quietly for Karl to hear. He has to say it again as he moves even closer. 'Mr Lagerfeld. Have you known Alexandra a long time?'

I feel most uncomfortable with this turn in the conversation, sure that Karl will have little interest in talking about me, but he answers very politely if non-committally. He is more interested in telling me about the hologram he has of his cat, Choupette, inside a glass lozenge dangling from his exquisite tiepin.

My chief aspiration for this meeting is to persuade him to speak at the *Vogue* Festival but there are too many people around to broach the subject, even though I'm sitting beside him at the desk. Right at the end of our conversation I bring it up, but he doesn't respond at all. I'll have to try again in another way.

When we leave, Richard says he's pleased, and how well that went, didn't it? I just feel relieved it's over. Constantly there is a split screen in my emotions, an awareness of what is good for the documentary and what is good for me. Not always the same.

I feel stuck because if Karl isn't going to speak I need to move on, but nobody will give me a definite answer.

As always, it's fascinating to see how the sketches and vision in the studio translate to the catwalk and this time the Chanel set is a Japanese-inspired wooden construction, situated in a faux-emerald grass-and-water feature, with a blue sky behind. It is a very calm collection, once the folderol of arrivals is over, conveying the idea of peace and the worth of nature. Cara Delevingne appears in Chanel biker boots and skinny trousers with her large dog and a crowd of minders and paparazzi. Once she takes her seat, the dog is removed by said minders.

For the rest of the day I move between showrooms and shows. At the incredibly beautiful Céline showroom, with its patterned marble floor and colourful flowers on stands, the PR, Annika, says that the American retailers are all talking about 'the crisis in retail'. Given their relentless desire for more and more collections to feed their stores and always something new to draw in customers, they might bear an element of culpability if there is such a crisis. This theme runs through the week. How many clothes do people want? Are there too many collections? She also says that the Chinese are now going on shopping weekends to Japan, which they treat rather as we would a weekend in Paris. A little retail therapy, a little culture – and currently the rate of exchange with the yen is in their favour.

27 January

One of the depressing aspects of the huge expansion of fashion retail is that so many shops are replicated all over the world. There was a time when different cities meant different shops. I would run to Anthropologie and Club Monaco when in New York and Isabel Marant and APC in Paris. But now they are all in London and, irrational as it may be, they have lost some of their lustre. Bringing back a shirt from APC in Paris was just more interesting than being able to buy it in Notting Hill. Even so there are often chinks of time to kill between appointments and looking in the shops is a way to pass it – a girl can drink only so many cups of American coffee, as black coffee is called here.

Schiaparelli is housed in one of the *hôtels* of place Vendôme, and when you look out of the grand third-floor windows, you can see all the gold suns as ornamentation on the balconies that were part of the original design, commissioned by Louis XIV (the Sun King). And that is why Elsa Schiaparelli (whose couture house has always been based in this square) created a perfume stopper of a large crystal sun for one of her scents. Our meeting with Bertrand Guyon, the designer, takes place in a room whose walls are covered with tobacco hessian, a fantastic background for hanging pictures, and I resolve to try this when I next move house. The walls have painted mouldings so you seem to be sitting in a set rather than reality and all around are wonderful pieces of furniture, portraits of the designer, and surreal works of art.

Sam and I go to see the Warhol exhibition at Musée d'Art Moderne, a good distraction from a flood of emails about a problem back at the office. In the National Portrait Gallery catalogue of *Vogue* 100, the last spread of pictures has the photographer Jamie Hawkesworth wrongly captioned as Hawksfield. It is a fantastically irritating mistake but the catalogues are now printed and polythene-wrapped. Jaime Perlman is so worried about upsetting Jamie that she has found a company somewhere in the north of England who will rewrap them all in record time and a team to come in and put a sticker correction into the whole printing. This turns out not to be practical from the gallery's point of view and they won't agree to Jaime's idea. By the end of the day a compromise seems to have been found whereby a certain number that are being sent out to the press will have the amendment in them. The question is when to alert the photographer to the error. I think the sooner the better: to delay breaking bad news is never a good idea. Jaime is less sure.

Emily, who is manning the ship, emails to say she thinks there is too much nostalgia in the Centenary issue. I find this mildly annoying as only last week she thought there was not enough and suggested a big feature tapping various people's memories of the magazine. Of course, the person I'm most annoyed with is myself for not being quite clear about what I'm trying to achieve, and not having time to focus on the detail as much as I should. It's easier when I'm in the office to get a clear overview rather than when I'm in the back of a car in Paris.

Emily is like a glamorous bluebottle buzzing around me with her inky hair. She has brilliant energy and is constantly fizzing with ideas. She is also relentless and emails me to say that the office is going to petition me about putting her idea of Justin Bieber on the cover; she had proposed it a few weeks ago but I wasn't keen.

28 January

There is a taxi strike in Paris this morning, a protest against Uber, and everyone's meetings are being delayed and cancelled. I'm meant to meet Alber Elbaz for breakfast at my hotel. He was fired from Lanvin earlier in the year and has been speaking out against how impossible he thinks the contemporary treadmill is for designers. I have just ordered coffee when a message arrives that he won't be joining me because of the strike. I call him straight away and he says his driver is frightened to pick him up from the outskirts of the city as the taxi drivers are stoning and chucking eggs at hire cars (I imagine his looks like one of the chauffeured cars we all use at the shows). I'm sad to miss him and immediately eat two croissants, which up till now I have avoided, to compensate for the disappointment.

The night before, Tom and Ruth Chapman of Matches.com gave a dinner for Vetements, the new cool brand on the block owned by Georgian brothers Demna and Guram Gvasalia. Demna has been picked to head up Balenciaga in a radical hiring since Vetements is a collective that has been working on the concept of street and everyday clothing and is deliberately positioned in opposition to the established big old houses. Even so, one of their hoodies costs

£415. This doesn't seem to be a deterrent as a huge number of stores want to stock them and the hoodies are completely sold out.

The dinner is held in a tapas place with long, high sharing tables where food arrives slowly, one dish at a time. The thinner guests slide it around their plates, stir it around the bowls, pick up a fork, then put it back down and generally toy with it, while the fuller figured get down to the serious business of placing it in their mouths.

Just before leaving Paris I visit the Musée de l'histoire de l'Immigration. It's a vast art-nouveau building with a carved stone bas-relief around its whole exterior. I wonder who paid for that kind of work at the time it was built. Upstairs there is a permanent exhibition on the subject of immigration, with old camera footage of arrivals and black-and-white pictures of immigrant communities in France – the Algerians arriving in Marseille, a group of Africans in a French square. One glass case shows the suitcase that belonged to a young man from India, with his six-sided photo cube of religious imagery, a cotton shirt, a razor, an orange plastic comb and a small framed picture. In the light of all the arguments about religious and secular identity in France, I had thought there might be some contemporary commentary on this but there was nothing. Still, it was moving and sad, and certainly made the point that migrant communities need to stay together when they first arrive in order to make the transition to another world, often without any family.

29 January

Unpacking rates pretty near the top of the list of my least favourite activities. There is something particularly unsatisfying about the pile of laundry, scraps of paper gathered on a trip, washbag to be decanted. It should reflect the happiness I always feel about coming home but instead the cases sit there reproachfully until they're emptied.

The Institute of Contemporary Arts is celebrating its seventieth anniversary this year and I have agreed to be part of a group photo of well-wishers. When I was in my late teens I spent hours there watching Andy Warhol films in the tiny cinema and browsing in the bookstore. Being there made me feel that I was the kind of person who went to the ICA – that is, arty, alternative, sophisticated, probably dressed in black. I hoped I might meet Patti Smith, or somebody just like her, if I hung out there. So I've always had a fondness for it. For a brief period in the eighties I sat on the council board when it had to decide whether to allow a body-piercing artist with HIV to perform in a show that required blood-letting. I seem to remember that I wasn't particularly keen on the idea, then realized I had *not* become the adventurous kind of person I imagined I would be when I was watching those grainy black-and-white films.

Before the shoot I meet Betty Woodman, the eighty-seven-year-old ceramicist, who is installing her show there from a roomful of wooden crates. She is a tiny, vivid figure, wearing curious cream tights with a mauve pattern, like bruising, and multi-coloured spectacle frames as she directs the unpacking. Those of us there for the shoot all gather outside the entrance on the Mall for the picture. Afterwards, Gregor Muir, the director of the institute, pulled out of a box a brightly coloured paper pop-art jacket that Peter Blake had designed for them in 1978 and gave it to me. Back at the office I ask someone to see if we could copy the idea of a paper jacket to go on sale at the festival. Who could we get to design something as good? Who would manufacture it for us?

Then Jaime and I go through all the pictures again of the duchess on Jaime's personal laptop. It's the first time I've been able to look at Josh's edit slowly with all the options. At times, as Jaime flicks them back and forth, it's like one of those spot-the-difference children's games – a strand of hair there or not, a finger moved or not.

At lunchtime I go to the hairdresser's. Just before I leave there, Sam arrives on the other side of the salon for the biannual cut I treat him to. I go up to say hello and he looks at me, confused. 'What's happened to your hair?' It has been blow-dried with big rollers so that the style will last, but I look like somebody out of a fifties sit-com. His comment concerns me so I spend the whole taxi journey back to the office tugging the curl down and negating a large amount of the time and effort the stylist put in.

All in all though it's been one of the days when I feel privileged to have my job. 'That sounds like a good day,' David says, as I fry sausages for supper as soon as I get home.

I've returned from my first sight of the hang of *Vogue* 100 at the National Portrait Gallery. It's completely wonderful and I simply can't wait for it to open and show it off.

You enter through the large double doors to the galleries and immediately ahead there is the flickering fashion film footage, which gives the show a powerful immediacy and makes you want to step forward into the rooms to watch: Cara Delevingne blowing pink bubbles, Karen Elson dancing in Bhutan, Edie Campbell as a mud-spattered jockey. To the left the walls have been painted a rich dusty blue-grey, which makes the space look very different from usual, and the long gallery appears slightly narrower. To the right are rooms of the work commissioned on my watch. I'd been concerned that the contemporary images might not stand up alongside the historical but the huge prints are luscious and compelling and utterly convincing as pieces worthy to be hung on those walls. Although there are some fashion pictures, in general the edit for this period gives a real idea of the culture of the age through the filter of *Vogue*.

Most of the work is still not hung and none of the big glass cases that will be installed have been filled with the planned prints and issues, but the enfilade of different-coloured rooms travelling back from the sixties to 1916 are *in situ* although still empty. It was a brilliant idea of Patrick Kinmonth's to stage it in this way.

Richard Macer and Charlotte Rodriguez, who were filming my first view, travelled back to the office with me and I was pleased that they seemed as excited by what they'd seen as I was. 'It's a real privilege,' Richard said, fiddling with the lens on his camera. He also said it was great to see me so pleased and happy, adding that it isn't something they've seen very often!

30 January

I'm 37,000 feet above the ground and travelling at 560 miles per hour, or so it says on the map in front of me on this flight to Milan. I'm also feeling thoroughly queasy, which is partly my flying anxiety and partly my total stupidity in waking up with a hangover from dinner last night. David and I went to my friend Flora Fraser's and I was so gripped by the conversation between fellow guests Charles Saatchi and former Lib Dem cabinet minister Chris Huhne that I drank way too much white wine. Charles, whether genuinely or simply to be controversial, described both Putin and Trump as 'magnificent', in his flat London accent. He considered their general 'magnificence' made the question of whether we were going to have a referendum on the EU utterly inconsequential since the only relevant conversation would be between those two. Chris is a passionate Europhile, and is looking extremely well in the aftermath of his jail experience. He didn't appear remotely rattled and was keen to hammer home his own pro-Europe stance. He asked Charles if he had ever done business with Russia. Charles said, yes, all the time, but he'd never been there. We left at the same time as Charles and his new girlfriend, Trinny Woodall. Just before he left, as we stood in the hallway, he grabbed me and pulled me under one of the overhead spotlights and peered behind my ears. 'You haven't changed,' he said, explaining that he was checking to see whether I'd had work done. Weird, undoubtedly.

As the flight was preparing for take-off the pilot warned that there might be a bumpy first part but it would clear once we were past Paris. In fact, it has been completely smooth and we are now somewhere above Lyon but I'm worried that the bumps have moved and are now an advance party just waiting for us to reach them. How much do I HATE flying? I want to go to sleep so that I don't know I'm up here, but like most frightened flyers, I also feel that it's only by my keeping vigilant that the plane will stay in the sky. I make the mistake of looking out of the window and see the Alps. Along with oceans, mountains are my second least favourite sight from a plane. How would one land in an emergency? When I first came to *Vogue* in 1992, I remember sitting next to Tom Ford on a flight back from Milan – he had just started designing for Gucci. He was incredibly kind to me as the plane jolted around and told me it always did that over the Alps: there was nothing to worry about. I've always been grateful to him for that.

The reason I'm on this plane is to go to Dolce & Gabbana's Alta Moda show being held tomorrow at La Scala. At this point no fashion show seems a valid enough reason to be hurtling through the sky. The pilot has just announced that there is very poor visibility in Milan and the stewardesses are now asking us to switch off all electronic devices in preparation for an auto-land. I realize this is, no doubt, normal procedure but it doesn't feel like that to me. It's also going to deprive me of my landing survival kit of loud music and trying to concentrate on a round of Spite and Malice on my iPad.

Of course, as soon as we land, I do a 180-degree flip and feel excited and very lucky to be in Italy. In front of me a woman in chinchilla is clutching cobalt-blue Kuwaiti passports. I wonder if she and the people I presume to be her husband and daughter are arriving for the show.

I'm collected by a driver and drop my luggage before going to visit the Pinacoteca Ambrosiana, an extraordinary and relatively little known Milanese historical treasure. Federico Marchetti, who is a benefactor of the place, has kindly arranged a private tour for me but I hadn't expected to be guided around by the president of the museum. First, he seats me in the old library where he tells me every book is worth at least a million euros and then we tour the galleries, with a very serious and pretty young woman guide. Highlights for me are the ancient books designed by the man who invented printed punctuation (I had never stopped to wonder how that had come about), a Caravaggio still life of a basket of flowers, and a Leonardo da Vinci portrait of the Duchess of Milan, with her beautifully styled hair tied under her chin. But my favourite is a lock of thick blonde hair said to be from the head of Lucrezia Borgia, who has always fascinated me since I discovered her in Jean Plaidy's brilliant historical novels as a child. Her stories were my *Hunger Games*, I suppose – the tales of royalty, intrigue, battles and romance every bit as compelling to my imagination – and with the added benefit of being based on fact.

A dinner has been organized for the evening and a change of plan has shifted it from a restaurant to Stefano and Domenico's Milanese headquarters. When I go down to the foyer a group of international press has gathered, along with Nicholas Cullinan, who has also been invited. The party is held in a series of rooms quite unlike most offices, the red walls hung with large screen-print portraits of the designers, along with rococo velvet chairs and candelabra dotted around. Plates of lasagne and pasta are handed out while tables are laden with trays of colourful small cakes and croissants stuffed with sweet creams. Italian fashion houses always hold carb-fest dinners, which are delicious but odd for a group of people who are unusually weight-conscious.

Dolce & Gabbana launched their Alta Moda shows four years ago. It is Italian couture and therefore, their theory goes, it should be shown in the country where it is made and which, in the case of this duo, it is inspired by. There are a large number of clients present for the two-day event, all in Dolce clothes and mainly from outside Western Europe: Dubai, Qatar, Kuwait, Russia, and several have flown in from Switzerland. What at first appeared to be an indulgence by the duo has turned into a twice-yearly experience that their clients clearly enjoy. It's an opportunity for total immersion in the world of the designers as well as effective marketing. They mingle and chat and they have even created bespoke handbags to mark the occasion, such as the one I find in my hotel room – a dusty pink embroidered velvet concoction. The number of orders has increased each season and the guests not only come to shop but to network and, of course, to show off their collection of the designers' clothes. If you have a wardrobe with dresses costing this amount you need opportunities to wear them, and here there is an audience of other people as interested in fashion as you are. Where else would a large part of the guest list be wearing transparent lace tops over satin bras and corsets, complete with gilded headdresses? One man I meet wears a chain around his neck with a jewelled hourglass in which miniature diamonds trickle through the waist instead of sand. To most of us, it's another world.

Today is the main womenswear show at La Scala and even the most cynical couldn't fail to be moved by the pair's excitement at being the first designers to show at this theatre, which has a huge emotional potency for the Milanese.

The audience are seated on the empty stage of the opera house and, on seeing the number of men wearing colourful Dolce satin pyjama suits, Nicholas, next to me, wonders whether they would be allowed on the school run in Harrogate where the headmistress has just banned parents from rolling up in pyjamas for drop-off. The models emerge from the back of the empty auditorium to an operatic soundtrack – Verdi, Puccini. Their clothes are, as ever, fantastical: bejewelled cloaks and vast headdresses, fur-trimmed opera coats and gowns embroidered to resemble the illustration of an opera programme, perfect black cocktail dresses and enormous tulle skirts with aprons of silk, illustrated with painted sketches of grand Milanese days gone by. It has absolutely nothing to do with clothes for real life, but while I'm sitting among an audience who are actually wearing some of these pieces it makes a kind of sense. There is an exuberance, pride and joy in the indulgence on display that is infectious.

Stefano and Domenico are utterly politically incorrect and constantly getting into trouble for upsetting someone or other, such as last year's spat with Elton John over surrogacy. I've become very fond of them, while knowing that they are capricious and the affection we have for each other could disappear in a moment if they don't feel appreciated by the magazine. But at least you know where you are with them.

We are moved off the stage and into the theatre for a short period, then the rococo space darkens and the stage opens for beautifully dressed tables to emerge for lunch. It's an incredible tableau lit by candelabra from above.

After lunch I go back to the hotel, and since it's a beautiful sunny day, I go for a run. The local dusty park is like parks everywhere on a Sunday afternoon, with parents gathered in the playground displaying a mixture of boredom, pride and anxiety as they watch their offspring tumble around. My iPod says I have worked off 360 calories, which won't even cover one spoonful of the risotto Milanese served at lunch.

David calls and says he's bought the food I asked him to get for next week and that he's pleased with himself because the Camden branch of the Lib Dems were collecting clothes for the Calais migrants outside our local farmers' market and he has given them some of his jeans, shirts and socks. I say I hope he's given them some socks that don't have holes in the toes since most of his do. To which he says that's typical of me, and asks why I have to say things like that.

FEBRUARY

3 February

Today is really quite horrible. It's one of those days when every text and email I open tells me something I don't want to hear. The combination of trying to achieve the right mix of Tim Walker's portraits for the Centenary issue – at the moment there are too many models and too few women working in other fields – getting the right guests for the big opening of *Vogue* 100 at the National Portrait Gallery, and confirming the speakers I want for the festival is beyond stressful. It's one step forward, two steps back. If somebody agrees to one thing, they're immediately followed by another dropping out.

It's at times like this that I feel as if I've been doing this job for too long. How often do I need to stress about the names on a guest list? But then I think, for example, of a young friend of mine who has just received a breast-cancer diagnosis and try to find a sense of proportion. Guest-list management is definitely hellish but it's nothing compared to being sick. Right now the number of people I know with cancer is making the landscape resemble a battleground with no way to dodge the cannon fire. There doesn't appear to be any logic as to who gets hit. The fact that I'm waking up in the middle of the night worrying about the contents of the Centenary magazine seems utterly ridiculous.

There is a lunch reception at St James's Palace in honour of the Landmark Trust. David and I hand in our phones, as is always required, and walk down the long, carpeted corridor and into a huge state room where the Prince of Wales arrives soon after us for a meet-and-greet. Small groups of people he might like to meet are corralled in advance for him so that he has a seamless path of conversation as he progresses through the room while bowls of chicken and mushrooms on rice are handed around on trays. There is a large amount of wine on offer although most people aren't drinking because it's lunchtime. It feels strange to see my generation all there, the men grey-haired and suited with their name badges pinned on and the women in long buttoned-up jackets and court shoes. One tells me that a friend of hers had looked at me and said disapprovingly, 'Well, she's just wearing a grey jumper. I suppose *we*'re all over-dressed.' But it was my *smart new* grey jumper!

Now I suppose we represent the Establishment. Where did that renegade youth go? I spoke briefly to the architect Amanda Levete, who is designing the new wing at the V&A and whom I remember at school in London as a much cooler, older girl in our unofficial uniform of striped Biba T-shirt under a Laura Ashley smock. I doubt her style of architecture is very much to Prince Charles's taste but even so she's here.

I didn't manage to speak with Prince Charles as I had to rush back early to the office to firefight and besides I don't know enough about the Trust to have had anything interesting to tell him. At the moment I'm not really interested in anything other than my own problems and achievements, which I readily acknowledge is not making me the best company. David is being saintly about this, although I must surely be on borrowed time.

Jaime comes into my office to say that the gold foil *Vogue* logo she wants on the Centenary issue is very expensive, and that Stephen Quinn, our publishing director, who, through advertising, makes all the money we spend, has put his foot down and won't pay for it. Jaime is a delicate figure with bleached blonde hair and usually very high black heels. She isn't necessarily very vocal but that doesn't mean she doesn't have extremely strong opinions, and I can see on this occasion she is cross and feels let down. I go into his office and negotiate, explaining that we really do need to make the cover look splendid, and although I don't really think that any dedicated *Vogue* buyer will be influenced by whether or not the logo is gold foil, I think it will add to the 'collectability' factor that will pick up some floating voters. Anyway, if nothing goes wrong, this issue will be hugely collectable and in its own way historic.

I offer to pay half of the costs out of my editorial budget rather than his production budget, which is where things like gold foil logos would normally be paid from, and for some wonderful reason he says he'll pay the whole lot. I love Stephen. He's one of the great magazine publishers of our age. Truly a magazine lover and completely passionate about *Vogue*. Sometimes he annoys me more than anyone outside my family, but more often he is the best and most enthusiastic business partner I could have.

4 February

I'm suddenly very nervous about whether we have the right mix for the Centenary issue. Maybe it *is* too historical and referential. I've been thinking about this particular magazine for so long but, as is my way, didn't plan anything until relatively the last minute and now I'm swamped by a lack of confidence about what we have. I know I wanted to look forward, not only back, but it's very difficult to think of anything completely contemporary that I feel sure is worthy of the mix. What is not going to seem random when someone looks back in a decade from now? But we probably do need to come up with an idea that is more about life today. The closest we have is the possibility of a story with Jennifer Saunders and Joanna Lumley around the *Ab Fab* film coming out this year. This has its own nostalgia but the film will be new. So far we haven't managed to find a photographer who can work with the dates they are available. With all the logistics involved in every single story, it's easy to forget that the end result is going to be exciting. Sometimes I have to force myself to seize a moment to feel pleased by a small achievement. Otherwise it's all about the problems.

We had a meeting about the phoney cover we're creating this morning, and it looked so good that I almost, but not quite, regretted that we weren't actually using it. Jaime had done a really elegant working of the number 100 on a matt white with a silver *Vogue*. I have suggested that Richard Macer film the meeting so that he'll be able to track the phoney story in the documentary, but when he asked me why we were doing a typographic cover I'm sure I sounded unconvincing, explaining that it was almost impossible to think of an appropriate person to put on the cover. It was true, though, that before I knew HRH had agreed I had indeed been planning something just like the one we were looking at today.

I need to get a final edit to Kensington Palace, and Jaime and I are going to come into the office on Saturday so we can use the printer and see the pictures full size before getting them something to see for Monday.

I have just been back to the National Portrait Gallery, and more of the exhibition is now installed. The illuminated three-sided Toblerones right at the entrance look just like the most delicious sweeties with their prettily colour-coded covers inside, and the forties room, with blood-red walls and blood-red lacquer-framed pictures by Cecil Beaton, Clifford Coffin and Lee Miller, is really gorgeous. Stephen and Jaime came with me and both saw it for the first time. Stephen, who has the Irish gift of the gab, was pretty well silenced by the spectacle, which was really very moving, and when we left, Jaime said she'd nearly cried. This whole thing is very emotional for us all, and as the days go by and the work gets greater and the focus tighter, it becomes even more so.

On top of this I must buy some new clothes. I have weeks of events and fashion shows coming up and nothing to wear. Clearly

'nothing' is a relative term as I have two cupboards full of clothes, but nothing I have is new and I'm meant to look like somebody who has new clothes.

5 February

In the taxi on the way home from the première of *Zoolander 2* (surely one of the worst films ever) last night, I read an email from Christopher Bailey announcing that he's changing the Burberry shows. Instead of showing spring/summer in the autumn and the reverse in the spring, the next shows will be of the clothes that will go immediately into the stores. And mens- and womenswear will be shown simultaneously. This is big news in the business. Many people have been waiting for an influential brand to take a step to change the way the fashion shows operate, and it looks like Christopher is the one to have prised the existing system open.

When I got into work today, everyone was talking about what it might mean. We had been about to post a story on the website about this whole debate, but looking at it again, in the light of this news, I saw that it was over-complicated and the emphasis lay in the wrong place. We hadn't planned to run it today but now we needed to get it up quickly and simplify it to make it more interesting and more relevant to more people. What was the effect of the Burberry announcement? Who would it affect and how? Working out how much we're writing for our own industry and how much for the considerably larger readership of the website is an ongoing question, and with issues like this, the call can be tricky to make.

Was this move the start of something that could, in the long run, affect magazines like *Vogue* quite dramatically? At the moment we photograph clothes two, three and four months in advance of publication. At its most basic summation, if the shows are to be about clothes that will be immediately in the stores we will have no advance sight of them and that will make it impossible for us to shoot our stories with them. Or we'll have to go to previews in the showrooms, which will be far less interesting than the shows.

Christopher and I are booked to have lunch together today – who would have known it would be such an important day to get the scoop straight from him? He has one of the biggest jobs in fashion worldwide and constantly experiments with new ways of selling, but he brings to mind the phrase 'bright-eyed and bushy-tailed'. He is always smiling, incredibly friendly and open when you meet him face to face, and he is such a contrast to the very tightly controlled, heavily 'copy-in' culture he oversees at Burberry where a million people are involved with any small detail. I had a doctor's appointment before lunch so he schleps over to the Chiltern Firehouse, which is near Harley Street, to accommodate me on a day when he could probably have done without the journey across town.

Christopher is very convincing and manages to appear positive and sure without seeming arrogant. Both at lunch and in the interviews I read today about this move he admits it is unclear how several aspects of the plan will actually work. But his overriding conviction is that there is no logic to the current method of showing clothes months in advance that no one can buy at that point. That all the excitement you can generate in a show is wasted (expensively) by people being unable to translate that immediate desire into sales. Imagine, he says, the show being live-streamed into Bergdorf Goodman and then the customer being able to turn round and buy what they've just seen. He also feels that production chains at all ends of the business will just have to speed up and, without saying it, clearly thinks that magazines will have to be part of that. It's obvious he wants his collections to feature in *Vogue*, and to gain the stardust that a wonderful shoot sprinkles on them, but it's equally obvious that he has no idea how this will pan out. I'm not sure he's right about this as a direction of travel but it's exciting that someone is shaking up the show model.

Discussion about this takes up most of the meal but at the end we manage a bit of personal chat, like his move to Gloucestershire from Yorkshire. His weekend commute had changed from him and Simon having a civilized drink on the evening train north to a five-hour drive with their babies and dog, which means the nearer destination makes more sense. And how we're loving *War and Peace* on the BBC and, in particular, Lily James acing in it as Natasha.

Back at the office Radio 4's *Today* programme is asking if I will be interviewed on Monday with the model Rosie Nelson, who last year headed up a petition about models being badly treated and encouraged to be unhealthily thin. The only point of my being on the programme is meant to be to publicize the opening of the National Portrait Gallery show but they obviously want to turn the conversation into a debate about BMI so I cancel. I have three television interviews after that and I don't want to start the day being harangued unnecessarily about something that isn't relevant to the exhibition.

Danielle Bennison-Brown is booked in to give me a presentation on *Vogue* Video. Danielle is new guard – very articulate and sure, another who obviously thinks she's walking with the dinosaurs but who appreciates what *Vogue* as a brand has to offer. She looks incredibly young with no make-up, straight hair, spectacles and chewing gum, but it turns out that her jeans, hoodies and sweaters are usually from the most expensive fashion houses or definitely the cool brands, like Céline and Vetements.

As she clicks through her laptop presentation my overwhelming thought is that I don't know how to put all those slides and bullet points on a screen myself. Like many things of that kind I'm reliant on someone else, a state of affairs I'm uncomfortable with, and once again I make a pledge to myself that I will do a crash course after all the Centenary stuff is over. It's the same with mobile phone numbers that I intend to memorize in case of a mobile-less emergency. Why don't I know Sam's and David's numbers by heart?

She explains her strategy, which is aimed at driving large numbers of 'millennials' to our videos. That word always makes me picture a huge army of robot-like creatures marching on the place. Surely people born in the late nineties aren't really as different as marketing terminology likes to make out.

Like everything digital, which I'd hope would bring something new and exciting, the scheme appears to rely on celebrity names with large social-media followings. It's so depressing that all the technological advances have, if anything, taken us backwards, encouraging a narrower and less intelligent focus for content. If we make videos featuring people with huge numbers of followers, they will theoretically post the video and we will benefit from their numbers looking at it. All well and good if what they're doing is interesting, but in the end it so often comes down to a pretty girl saying whether she prefers flats or heels, coffee or herbal tea.

There is room in the strategy for more interesting videos but, due to the prevailing click-bait mentality, they are regarded as second division since they won't attract anything like the massive numbers needed to make an impression in the digital universe. Intriguingly one of the things Danielle's department has learned is that if you have an online series it's best to put it up at a regular time every day or week. Given that television is now resigned to people watching their favourite programmes as much by catch-up as by the schedule, it strikes me as a curious inconsistency.

One of their thoughts is to do a *Lunch with Vogue* series, as a format for filmed interviews, but she tells me this is unlikely to include models since, ludicrously but predictably, IMG (one of the biggest model agencies) has a contract clause that forbids filming any of their girls eating.

Right at the end of the day I discover that the costs on Tim Walker's Hall of Fame portfolio are now dangerously high and he is proposing a truly wonderful idea of a picture of Kate Moss turning into a dragon based on a 1920s illustration. The budget for that one shot is coming in at nineteen thousand pounds because of the cost of creating the dragon, so it's totally out of the question. I need to talk to him. He's doing such a great job, from the little I've seen so far, and is putting so much time and effort into this story that I don't want to be a downer. But we don't have that money.

6 February

I have a completely free Saturday, apart from working on the June cover for a bit in the office, and decide to go into the centre of town to look for some new clothes.

I am breaking my own rule of avoiding shopping for special occasions as invariably I don't find what I want, and probably don't even really know what that is, which makes the catch even more elusive. I find myself on the fashion floor of Selfridges, which stocks every conceivable designer, utterly lost as to which direction to turn. Problem number one is that I don't know where to find anything. I am the editor of *Vogue*. Surely this should not be happening. I should know the map of Selfridges' fashion floor like the proverbial back of my hand (incidentally, does anyone know much about the back of their hand?). I decide to approach it as I would an unfamiliar supermarket and search via categories. Categorization and classification was one of the few things I enjoyed in my social anthropology degree – what can be paired with what through use, familiarity or genesis? It kind of works when you're trying to find mustard or paella rice but less so with designer clothing.

I'm looking for the Japanese designer Sacai's second line, which I hope to find by asking at the main Sacai section. My classification strategy fails at the first hurdle since it doesn't occur to me that it will be sitting next door to the Italian fashion house of Moschino. Sacai is a fairly conceptual Japanese brand and Moschino almost the complete opposite. As I arrive at the corner, I'm greeted by a young man called Caleb with 'Hi, Alexandra.' On seeing my blank look, he tells me he did an internship at *Vogue*. 'I called in some pieces for the Galliano shoot with Kate Phelan,' he tells me, with great pride in the memory. That shoot was with Tim Walker a few years back just when Galliano was emerging from his exile post leaving Dior, and we agree that it was a very 'special' shoot. 'What are you looking for?' he asks.

'Sacai Luck?'

He says he doesn't think they carry it any longer but the brand manager is in today and he'll check with her.

While waiting for this information I wander off through rails of Victoria Beckham dresses (the amount they stock means she must do very well for them), which are next door to Stella McCartney. In the department-store world the issue of 'adjacencies', who each brand sits next door to, is vitally important to both them and the store. Some brands won't agree to be stocked if they don't feel their neighbours are quite up to scratch or reflect on them in the way they wish. It's a bit like buying a home, I suppose. Anyway, Victoria has Antonio Berardi and Roland Mouret in her neighbourhood, with Stella across the way, and opposite Stella there was Saint Laurent, so that seemed a fairly prime position to me.

I find two dresses I like on Stella's rail but not in my size. I return to Caleb, who confirms that there is no Sacai Luck in Selfridges but he has read my first novel, *Can We Still Be Friends*, and passed it on to his mum. I thank him and, like all novelists, don't miss the opportunity to alert him to the fact that my second will be out in paperback in a couple of months.

On the way to look at Stella's dresses in her own store I drop into Jigsaw, which has really good, well-priced, easy clothes and I could do with a few pairs of their trousers, which fit me well. As I riffle through their rails a man comes up and says he thinks he knows who I am – aren't I editor-in-chief of *Vogue*?

'I saw the shoes and I thought those are quirky shoes. It's nice to see something quirky on a Saturday afternoon.' I'm wearing a pair of huge white Stella brogues that she gave me. I agree that they are kind of *quirky*. It's probably a rare occasion that I'm wearing something that someone like him would expect to see on a Saturday on an editor-in-chief of British *Vogue*. Even so I can't find anything to buy there today.

When I reach Stella's shop I discover both dresses in my size but they couldn't fit me worse, most disappointing as they are lovely – one in black with embroidered silk flowers and a low neck and the other a flower-printed dress with daisies.

Jaime is in the empty *Vogue* offices when I arrive and we look through all of our edit of the HRH shoot again and I ask her to put a gold logo and 'HRH The Duchess of Cambridge' on our favourite cover options. When you put on the *Vogue* logo, it changes the image hugely in a way I can't quite analyse. Some of the best photographs don't work in that context because covers must have an immediacy that often a more intriguing and rich picture doesn't possess. It's great to see them all printed out, which we can do because no one else is around, and for the first time, I get a sense of what the story may look like in the magazine.

★

I meet my mother at Piccadilly Circus to see *Janis*, the Joplin documentary, which has just opened. Mum doesn't know much about her music but says she knows Joplin 'came to a grisly end'. I don't know much of her music either. At the time she seemed too shrieking and noisy for my taste – I preferred mellow stuff like Carole King's *Tapestry* and Melanie's *Candles in the Rain*. But the film makes me want to listen to all her albums with a new appreciation of that incredible bluesy voice. Her clothes throughout are wonderful, and although she has a plain if expressive face, she has a wonderful figure with long slim legs and small breasts. There is one shot of her in concert where they home in on her feet moving. She's wearing a metallic-knit flared trouser suit with gold shoes that looks like something fresh out of this season's Gucci.

As I type this diary, an email comes through from Scarlett Conlon who works on our online team alerting me to a piece of breaking fashion news. Vetements have just announced that they are to abandon the conventional ready-to-wear schedule to show their collection, nearly three months earlier, at the same time as couture. It's interesting and possibly a bit crazy that a new brand with very much a cult following is being paid such attention but these are febrile days in the industry and it definitely feels as if another building block of the fashion calendar is being pulled from the bottom. By the end of the week I may be standing among a collection of bricks needing to be rebuilt in an entirely different configuration.

9 February

Last night was the patrons' dinner at the National Portrait Gallery, and it was the first time the whole show was open to view. It looked brilliant. David and I were invited and I kept wanting to tell people I didn't know what to look at and urge them to my favourite covers and articles in the glass showcases. Just as we were all moving upstairs to dinner I spoke to one man who said he had only come this evening for his wife and had thought he would be bored since he wasn't a fashion kind of person. But he wasn't bored at all. He was really impressed. That was wonderful to hear.

Now it is all there in a really rich and fascinating mix, from the Lee Miller war images to the projection room that mimics the way that, until the nineties, we would view transparencies, the audible click-click of the projector as it went through a box of 35mm slides, to make a final choice. Nick Knight came to the dinner with his wife, Charlotte, and I rushed them into the lightbox room where three of his pictures glow on the wall, a spiral of pink like a dress turned into powder, a mouth painted deep purple with a Mikimoto black pearl between white teeth, and Christy Turlington in a sequinned fuchsia mini-dress we shot one couture week in the sculpture garden at the Rodin Museum in Paris. I remember we called the story 'She is D.I.S.C.O.' after an early eighties song. Nick looked suitably impressed by his own contribution, which has been pretty substantial over the past two decades. Not only, I thought, pleased with his work, which he usually is, but pleased to see it included there.

At dinner I sat between Nick Cullinan and Leon Max, with whom I'm hosting tonight's big private view. Leon and Yana had spent Christmas in Mustique and they had clearly enjoyed all the social razzmatazz, though he said he nearly died of boredom in the first week when hardly anyone else was there. He wants to build a modern house from scratch and is putting aside two hours every week to work with an architect on ideas. But not on Mustique. The house he wants to build wouldn't work there. When we stayed with him at Easton Neston for a night last summer, he had shown us round the gardens, pointing out plans for new landscaping. I asked him how it was going and he showed me some pictures on his phone. I had really wanted to ask him what he thought about his life now, so very different from his childhood: the journey from the Soviet Russia of that time to private jets, stately homes and the fashion business is like the plot of a blockbuster novel. But just as I was about to get to this subject we all turned as the next course arrived. Leon had Zaha Hadid on his other side in an enormous ostrich cape so she looked just like Big Bird.

I spent this afternoon moving yellow and green Post-its around on a paper seating plan. Leon is giving a dinner in the Victorian galleries after tonight's party and Sacha, who has been organizing most of it, has been driven to her sickbed by the stress of the whole thing. As per usual, around lunchtime people who said they couldn't come originally had changed their mind while others dropped out. It was an impossible task: as soon as we thought we'd nailed it, there was another change. Lara Stone is coming. Ten minutes later she isn't. Juergen Teller, who has flu, is now going to make it. Photographer Alasdair McLellan can now come but Natalie Massenet drops out. Someone should invent a game app – Party Planning. It could beat Candy Crush.

At home I have my make-up done by Amelie, who has to work around my trying to read the seating plan on my phone as Sacha, who has forced herself from her sickbed, and I rework it with the latest changes. I ask Amelie if she can paint the lip liner a little above my lip line to give me larger lips. 'You mean like Kylie Jenner?' she asks.

'Exactly,' I reply. I have no idea what Kylie Jenner's lips look like.

When I finally check the mirror I have the kind of lips Ivana Trump had in the eighties, huge and glossy. With heavy eye make-up, too, I bear a distinct resemblance to a different Jenner. I tell Amelie that I can't do the lips *and* eyes thing and rub the lips off. She asks me who I'm most looking forward to seeing tonight. But it's not like that. What I'm looking forward to seeing is the culmination of years of planning and discussion come alive with guests.

We have invited so many that the galleries should be full and buzzing.

10 *February*

Sam and I travelled together to the National Portrait Gallery, and by the time we arrived the place was already packed. My godson Harry arrived just after us with his friend, and in front of me, Nicky Clarke was reminiscing about the night of *Vogue*'s 75th anniversary, when Gianni Versace appeared in his brand-new hair salon. Most people were drinking in the entrance hall rather than going into the exhibition so I headed into the show to drive them through, and for the next two hours it was like a carousel of faces and greetings from my past and present. Penelope Tree, now in her sixties, looked so beautiful and serene in a high-waisted printed silk dress, with the same fringe and huge eyes that made her a famous model. Jerry Hall was gliding regally around the central gallery, sadly without her betrothed Rupert, but posing for the photographers with the mega-smile she can switch on at whim. Mario had said he would be bringing five assistants with him and was flanked by his entourage of good-looking young men in suits to whom he introduced me.

As I stood beside the enormous Snowdon blow-up of Hockney in his studio, the American man-about-fashion-and-art Derek Blasberg appeared with Dakota Johnson, who was on our February cover. We interviewed him for the last December issue and he had agreed to try to bring the actress, whom he was escorting to the première that night of *A Bigger Splash*. She's taller than I had noticed at the Gucci dinner, and wearing a gold goddess gown. Photographers are swarming around the pair. He introduced us and I mentioned that I'd just watched *La Piscine*, the sixties film that was the inspiration for *A Bigger Splash*. Just at that point my mother and brother came into view through the crowd. I was torn between continuing to talk with Dakota and greeting my family and couldn't quite work out how to mix the two. So I left her, saying I had to say hello to my mum. I hope she understood.

The night is almost impossible to write about as there was so much to experience, so many people to greet: Zandra Rhodes, with her violent-pink hair, who is always so friendly and enthusiastic, my oldest friends from outside fashion, whom I tried to talk to but was continually distracted from, the photographer Peter Lindbergh from Paris, who has taken so many great *Vogue* pictures, including the famous group supermodel cover in 1990. Snowdon's daughter Frances was there, representing him as he is now a little fragile for such a crowd, and I spoke to Diana Donovan under one of her husband Terence's great shots. Only Bailey was missing, even though we'd given him his own wall of images. Regan Cameron, who has shot a number of celebrities for us, said he felt so emotional about his illuminated portrait of Kate Winslet.

Emotional, that word. Everyone was using it. Not happy or sad or disappointed or excited, but emotional. And probably for many of us the emotions are mixed. A sense of melancholy over the passage of time. Pictures that we remember seeing when we were young – where have the intervening years gone? The usual toll that time has taken on many of the crowd, displayed on the walls not only in their physical prime but invested at that point with the lustre of *Vogue*. And at the same time I saw real pleasure in the rooms that came from a sense of achievement, in artists, subjects or *Vogue* staffers, and from others in simply being there, in the midst of it all. But for some, perhaps, there was a more complicated reaction to having once been part of the world that is *Vogue* and not being part of it any longer.

The dinner afterwards was at one of the longest tables I have ever seen. What was originally going to be for about thirty people had expanded to around eighty, and I wasn't prepared for that many. Friends of Leon, such as Annabel and William Astor, and Richard Caring, a few retailers, like Alison Loehnis from Net-a-Porter, photographers and models. It was oddly stressful, possibly because I was still buzzing from the party downstairs and not at all relaxed. I had to give a short speech to thank Leon in particular, but realized that what I had planned to say would have played better to a much smaller group than we now were. I had no notes and hadn't prepared it well enough. So I bungled it, really. Leon's impenetrable demeanour gave no clue as to what he was thinking.

I had placed *Mail on Sunday* editor Geordie Greig on one side of me and Mario on the other. Geordie is one of nature's great operators and by the end of dinner was suggesting to Mario that he fund a scholarship in his name and that Geordie and I would both give a party to launch it. He clearly finds his job fascinating in terms of the power as editor of a national paper, then difficult when people he knows become news stories and won't like what is going to be published. He said he always calls them in advance to let them know. Geordie used to edit *Tatler* and has never liked falling out with people – a tricky trait in his new role. David was further down the table and enjoyed himself talking to Sophie Hunter, who told him she'd met her husband, Benedict Cumberbatch, in a loo. Technically re-met, but it makes a better story if we leave it as met.

I give myself an extra hour in bed this morning as a post-party present. When the alarm goes at eight David has already got up. I reach for my phone and read some thank-you emails and texts. Today feels odd. I don't quite know what to do with myself in the aftermath of what was a brilliant launch.

There is dire news from the New Hampshire primary. Hillary is being rejected by young women and Trump doing ludicrously well. I think Trump is being underestimated. When I go downstairs,

David has managed to find the one slightly sniffy piece about the show by Jess Cartner-Morley in the *Guardian* and waves it at me as I drink coffee. Robin Muir, though, has sent a link to a wonderful review in the *Telegraph*. I can't expect everyone to love the show but it feels very personal to me. It's not about my own contribution to the magazine. It's about the whole thing of *Vogue*. The 'thing' that I'm taking care of.

I speak to my mother, who says, 'I'd made up my mind that I wasn't going to like the picture selections and you wouldn't have my favourites,' but she seems, broadly speaking, to be pleased by what she saw. She also tells me that when a friend from my early childhood, Rebecca Fraser, had given her a hug, she'd said, 'Who would have imagined this when we knew Alex aged four?' Exactly. I'm so lucky still having a mother around who remembers me aged four, even if she can say annoying things like the above.

Emily is about to leave for New York Fashion Week, which she is attending instead of me as I'm too busy to leave the office. She is very worried about the documentary and tells me that Richard Macer had said earlier in the week something along the lines of 'You look very nice in that,' and she had felt it was an inappropriate comment for him to make. I find that extraordinary, and can't understand how a man complimenting you on what you wear in a work environment is anything other than pleasant or, at worst, irrelevant. But she thinks it was in some way patronizing. Christ, poor men. Later I report this to David, who says he's always telling the girls in the *Tatler* office, where he works part-time, that they look great in something they are wearing, and that they thank him and appear to be pleased. Perhaps they feel like Emily and think it's creepy, and he just doesn't realize.

11 *February*

I woke up with a stomach bug that will almost certainly be related to the come-down from the excitement of the launch. I had a day to luxuriate in it and to appreciate the wonderful flowers I was sent but now it's on to the next thing or things. There is a deep frost in the park, which covers some of the shrubs in sparkling white while others are still green, but the grass is crunchy with ice, which makes my run more pleasant than the other day when all the crocuses were flooded by Storm Imogen the previous night, poking their lilac heads out from the pools of dirty water.

It can be hard to remember that there is anything other than the Centenary to focus on, but there are, of course, more issues of *Vogue*. We hope we've nabbed Renée Zellweger for the cover of the following one, our annual Ageless Style issue, to tie in with *Bridget Jones's Baby*, which she has finished filming.

The Ageless issue is regularly one of *Vogue*'s best-selling of the year. When I first thought of it, I didn't want it to be completely about fashion for the older woman but about the idea of style, no matter what the age. Fashion and age is one of those hardy perennials that can be looked at again and again. Are there age limits on certain items? Do older women want to shop in the same places as the young and vice versa? What styles are the most flattering as you age? When you are young you never think about whether older women can wear the same things as you, but as you age, you may wonder whether it's okay to wear the same. If you like something, shouldn't you just wear it and not be concerned about age appropriateness?

I have noticed that women with daughters are much more focused on this than those of us without. I suppose they have a flesh-and-blood example right in front of them of how much better something will look on a younger body, and daughters can be piercingly cruel when they think their mother looks silly or is trying to be too like them. I'm not sure many sons notice what their mother wears.

Anna Cryer, who took up the poisoned chalice of festival organizer, is now heavily immersed in the festival details, and we go through plans for the ticket sales again. She emphasizes that since we need ticket revenue to pay for the whole thing we should maximize it. The issue, as with selling anything, is the price: what will people be prepared to pay for each event? Should all the talks be the same price? But, unlike selling apples or pears, skirts or shoes, here we're selling human voices: it's difficult to calculate and risks upsetting people if they feel they're not valued as highly as some others.

I look at her new plan, which generates more revenue, but then she alerts me to a structural detail that means it is going to cost us more. I'm faced with the frustration of having found a way to make more money, only to have to spend it on higher production costs. In the end I say grumpily I don't want all our quite minimal profit to be spent on this new proposal for a higher-spec lacquer for the make-up tables. Anna is like a head girl in an Enid Blyton story, with wonderful white skin and curly mouse hair, that she winds round and round her fingers as she looks at the endless spreadsheets. She is purposeful and cuts to the chase, and is particularly useful as she has not worked on the festival before and often sees things with a clarity I don't have. She also has the most wonderful laugh.

I call Juergen Teller to talk about his appearance at the festival. Juergen is an interesting example of a photographer who has been uncompromising in his revealing and often brutally exposing work, yet who is commissioned by fashion houses Louis Vuitton and Céline. His women are rarely conventionally beautiful or glamorous. I want to question how he thinks about fashion as opposed to his private work. I know he will say that it's all the same to him, whether he's photographing himself and Charlotte Rampling naked, or his mother in a wood, or a model for Louis Vuitton, but I also know that even for Juergen there will be constraints and collaborative elements that mean his own work is different from his commercial work.

He's just shot the cover for Elton John's new album and he tells me that Elton's money enabled him to buy his first home: he used to work in the music business and met Elton, who took a shine to him and kept hiring him to take more and more portraits back in the eighties. Eventually Juergen took his then girlfriend Venetia Scott along as a stylist, and Elton didn't ask him back again. By that time, though, he had paid Juergen enough to help him buy the building, in what was then a scuzzy North Kensington backstreet, which he has expanded into a house and office with his wife, Sadie Coles.

Just before I leave the office I get an email saying that Alessandro Michele has agreed to talk at the festival. What he's doing at Gucci is currently a big story in fashion so this is fantastic news. It's particularly good to get it at the start of the weekend as I know I'm now quorate in terms of agreed speakers and therefore I should be able to relax. When I get home the house is empty and freezing cold. Even though the boiler is theoretically fixed, half the radiators simply don't throw out any heat and, of course, today the temperature has simultaneously dropped. I go next door to ask to borrow some chairs from my neighbours, Charles and Virginia, for the birthday party I'm giving my sister on Monday, then come back and make roast vegetables and calves' liver for David and me.

After dinner we look at a map of Europe so he can show me where the island of Ponza is. We're thinking of going there for a few days after the *Vogue* conference in Évian this June. I trail my fingers along the page from a patch of water, which I assume is Lake Geneva, down through France and Italy, but David tells me that the lake I'm pointing at is in fact in Hungary not Switzerland. Not for the first time, I'm appalled by my lack of basic geographical knowledge.

13 February

I had meant to spend today in pyjamas with the only plan to finish the really quite brilliant novel I'm reading: Emma Cline's *The Girls*, based on the Manson gang story. But when I wake, David and I both agree it would be interesting to go to the pre-Bafta brunch that the film producers Eric Fellner and Tim Bevan of Working Title are hosting. So, it's off with the pyjamas and on with my new Gucci loafers and a borrowed animal-print jacket from American designer Adam Lippes. The brunch is incredibly good fun and that format, whereby you can just drop in and leave when you want, is much preferable to the long, seated dinner. But, then, this particular brunch also has the tail wind of Movieland propelling it so that Eric hangs at the door with Eddie Redmayne (Working Title produced *The Danish Girl*), the latter more schoolboyish than imaginable in a maroon crew-neck school-uniform-style sweater that only a British man would wear. All over the room people of both sexes are swooning over Michael Fassbender. The Chiltern Firehouse is crammed and only rubbernecking is possible as you can't move far.

I spot Bailey in a corner with his wife, Catherine, and Antony Gormley, so I push over, first to thank Antony for coming to the National Portrait Gallery opening, and second, to talk to Bailey about the *Ab Fab* shoot we've asked him to do. He hasn't seen the exhibition despite the wall dedicated to his work, which I assume is to show us that he doesn't care about *Vogue* and to emphasize that he considers we need him more than he needs us. Antony says that the black-and-white pictures make the exhibition, and Bailey replies, 'Oh, you mean my work,' with a cackling grin as Antony pulls up photos of the show he has taken on his phone. Instead of Bailey's pictures, he flicks through John Deakin's portrait of Dylan Thomas emerging, like another tombstone, from the ivy in a graveyard and Deakin's head shot of Francis Bacon, or 'Mr Pig', as Bailey calls him.

The food comes round in minuscule bowls, along with champagne mimosas, and it's all got an LA look, with everyone dressed low key. Sometimes these parties can be depressing and feel as if they're just for show, but this is a proper gathering with lots of chat and gossip. I end up talking with writer Peter Morgan about the Queen. He's spent so much time thinking about her, first with his play *The Audience* and now with *The Crown* mega-series, and concludes that the secret of her success is that she is a blank canvas on to which people can project what they need. It's a bit like how we've used Kate Moss, as somebody who transcends the individual and is more a representative of an idea and an era, although there any similarity between the two definitely ceases. I don't agree with him, though, as I'm much more of a monarchist than he is and think the royal family are crucial.

Valentine's Day, and David and I are going for a treat lunch at Spring in Somerset House and to look at the Courtauld collection, which I have never seen. I am becoming obsessed with the reviews of the *Vogue* 100 exhibition, and whizz through the papers looking for mentions of it and not bothering with the things I normally enjoy. The *Mail on Sunday* has an absolutely pathetic piece about it by Liz Jones, and I feel like contacting Geordie and asking how he could have allowed such a predictable and self-referential piece to be published. We spend nine years working on an exhibition of 100 years of culture and Liz's double-page spread is about how the pictures make her feel inadequate. Why do I read the *Mail*? Last week the *Daily Mail* had a double page of broadly negative comment by Sarah Vine, saying that the exhibition served to show fashion had lost its sense of style. But in general the reviews have been glorious and made the point that this is not an exhibition about fashion but about how the culture of the age has been shown through the prism of *Vogue* and fashion photography. Great pieces in *Time Out*, the *Evening Standard*, the *Daily Telegraph*, Saturday's *Times*, the *New York Times* . . . I take all comments personally.

17 February

Last week ended well so this week I'm certain that something difficult will happen as a reproach to me for feeling too relaxed. It's my nature to think that there's a problem hiding round the corner just about to leap out and say, 'Boo.' Organizing all the different strands of the Centenary is emotionally exhausting. One thing goes well; another veers into difficulties. Mario Testino's Decades shoot arrives and is luscious. A different British model is representing each decade, from Stella Tennant in Edwardian-style McQueen, to Jourdan Dunn in contemporary Margiela by John Galliano. All the pictures are good and just what I wanted, although we need to find a slightly different choice for the fifties. David Gandy appears suitably caddish in a white tux, but Karen Elson in a tulle gown looks a little hard.

We still have the final Tim Walker portraits to nail. Tracey Emin has twice cancelled even as he arrived at her house. I would really like to have her in this story for the magazine but Tim is getting a bit fed up. David Beckham's people want a number of different concepts from Tim to propose to David, if he is to agree to be included. I know Tim wants to shoot him on a football pitch, kicking a crown into the air, which would be wonderful. But I have a feeling David might not think so.

My fashion director, Lucinda, walks into my office saying she had a great meeting with Bailey about the *Ab Fab*. They haven't worked together before or, anyway, not for many years, and I was worried about how they would get on. He told her he liked the energy of the unexpected and asked her why she hadn't had Botox.

We have our monthly circulation meeting and start making plans for what we hope will be a high June Centenary issue sale. The circulation team are projecting about a 25 per cent rise in year-on-year newsstand sales, which is a big ask. Some magazines' sales figures are based on about a third free copies or bulk (highly discounted sales), but we focus on our newsstand, which is mainly full price. We never bolt on free gifts but last year we reduced the price of the magazine on a few issues in some areas. It's extraordinary how a price reduction of a pound makes such a difference to sales figures. I always feel maddened when I see someone reading *Vogue* at the hairdresser's. 'Why don't you buy your own copy?' I want to say, as I glower at them from my hideously unflattering gown.

The duchess is meant to have been shown all the edited pictures but I haven't heard anything, which is worrying me. I come home mid-afternoon to prepare for the birthday party I'm giving my sister Nicky, who has just returned from Los Angeles, and start moving furniture around, stuffing tea lights into holders, then become obsessed with the idea of making guacamole so I have to find avocados and coriander. Sam's friend Joe arrives to cook the dinner, bringing three almond-and-orange cakes for pudding. I don't know how it happens but there's always a moment when, having thought you had everything under control, you discover there's a massive amount left to do, and suddenly I have only half an hour to get ready for another private view I'm hosting at the National Portrait Gallery, this time with Stephen Quinn and Nicholas Coleridge. When I try to have a quick bath the hot water has run out.

As David arrives back, I leave the house, screaming instructions to him and to Sam, who has determinedly spent the afternoon not helping in any way, just lying on the sofa vaping.

By the time I get to the gallery the private view is already full, this time with many Condé Nast staff and a lot of our advertisers and fashion-house representatives. It's wonderful to be able to show them around and discover bits and pieces I haven't seen. Wolfgang Blau, who has recently joined the company to work on our digital arm, spots an article from 1917 all about the fear that the gramophone could wreck our relationship with music, and points out that it could easily have been written now if you exchanged iPod for gramophone.

By seven thirty I have to leave, as everyone is meant to be arriving at home at eight. I get into the car and find a text from Rebecca Deacon, saying she's on her way to the party and hadn't managed to show the pictures to the duchess that day. I'm not going to be there to look after her, which makes me even more nervous, and I suddenly find the juggling of everything impossible and struggle to switch back into being sister/hostess.

At home, my brother, Jason, Nicky, David and Sam are having a nice time chatting, but I arrive whirling anxiety and hurling orders. Why is there no wine poured into glasses? Why are the lights too bright? Why is the kitchen door wide open? (Answer: because Joe is filling it with smoke with his char-grilling.) The house begins to fill with arrivals.

By midnight I've relaxed and have had a great time.

18 February

Bailey calls to say he thinks Stephen Fry should be included in the *Ab Fab* story and then, completely randomly, adds, 'By the way, fifty per cent of dyslexics can read.'

'Whoa, where's that come from?' I answer, trying to understand the connection between Fry and dyslexia before realizing there is none.

'You said to me you were surprised that if I was dyslexic I read so much.' Which is true. I did say it to him, several years back when we were talking about reading. I tell him I know that people who suffer dyslexia can read, but often it's hard for them. 'Yes, it is hard. I can't see the spelling. I see the word. It's like Chinese characters. You know, in China its two per cent for dyslexia. Here it's ten,' he replies.

*

Finally I get to speak to Rebecca Deacon and the viewing has gone well. I have suggested a number of different cover shots, mocking them up with the *Vogue* logo. Covers are such a complex beast. Often the picture you like best doesn't work so well on a cover – the eye contact isn't quite there, the attitude somehow not strong enough to jump out of a newsstand. Even though we haven't got a firm decision between us on the choice of cover image yet, it's a huge relief that the duchess is happy with them in general.

There's another (my last) private view at the gallery tonight and I meet Nicholas Cullinan with a memory stick of the pictures to show him. We go into his small office where I lay paper printouts on the table and talk him through them, but I want to show him the images on a computer screen where the details will be better. We jam the memory stick into his desktop where it fails to register. After several tries at pushing it in and pulling it out Nicholas summons someone to help. But we can't let them see the contents of the stick so it's a very awkward few minutes while the aide explains that because the memory stick came off a Mac it won't work on Nicholas's Windows but he'll try to find a laptop in the now empty building.

Time is tight as Nicholas has to be downstairs to greet guests for the private view across the road, but a laptop is quickly found in the empty offices. I try to open the stick, and *again* we can't get into it as it needs a password, which Jaime hasn't given to me. I cannot believe that I have these historic images and I'm trying to show them to the director of one of our national institutions and it's such a fuck-up. Time is ticking by and Maria Balshaw, who is taking our exhibition to Manchester Art Gallery in June, has arrived downstairs to meet Nicholas. I track down Jaime to get the password, and finally I can show him – by which time we're both hysterical with the almost surreal incompetence of it all. He loves them.

*

David and I go to our friend Christopher Sykes's film club where he is showing *The Man Who Fell to Earth,* which I have never seen. David Bowie is beautiful as the alcoholic alien but it's unquestionably too long and probably appeared better when it was released in the seventies. At dinner afterwards in a nearby Turkish restaurant the group is talking about Jerry Hall marrying Rupert Murdoch. One of our party knows her and says she is over the moon and is telling everybody who might be in any doubt, in that famous Texan drawl, that 'Rupert is real *hoooooot.*' A heavenly rumour emerges that we all desperately hope to be true, that Wendi Deng is now having an affair with Putin, but that does seem less likely and almost certainly libellous.

19 *February*

It's three fifteen in the morning – the darkest hour. What I call the night train has just gone past, the one that is meant to carry nuclear waste through the city from north to south. When we first moved to this area, everyone told me about this train and its cargo but I have no idea if it really exists. My brain is whirling with a carousel of people who have no place in my consciousness at this time of day but nonetheless appear to be firmly lodged there, David Beckham, Rihanna, Alexa Chung, and then, in the rare moments when they shift, I'm thinking of clothes for the next three weeks of fashion shows and whether I already have lung cancer from smoking since I was thirteen.

Beckham is there because I so want to have him in the Centenary issue and the picture is still a week away from happening and therefore has a week *not* to happen in; Alexa, because she came into the office a couple of days ago to discuss doing something different from an interview for the festival. Fiona Golfar – who often has clever ideas – thought we should ask her to do something more reality/entertainment based, such as auditioning members of the audience for 'How to be Alexa'. Understandably she didn't like the sound of that and said she wasn't sure how desirable it was to be her anyway. Instead we're thinking of a way for her to steer a panel with a couple of other people. Maybe she and her friend Derek Blasberg can do a kind of live advice clinic.

I saw her tonight at the launch of her M&S range, which consists of more or less updated reproductions of original designs she discovered in their archive. There was a gabardine navy trench coat that anybody would want (Alexa has reworked it in khaki) and a pair of wide-legged bright yellow trousers that she is delivering in a more commercial white and navy. Odd to think that M&S had really quite out-there designs back in the fifties.

Rihanna has claimed her place in my brain because just before I went to sleep Jaime texted to say did I know that our world exclusive on her for the May cover has been bust by American *Vogue* parachuting her onto their April issue. She suggested that we swap Kate Moss and Rihanna so we don't come second. Although all the *Vogues* are part of the same company we are also internally competitive with each other when we need to be. It's a good idea if we can do this logistically but we are less than three weeks away from being on sale and I doubt we have time to change the cover, the inside story, the contents page, the editor's letter and the magazine's general pagination. It's infuriating to have an agreement breached like this but agents are tricky customers at the best of times and will always find ways to argue that 'exclusive' applies only in some arcane way that you can't possibly have imagined. I have no idea if Anna Wintour knows we're meant to have an exclusive, but even if she does, I doubt it would factor into what she wants for her own magazine.

This is not what I want to be thinking about in the middle of the night and I am usually the very lucky person who easily finds refuge from worries in sleep. In fact, the more worried I am, the more I sleep.

Today's meeting at Kensington Palace is also fizzing in my brain. I am taking a final series of cover options over there. I do feel a heavy responsibility for this picture as I know it will be shown all over the world and will become truly iconic, rather than in the lame overused sense of the word as it is so often applied. The way we portray the duchess will become part of the public's perception of her. I want to do her and *Vogue* proud, and for it to be memorable but also reflect *her*, rather than a construct of her. There is now a number one cover option, which originally I hadn't favoured, because she is in a slightly autumnal Burberry trench and we publish in May, but I've been won over by the wonderful, genuine smile, which she truly has in this picture. And by her direct gaze at the viewer. I had thought that the check shirt would be the winner but I don't feel any of those shots quite have it, and neither, I think, does Josh.

My driver to Kensington Palace has strong opinions on the royal family. He tells me that his paper says it was only yesterday that Prince William started work after Christmas. I ask him what he thinks of the duchess.

'I think she's lovely, meself. Yeah. I think there's love there between those two and if there is, good luck to 'em. The shit they have to put up with. I wouldn't do it for all the tea in China.'

Nicholas Cullinan and I meet the team to look at this new suggested cover and, again, at the images. I meant to bring my laptop, bearing in mind the trouble we had in Nicholas's office, but this time, even though there's a small Windows laptop on the banqueting table, the memory stick works. I open the cover and there's an immediate agreement on the picture. It's like hitting the perfect tennis stroke when you know you've got it right in the centre of the racquet and you can scarcely feel the ball.

But the picture still has to be approved by the duchess, who isn't there, and I don't yet have any feeling of security. The very last deadline is approaching if we want to use gold on the logo and put it through the best possible repro process so that it really shines and is perfect. We work on for an hour, assuming it is, and discuss the installation of the picture at the National Portrait Gallery, a potential viewing and the date of *Vogue*'s publication.

When I get to the office I run into the art department to ask Jaime if she has discovered whether we can logistically manage the Rihanna/Kate cover-story swap. Overnight I've become convinced it's the right thing to do and, as it happens, Kate Moss would hit the newsstand just as the Rolling Stones exhibition opens. I'm buoyed by a sensational sales figure for March: it's the best we've had for some time and I feel as close to invincible in my decision-making as I can be. But there is a huge amount of work to do to effect the swap in time. First I have to convince Stephen that it's the right thing, even though it will cost several thousand pounds. I run into his office with my iPhone showing the Rihanna cover I want to use and say, 'I don't often ask you to do something for me but I am now.'

'The answer is *no*,' he says convivially. 'You women are always trying to twist me around your little fingers. What is it?' I show him the picture, which hasn't been cleared through our traditional cover meeting process, and explain that it will have a better chance if we move it to April because our exclusive has been breached. He immediately says yes. I love him.

I have to rewrite my editor's letter; the contents page, the stockists, the page numbers and the cover lines all have to be redone in twenty-four hours. Of course, this is the first day of London Fashion Week and all my fashion writers are at the shows, and other staff members are off because several people don't work Fridays. The office is only a third manned and I'm crashing around like a madwoman trying to get this done in time. But everyone there gets behind it and does what's needed.

I email Nicholas Coleridge, who is in Mumbai, to tell him what's happening, and that I've had to make a unilateral decision on the cover image and he's very supportive. It's not often on *Vogue* we have to move so quickly and I realize how much I enjoy the speedy decision and surfing the adrenalin of having to throw everything up and move it all around.

By the early evening I still don't know what our Centenary cover picture is going to be. My first fashion show of London Fashion Week is Charlotte Olympia at the Roundhouse in Chalk Farm. There are two signs outside the show, one saying 'Press', the other 'Guests', as if we the press are not guests. This irritates me, which I recognize is a sign of my stress and I decide it's not worth getting worked up about – but I am. It's Charlotte's first show and she has a round black catwalk and the models are all dressed in black forties vamp mode to showcase her metallic shoes and bags. They look like versions of her, with Veronica Lake waves, pale faces, deep red lipstick, and the shoes are retro glam. So many British shoe designers have taken this exaggerated, almost theatrical route. Sophia Webster's designs have a cartoon clarity, Nicholas Kirkwood's are almost pieces of architecture, and Charlotte fits into the mode, with her vivid embroidery and camp sensibility, towering platforms and curved heels.

20 February

I thought I'd ordered enough provisions to keep Sam and David in food while I'm on the road next week but when the delivery arrives there seems to be only loo paper, Fairy Liquid, almonds and salami. Clearly their dietary requirements have slipped low on my priority list. I wonder what the delivery guys think as they load people's orders into bags. Do we fall into area clichés? Does the woman in Queen's Park tend to buy burrata and the woman in Clapham mozzarella? Can they tell if they're delivering to a man or a woman by the shopping list?

Fiona Golfar sends me a picture from *The Crown* shoot she did last week. It's first-rate, with Claire Foy, who plays the Queen, in a red dress. She's wearing contemporary fashion but the styling and the location give a feeling of the period and the person she's acting. I immediately call to say how good I think it is and Fiona tells me she sent me that one because she knew I'd like it.

'So what are the others like?' I ask suspiciously, which, as the words leave my mouth, reminds me of one of my father's favourite Jewish jokes. Mrs Goldberg gives her son two ties for Christmas and as he comes down the stairs for dinner wearing one, her reaction is a reproachful 'So you didn't like the other?' Frequently I feel I'm becoming more like Mrs Goldberg by the day.

Photographer Jason Bell shot ten pictures and only had about fifteen minutes per picture, but it was tough because they had to ditch the production company, which was costing us too much. It was all hands to the tiller, and even Fiona's espresso machine had to go from her home in Shepherd's Bush to the stately location.

Because it wasn't a conventional fashion shoot many of the fashion houses were much less helpful than they might be over lending clothes, which is a ludicrous side of this business. The pecking order – who is a *cool* editor, who is a *cool* photographer, which is a *cool* magazine – is all very well, but sometimes I feel that the industry hasn't caught up to the fact that people don't want to see clothes only in *cool* fashion pictures but in a context. This attitude is also completely mad when houses lend to street-style girls to be snapped by hordes of Japanese photographers as a way of marketing. Yet they won't, for instance, want to lend something to be worn by a head of pathology in a hospital. It's one of my bug-bears. How are we meant to inspire young girls to be judged on criteria other than physical appearance when worlds they admire, like high fashion, don't encourage the notion that you can mix being a fashion plate with working in other fields? As I write this, I think maybe we should do a whole issue on the subject – no models. Perhaps for November. We could call it the Real Issue.

There is a huge sense of change around everything at the moment. Certainly in my own professional world, with questions over rejigging the fashion-show schedule and the role of the shows, but also in the wider world. Today David Cameron announced the referendum date, and in the States, Donald Trump continues to surge ahead, which is movement of a kind, if a terrifying kind.

I expected the controversy over the shows would be hovering above London Fashion Week but in my first full day of London shows there was little evidence of it. Jonathan Anderson again showed a clever, modern, futuristic collection that lit the touch-paper for the London shows. Jamie Hawkesworth was seated opposite me and I was reminded how irritated I was with him months ago over the painfully time-consuming business of fixing a shoot and today of how charming he is in person. He had even called to apologize. He didn't seem to be at all worried about the error in our catalogue that had caused such anxiety in Jaime. I didn't recognize him immediately, mainly because he's cut his hair but also because I get show myopia where everyone becomes part of a colourful fleshy blur.

He said he had just been in northern Italy shooting a project about beavers. I assumed this was private work but apparently not – it was being done for a client even though he hadn't actually seen a single beaver. I'm curious! But it was nice to speak to him and I suggested he might shoot David Beckham for us. Tim Walker is still scheduled to do it but I have a strong suspicion that won't happen so I'm eager to have a Plan B. He seemed keen and said it would be interesting shooting a good-looking man as he tends to avoid good-looking people.

Often when I ask someone face to face to do something they say yes, and then when others get involved, this changes. It's never easy to tell if that is because they prefer not to say no if put on the spot, then get someone else to break the news, or if their agent doesn't want them to do it or if, in fact, their diary really does prevent it. Anyway, fingers crossed for this.

I didn't go to many shows today but there was a dinner to launch Marc Jacobs's new range of make-up in the evening. It was in a new Mayfair restaurant called Parc Chinois, which, as its name suggests, is Chinese-designed in a very Suzy Wong manner, with lanterns and deep red lighting and dragons. Rather fabulous – or, at least, the basement was, where the party was held.

I hadn't seen Marc for a few years so it was good to say hello and talk, although it was only brief as more and more people kept arriving to do the same. I was sitting next to his CEO, Sebastian Suhl, and across from the actress Naomie Harris, whom I'd seen a few months back in *Spectre*. I asked her what it was like to be in a Bond film and she said she'd enjoyed *Spectre* more than *Skyfall* – fewer stunts. Even though they have stunt doubles the actors still have to do the last bit of the stunt, she explained, the falling over or what-have-you, so they still get the bangs and bruises. She was, unlike most actors, interested in everybody else and asked questions. Beth Ditto performed Bowie's 'Let's Dance', which was a great moment, and then I hauled myself out with the knowledge that I had twelve shows to get to the next day.

21 February

The first show today, Preen, was held at Tate Britain, and because the museum was still closed at that time in the morning, we were taken through the completely empty Turner galleries to get to the show space in the Duveen Hall. Frustrating to be just passing through when it would have been such a delight to linger.

I like Preen. Justin Thornton and Thea Bregazzi, the designers, have a real talent for mixing print and fabrics. I would love to wear some of their catwalk looks but I think now I would look like a bag lady. What appears delightfully creative and wild in your twenties is really hard to carry off in your fifties, however much you don't want to stick to beige and navy.

No chance of that in the world according to Anya Hindmarch, whose show, PXL8, was all about the cube motif, illuminated squares of vivid colour and playing on pixellation in leathers, furs and even crystal trims. It was clever and must have cost a fortune, and presumably they find it worth it, since every season Anya puts on some kind of extravaganza to show off her bags.

There are shows every hour on the hour today and it's quite demanding. But it's really interesting to meet the Labour mayoral candidate Sadiq Khan, whom Caroline Rush, from the British Fashion Council, who is caretaking him, introduces to me. He says he's just been to the National Portrait Gallery show with his daughter and is very complimentary about it, which naturally, instantly means I like him. He's smaller than I imagined, with neatly cropped silver hair, a firm handshake and eye contact. I can't remember exactly what date the mayoral election is and suddenly panic that it's the day our Centenary issue is published, but it's on 5 May, a couple of days later. 'Not that I'm counting. Seventy-four days from now!' he says.

He also mentions that Zac Goldsmith has just announced his support for Brexit (predictable, considering that his father, Jimmy, founded the anti-Europe Referendum Party back in 1994), and clearly feels this will help his own cause, given London's racial and cultural mix. I'll be amazed if Sadiq doesn't win. He would probably have had my vote anyway, but now I've met him I'm impressed by how valuable he feels culture in its widest sense is to a big city. I make a note to see if we can get both him and Zac to give us their views on what fashion means to London for a piece for the website.

The McQueen show is in London because of Sarah Burton's pregnancy, and a huge crowd gathers in one of the big horticultural halls off Vincent Square. It would be marvellous if McQueen returned permanently to London but there is something about the way the show is staged, very simply rather than in some incredible London building, that makes me think this is not the plan. However, the clothes are ravishing – a very romantic and feminine collection infused with a dreaminess. They are all fantasy – and many reference ideas that McQueen himself had – but it's peacefully arresting rather than disturbing.

I rush to the office to change for Browns founder Joan Burstein's ninetieth birthday party, The place is empty since it's Sunday evening. I hate dressing for parties in the office loo. I like to take a bath and decompress, slough off the work day and step into a different mode. The Vogue House loos do not encourage this and the lighting is extraordinarily unflattering, too. I have a new dress that Osman has made in a splashy black-and-white rubberized cotton and it fits perfectly with a full skirt that goes some way to making me feel festive. I arrive just as everyone is being moved into dinner. What a lovely evening, mixing the designers Joan has worked with through their careers, like John Galliano, Rifat Ozbek, Manolo Blahnik, Alber Elbaz, with her family (literally about two dozen grandchildren), many of her old friends and a few professional people like me. She has a swing band and each table setting has a special paper bag to take away the table flowers.

I sit next to David Hare with his wife, Nicole Farhi, on his other side. We talk about theatres (the actual buildings) and he tells me how Denys Lasdun won the design of the National Theatre by drawing the curved amphitheatre of Epidaurus on a napkin for the

National's then director Laurence Olivier, and saying he would want to design something like that. Epidaurus is not the first place that comes to mind when I'm at the National, which David says is technically a terrible theatre. I have very mixed emotions about David, who is vitriolic about my father as a theatre critic but whom I admire as writer. Nicole has given up fashion and now works as a sculptor. It's interesting that even her style of dress has changed and she's in some flowing caftan-like outfit rather than the tailoring I associated her with when she was a designer.

22 February

Throughout the London shows I have my phone in my hand all the time as there are so many problems to deal with now we are in the last few weeks of getting everything in for the Centenary issue. I can't bear to put it away – it's both worry beads and a fire alarm alerting me to the constant sparking of dilemmas. Small fires are springing up all over the place but there is only so much I can do to persuade people or to encourage them. This issue is incredibly important to me and I feel compelled to push as far as I can.

Today I have Richard back in the car with me, pointing his camera at my profile and asking questions, then saying, in what is surely faux-confusion, 'Oh, sorry. Did you not want to talk about that?' Or 'Oh. Was that a difficult question for you? Sorry.' This, even when I have just told him the reason why I might not want to discuss something.

I'm trying to be as honest and open as possible for the film but there are times when to do that completely would simply be too hurtful for people or would cause long-term problems. He wants to know why we swapped the covers and I try to explain about our perceived exclusivity but I don't want him making it look as if there is a personal battle between Anna Wintour and me. I can see that for him this is a tempting, meaty story, and he is quite short of those. There are insights that might be good for them but I didn't go into this project to commit professional hara-kiri, although occasionally I feel I may have already done that.

I get exasperated and run into Sophia Webster's presentation of her shoe collection. It's held in St Barnabas in Soho and is a Gothic installation with a Beetlejuice theme, worn by girls holding little clutches with motifs like 'Bored to Death' and 'To Die For'. The collection has a darker sensibility than what I think of as her more usual upbeat bubblegum approach. She doesn't yet know she has won the British Fashion Council/*Vogue* award, which will be announced in March, and, looking at this presentation of incredible shoes, I feel we made a good choice. It amazes me how these young designers continually come up with new ideas and push on in such an upbeat way.

The David Beckham photo-shoot saga continues as his art director has come back and said now that he really *would* like to be shot by Tim Walker but wasn't prepared to kick a crown around as the shoot concept. Tim is worried that he won't be able to do anything original enough to make him interested in taking this picture, so one minute it's off, and back on again the next. Robert Spensley, who is driving me around town for the shows, says, 'Why don't you paint him gold?' which I think is a brilliant idea – Goldenballs crossed with an Oscar. We could even do one of Tim's table-top portraits like the now famous one of McQueen posed with a skull that dominates one end of the National Portrait Gallery show. I can't get Tim on the phone to suggest this and time is running out.

Jaime calls to say Richard Macer has said he's going to ask Anna what she thinks about the Rihanna cover swap, which is not what I want as that will inevitably mean Rihanna's whole team getting involved. I'm furious that, having been taken into our confidence over this, he is now betraying our trust. I call him to say I'll pull the whole film. It's a horrible morning.

Burberry is held in a new format and we sit on little turquoise benches in concentric circles listening to Jake Bugg strumming as the girls walk. There is only so much you can do with a trench but Christopher seems to keep up a high standard of new ideas and the accessories are strong.

After Burberry I try to find a chicken to buy for dinner tomorrow night. It's the only gap in my schedule for the next thirty-six hours but Knightsbridge is not big on butchers. There's Harrods Food Hall but I baulk at what it would cost there and the place is so large that it would take me ten minutes just to find the chicken. Thank heavens for Google. Robert finds a butcher a bit off our track in South Kensington and we race over. Done: one chicken and a dozen chipolatas. It would be easier to order in a take-away but I know that to cook roast chicken for Sam and David the night before I go to Milan will make me feel better about myself. It will be a kind of reconnection with the person I am when I'm not working and whom occasionally I lose track of.

23 February

I had supper with my friend Jane Wellesley last night. She reminded me as we sat down that 22 February was the anniversary of the day our friend *Sunday Times* correspondent Marie Colvin was killed in Homs. I'm so speedy and self-obsessed right now that I can't emotionally engage in the memory, apart from saying it was good we were together tonight, but I clearly recall stepping off the early flight to Milan on that morning and getting millions of texts saying, *Call*, then learning the news and bursting into tears in the passport queue.

I ordered pizza, which I never usually allow myself, and wake this morning filled with fury at myself for the indulgence, which has made me feel slow and heavy. I try to run but it's a real struggle and I give in after four kilometres, listening to the *Today* programme's item on virtual reality. If their report is true, this whole business of fashion shows will be irrelevant in a couple of years as we will all be experiencing them through a headset.

When I get home there is a text from Tim Walker, saying he is passing on David Beckham as he doesn't feel confident he'll get a good picture. I try to encourage him to continue and suggest the gold idea to him. He agrees that I can talk to Beckham's art director, the main point of liaison here, and he's also keen to shoot him in the nude, splitting him up into a series of body parts, which could be brilliant. Take a beautiful man apart and put him together in another sequence.

As I describe these possibilities to Beckham's art director, I add that I know we're not making things easy but we just want something that will work with the other portraits and be really memorable. But time is running out. As soon as I close the call, Bailey rings to say that Lucinda has asked if he would include Victoria Beckham in the *Ab Fab* shoot, which he doesn't want to do. Do I know, he barks, if Lucinda understands what it's like working with him? Somebody tells me that it was a full moon last night, which may or may not have something to do with this pandemonium.

My phone rings again straight after Bailey hangs up. It's Naomi Campbell, whom Tim was meant to shoot for the issue but she stood him up and is now upset that she isn't in the mix. 'I was ill. That's why,' she says, adding threateningly, 'It's not going to look good in the press if I'm not there.' I try to explain that the shoot was fixed for the day in question and we were not given another day with her as an option, so it's now impossible to do much, especially as she's leaving for LA tomorrow. I'll look into it and see if there's any way of squeezing in another shoot. I send her over some tickets for the National Portrait Gallery exhibition, which she hasn't seen and where she is well represented, and get a sweet text later thanking me and saying it was 'amazing' with lots of emojis I can't interpret.

I'm at home in the kitchen when I get a text from Rebecca Deacon saying we have the go-ahead on all the pictures. I call to thank her and talk it all through. I don't feel the relief I should, which is weird.

24 February

The last couple of days have been the most stressful of my professional life. The more stressed I am the more my fear of flying takes hold and I have nightmares about having lost something, which I can't find no matter how desperately I search (no need for dream interpretation there). When I wake there's the fizzing terror I always used to have before a flight and have now usually got under limited control. Outside there is a thick frost and the sky is salmon pink as I'm driven to Heathrow through the early-morning streets before the traffic has built up.

I thought I might even look forward to being in the air today as that would be a couple of hours when no information about work could reach me, but it hasn't turned out like that: I'm frightened. As I order my usual sedative of white wine, at nine in the morning, I'm embarrassed by the glance of the man in the seat next door, who obviously thinks I have a problem. When we land a cheery face greets me from further back in the aisle of the crowded plane. It's Peter Soros, who was married to Flora, one of my oldest friends, and now looks totally different, with a short grey crop as opposed to the dark 'fro I associate with him. And he's become very slim. 'What are you doing in Milan?' I ask.

'Oh, you know, the three Fs,' he says, in his American accent.

'Fashion? But the others?'

'Furniture, fittings and food,' he quips. He tells me he's lost thirty-five pounds so all the suits he has ordered from his Italian tailor have to be altered. He introduces me to a friend he has with him, who works in the financial sector, and they offer me a lift into town, which I have to refuse as I need to wait for my baggage. I watch them stride carelessly ahead, luggage-free, while I'm marooned at the carousel. Oh, the bliss of carry-on bags only – something I have very rarely achieved. For this five-day trip I have two large cases. As I wait, I receive a text from Rebecca reiterating that the duchess has completely cleared the cover and story. My legs shake with relief as I haul the huge cases onto a trolley.

Once again we've all taken the same plane to arrive in time for Gucci, which this season is a little harder in tone, but essentially has the same feel as last. There is crashing sound and strobe lights, which are uncomfortable as a backdrop, but the clothes have the individuality that most of us liked at his last show. Heavy embroidery, rainbow colours, a total mash-up of references, from the *Grey Gardens* headscarves to boys with sixties pudding-basin haircuts, mythical flora and fauna, street style, floating chiffon gala skirts and garish-coloured tights. Accessories have been piled on everywhere, with a zillion bags that will do big business for the brand next autumn.

Last season Alessandro brought us the furry backless loafer but in this show he teams most of the looks with shiny high heels. It's like the most glorious dressing-up trunk filled with glittering treasures – and how can one fail to be excited by that? After the show I go backstage to congratulate him but also to thank him for agreeing to speak at the festival in a couple of months.

25 February

I have a moment of pure pleasure at being in Milan in the crush at a coffee bar, waiting for my macchiato. The baristas' performance, as they reach for the white china cups while manipulating nozzles of steam into the milk and shouting across the counter, is almost balletic. This trip I have a new driver, Andrea, who doesn't understand anything I say. His English is non-existent, apart from 'please'. Worse, he's unable to tell me he doesn't understand. I tried to learn Italian a few years back and have some vocabulary but no grammar so neither English nor my Italian works for him. Having a driver might seem indulgent but it's the only way to get to all the appointments and shows on my schedule. We communicate in pidgin managing only *'il traffico e bruto'* and how we are now *'molto tardi'*. I am on edge as he drives with only one hand on the wheel and in the other his phone with a low-fi sat-nav system that doesn't appear to acknowledge the one-way system that dominates the city.

The big show of the day is Prada. Every season their space is transformed into a different set, and tonight we're in a kind of old marketplace with wooden floors and balustrades, the light-bulbs above covered with rather chic wire-mesh hoods. As usual the show is layered literally in terms of clothing but also in ideas. There are heavy coats and capes, cinched with broad white cotton corsets/belts, Argyle-print woollen tights and white sailor caps. Beautiful embroidered velvet dresses and drifting organza are rooted with heavy flat lace-up boots. The girls carry bags slung across the body and have the red lips and cowlick hair that Miuccia often favours. The applause at the end is greater than I have heard for any show here. It's very much a Prada classic hits.

26 February

Andrea and I have given up trying to communicate verbally and have resorted to Google Translate. Early indications are that this is not hugely successful since predictive texting means that, in a hurry, we're showing each other mumbo-jumbo on our phones. After waiting for thirty minutes after the Emporio Armani show in the middle of a roundabout, I lose my temper and call Laura Ingham, our maternity-cover executive fashion editor, who is organizing us here, to ask if she can get someone who speaks Italian to explain to Andrea how to do the job? They do this while I'm in the car and I'm relieved that he seems perfectly happy to get the call and is not at all put out at the criticism. From then on, there is a huge improvement and I start to arrive at places on time.

The meetings are more important to me than the shows. They're active rather than the passive experience of looking at the fashion. Gucci's Robert Triefus and I meet up at the new Mandarin Hotel where every surface is covered with vast glass tubes of orchids. Robert has been working in fashion since I started at *Vogue*, first with Calvin Klein, then Armani and now Gucci. He's always convincing in what he says and is able to convey the message that his company is not happy with what we're doing without it sounding pathetic, bullying or hectoring. Luckily that isn't our conversation today and we discuss the format of Alessandro's talk at the festival and their upcoming Cruise show in June at Westminster Abbey. I asked how they managed to nab such a top location for the show and he said he thought the abbey was as pleased to have them as Gucci was to have it there. Sometimes all you have to do is ask – and, I imagine, make a substantial donation.

Later that afternoon I meet with Miuccia in the Prada headquarters at via Bergamo. Outside is a traditional frontage – stern, with a small wooden door in the stone façade – but inside it is Prada world, with the big steel Carsten Höller slide just outside the automated entry gate, clocks with five time zones in reception and a vast, empty courtyard. We arrive together and walk to her meeting room, with its one white table, chairs and more empty space. If I could choose to look like anyone it would be her – the Roman hawkish nose, tanned skin and streaky tawny hair. She always looks wonderful, with a style that defies age and categorization and, no matter how extreme her clothes, she's never anything other than chic. Today she has a long brown leather coat that she showed in menswear over a print shirt from yesterday's collection. Bare tanned ankles appear from her black brogues and, as always, she's wearing stonkingly beautiful earrings – large ruby-and-diamond drops.

We discuss politics – the craziness of what's happening in the States, whether the electorate will ever warm to Hillary, even if they think she's doing the right thing. Miuccia feels the Republicans are frightened by Trump, and I tell her that in the UK, people I would never expect to do so are considering voting for Brexit. She says that when people feel threatened – by immigration issues, war, the economy – they always become more conservative and turn in on themselves. Somehow this leads to a conversation about young women today.

Some of the reviews of her previous night's show included quotes from her about contemporary women's lives and she looks genuinely pained at the possibility that a younger generation is falling back to a more traditional role stereotype. Certainly I notice that a lot of younger women simply don't want the life of their mothers, who worked full time and had no time for themselves. I tell her that my mother always said you can have only two out of three – work, family and social life. Miuccia says for her it is work and family. I think I more or less have the three but with only one child and no husband to have expectations of me, it's possibly easier for me than it is for many people. I think it's different being with David from being married. Either of us can just walk if we want.

The press and buyers move around the city, like a vast shoal of fish, between the shows, either in huge old palazzi with gilded ceilings and chandeliers, or more industrial spaces. At Tod's I sit near Lisa Armstrong from the *Telegraph* and Anna Murphy of *The Times*, who are both wearing silk Dolce & Gabbana pyjama bottoms. Stefano and Domenico have given them to editors, and although they both look rather dashing, Lisa in sea green and Anna in amethyst silk, I'm not entirely convinced about them for workwear in February. 'Well, probably only in Milan,' Anna admits. 'What goes on tour stays on tour.' But Lisa is convinced that pyjama wear is a going concern for the spring.

Although these are gifts, it is a myth that they influence the writers and make them beholden to the designers. If anything, it works almost the other way and the journalists feel they should wear what they're given to be respectful. At my company we have a policy of paying a sum to charity for anything we accept, which concentrates the mind as to what you really want. It's not the retail price but you have to give enough of a charitable donation as to make sense. If we don't want the gift, it joins the sales we hold throughout the year with the proceeds for charity. The idea that the fashion system survives through this kind of payola is nonsense. In all honesty, most of us have enough handbags to last us for life and being given another is in no way going to influence our opinion.

27 February

The temperature has fallen, and as I open the windows onto my terrace, an icy blast fills the room but succeeds in waking me from the vacuum-packed stupor of too many nights in hotels. I have brought one of my favourite books to Milan, Joan Didion's *Slouching Towards Bethlehem*. Waiting for the Bottega Veneta show, I flick to the front where I have inscribed my name and the date '1/10/75' in this now tatty Penguin paperback. When I wrote that I would have been eighteen and probably thought I could be Joan Didion. Now I know I will never be her.

There is a wonderful essay in the collection, which I read regularly, called, 'On Keeping a Notebook', which, for anyone like myself who does so, is spot-on and quite rightly observes that the notes one makes, the random scraps of conversation, description, *aperçus*, all basically feed back into a kind of self-obsession.

They say more about your interest in yourself than they do about the thing you have written down. Why did you notice it? What did it mean to you? I suppose in some ways this diary is exactly that.

I love Bottega Veneta and wish I could afford the clothes. Across the runway I notice someone in a very expensive Gucci skirt I was considering buying. During the fashion weeks you see a lot of people in designer clothes, some looking terrific and others awful. I'm pleased that I've just saved myself a great deal of money as I know now that if I'd bought it I would only see this other person wearing it and worry that I might look like her. I write this in the full knowledge that sometimes other people will be feeling that about me.

In the afternoon I visit the Ralph Lauren palazzo, which is exactly what it sounds like – an American fashion designer's interpretation of a palazzo. There are white-coated butlers on hand and white-covered sofas in the upstairs 'private room' where the really wealthy customers can shop, if they wish. I ask Sadie, the PR, who is showing us the collection, when the Ralph Lauren research wing at the Royal Marsden is planned to open. In 2014 I was a trustee at the hospital and introduced Ralph Lauren to them for a fundraising initiative at Windsor Castle. Mixing foundation hospital, luxury fashion house and British royalty was at times a real car crash of cultures but the happy ending was that Ralph, who has a history of supporting breast cancer initiatives, contributed a very generous amount to the hospital's work.

If I could have my way, his visit to the opening of the wing would tie in with my gala dinner so he would come to it, but Sadie says that, as yet, the date is still not fixed. I'm starting to feel like a sheep-dog herding my flock from a very large field towards some gate that opens on to who-knows-where. Everywhere I go I'm asking someone to do something for me.

Milan is filled with families who work together in the fashion business, and the designer Luisa Beccaria is from one of these. Luisa is a whirling dervish of chatter, persuasion and conviction, and designs a collection of very pretty eveningwear. They are the kind of clothes that you need the lifestyle to go with – pastel chiffon gowns, embroidered cashmere, tapestry-stitched velvet dresses. She texts me to ask if I'd like to come for a drink at her new home, which I most certainly would as I'm curious to see it. Four nights is my tipping point in any fashion city for the shows and I crave a moment when I'm not in my hotel room, car, on a bench or, as I just said, asking someone to do something.

Luisa's house, like many in the centre of Milan, is completely different inside from out, where there is only a forbidding double door in a stone façade. Inside, it is built around a courtyard and on each storey there is a beautiful enfilade of rooms with parquet floors. Luisa is married to Lucio, aka Prince Lucio Bonaccorsi di Reburdone, a seemingly saintly figure who brings out supplies of Prosecco, and smoked salmon on slivers of bread. He smiles genially before chatting to the parade of beautiful twenty-something children they have produced, coming in and out with shiny dark hair, flicking through their phones and planning their Saturday evening. Luisa is the kind of woman who is untouched by political correctness and can say of her family's sleeping arrangements, 'My son, he put himself in the room for the Filipina at the bottom,' without a second of discomfort. Several years ago she told me that wealthy Italians were sending their maids to shop in Geneva to avoid showing credit-card bills in Italy.

Just before I leave, Hamish Bowles arrives. I ask him about the next show – Philipp Plein. I don't know much about the designer although I'm aware, like everyone else, that he's very flamboyant and is making a lot of noise, opening stores everywhere. Hamish isn't going to the show tonight but, he says, the last time he did, a huge fireball flew past my French *Vogue* counterpart, Emmanuelle Alt, and missed her by centimetres. He has also heard that Plein initially made a fortune out of clothes rails and crocodile-skin dog baskets, which is an intriguing combination.

Fashion loves a mysterious fortune, and when I arrive at the show, which is held in the exhibition space La Fiera outside the centre, I realize that Plein is Willy Wonka. The same mystery and sinister toys. The vast hall is filled with flashing lights that climb mirrored panels, and when it is eventually filled, an hour late, huge trucks appear with a noise like gunfire and flames blazing from funnels. The models walked so fast it was hard to see the clothes but they looked like regulation kit for the new world of wealth – Russia, China, Korea. They love expensive furs, elaborate trainers and beanie hats.

I rush out quickly to try to get to Mario Testino's party for his special edition of Italian *Vogue* but am defeated by the huge crowds at the door, my own weakness of spirit and my desire to get to bed.

28 February

Sundays in Milan are usually very quiet and not normally as wet as this. The rain hasn't stopped for a second and the cobblestones are soaked. It is as if God has opened the sluice gates. I let myself sleep an extra hour, then head off to Marni, which I usually enjoy and which is styled by my colleague Lucinda Chambers. I see so much of Lucinda in the show – her love of utility colours and earrings. Then I go to see Luisa Beccaria's collection in the showroom, where she introduces me to her immaculate mother, with coiffed grey hair, slim and in black, so different from Luisa's wild black locks and always pastel colours. The last time I was in this area it was a baking hot September lunchtime, and there was a street market. I bought three enormous vintage linen sheets for forty euros each, and use them as tablecloths at every party we have. When somebody spills red wine and an ashtray it doesn't matter as the rough warp of the linen makes it easier to get the stains out.

29 February

Armani's show is held in his Tadao Ando-designed theatre, a brutal concrete structure, filled with black-suited men and women – an Armani army. Backstage I have a quick meeting with the designer, who is sitting alone at a table flicking through the Italian morning newspapers, which, because of deadline timing, haven't managed to print the Oscars news. But he is in a great mood as Armani clothes were on so many of the big stars of the night: Charlotte Rampling, Cate Blanchett and, of course, Leonardo DiCaprio, who is a loyal devotee and has been wearing Armani since he starred in *What's Eating Gilbert Grape?*

Just before their shows is not normally a good time to meet designers as they're focused on the presentation ahead but Armani seems relaxed and chatty. He talks briefly about the collection that he's about to show: it's called Black Velvet and features a lot of exactly that. He says how much he likes velvet, the texture and the way the light plays on it. Around him more people collect and I can see many of them checking pictures of Oscars Night on their phones. He's in good shape, a muscled torso obvious underneath the thin crew-neck blue cashmere sweater and loose trouser he often wears. His is a fox face – deeply suntanned with small sharp teeth and still bright, pale blue eyes.

Many of the leading designers in Milan gathered for a lunch on the opening day, for which I didn't get out in time. They were joined by the prime minister, and Armani is pleased that Renzi had given him a name check. 'Of course he would,' I say. 'After all, you are the biggest and the oldest designer in the country.'

'Oldest? *Decrepito?*' He reels back in faux-horror. He's said to speak no English but I'm pretty sure he can understand quite a lot. I'm always gratified that so many of the designers struggle through in my language and always also feel so pathetic at my own inability to communicate reasonably in theirs.

At the end of the meeting, I ask him whether he'll be able to come and celebrate with us at the gala dinner. He says he will, nodding at his aide-de-camp to log it into the diary. This makes me very happy as I go and sit alone in the empty auditorium to wait for the rest of the audience to arrive.

I manage to catch an earlier flight back than I was booked on, which is an achievement for me as I'm very superstitious about changing flights. But the possibility of an extra hour or so at home this evening to unpack and get everything sorted out pushed me on to make the switch when I got to the airport early. In the car home from Heathrow I saw a London I very rarely see as I'm always at work at this time in the afternoon. The pavements are filled with toddlers collected from nursery and the bus stops lined with push-chairs and the elderly. There are many grandparents holding young children with one hand and shopping bags with another. I find the hours between four and six very alien, not somewhere I'm comfort-able. The only time I was a part of this world was when I was on maternity leave and then it depressed me. I don't know why but it always seems so empty and oddly silent. Today even the trees were completely still in the park outside as I unpacked. I suppose I'm institutionalized to office life. But now I think maybe it was because when we came back from school there was often no one at home for a while. The flat would be dark and only really came to life when my mother returned from work or my father appeared. Or, alternatively, my aversion to this time of day has absolutely nothing to do with any of that.

MARCH

1 March

It's my mother's birthday today and I haven't had time to buy her a gift. I've warned her of this and, of course, she said no matter, but I think everybody likes to have something to unwrap on their birthday.

I get my hair cut by George Northwood, who has just got off the plane from Los Angeles where he was styling Alicia Vikander's hair for the Oscars. He was there for only two days and watched her winning her Oscar for Best Supporting Actress in *The Danish Girl* from her hotel room. When I say he must be completely exhausted, he answers that it's better to come into the salon and be with people or 'If you go home on your own, it's a bit like "What was all that about?"'

Today I had the first run-through of all the visual material for the Centenary issue. It's exciting. There are wonderful illustrations from the 1920s magazines and new fashion illustrations we have commissioned from contemporary artists, like Natasha Law and Quentin Jones. Then there are the enchanting personal pictures of designers as children or, at least, in their youth. I love the picture of Armani sitting with his brother on a beach, his beautiful mother in her swimming costume, and the one of Tommy Hilfiger in his flares as a young man. Then, in a section for people's memories of *Vogue*, there is a great picture of Helmut Newton, Manolo Blahnik and Anjelica Huston to go with her recollection of the shoot. Helmut and Manolo are wearing practically identical white loafers.

The David Beckham saga continues. He has offered us alternative shoot days but nothing seems to be working out date-wise with possible photographers. There was a marvellous moment when we thought perhaps we could parachute him into the *Ab Fab* shoot but then it turned out he would be travelling. At the end of the day Jaime comes in triumphant to say that finally, finally, we have an agreed time between him and Jamie Hawkesworth for his portrait. Shortly after that an email comes through to say that the *Ab Fab* PR doesn't want us to use Georgia May Jagger as the model in the shoot – which has been arranged now for weeks. They appear to be objecting on the grounds that she is not in the film, but we had never committed to using a model from the film and I am not keen to turn this into a huge promo. One up, one down, and so it goes. If we can't use Georgia we probably won't do the shoot, which will be a shame after a lot of work. But to start trying to agree on a different model now is insane. We need to use somebody we shoot for the magazine to make sense and, as far as I can tell, their suggestions don't fit that criterion.

2 March

My mother's birthday dinner was lovely, and I drank a lot of the delicious red wine that my brother-in-law Con ordered. I managed to get Mum a present in a late dash to Liberty, and she seemed pleased with the silk top and Liberty-print wallet. She's going on holiday to Sicily soon and sometimes it's nice not to carry a bag and just have something slim to put a credit card, cash and a phone in when you go out at night. Mum told me how much she enjoyed looking again at the exhibition, then added, 'But if I could be allowed a criticism –' I interrupted and said she was *not* allowed a criticism: I just want to bask in unadulterated praise. A few minutes later I couldn't resist hearing what point she was going to make, which broadly seemed to be that the newer portraits were not as strong as the older ones. Mum looks wonderful, with keen eyes and lovely skin, nothing faded about her even at eighty-nine.

Reading the papers this morning, I ask David what the difference is between migrants and immigrants. I feel foolish for asking but now that 'migrant' has become such a tainted noun I'm trying to work out the exact criteria for this tarnish. After all, my dad was an immigrant from Canada after the war, and his parents left Ukraine for Canada around 1911 to escape the pogroms.

Despite March's arrival it's suddenly freezing and I notice green mould accumulating on all the windowsills and on the wall of one side of the house. I'm waiting for Joseph the builder to arrive to discuss building a new garden shed just outside the kitchen and he can look at the mould as well. David isn't very interested in mould on windowsills so as I make up I observe that the problem with my face is the deep lines under my eyes. He shouts from the bathroom, 'We've moved from problems with your house to problems with your face. Is there no single aspect of your life that you will *not* worry about?' By the time I leave for work I have found some resolution to the mould, and in two weeks I should have a very fine shed, but the lines under my eyes are another matter.

I have asked Erdem to make me a dress for the Centenary gala and today we have our first meeting. He works out of a studio in Bethnal Green above the Rich Mix cultural centre. I love his personal office, which is crammed with beautiful books, and there are always pictures stashed against the bookshelves, waiting to be hung or framed. He has been bidding by phone on an illustration in an auction at Sotheby's but it's gone for ten times the estimate. He thinks that's because the artist was Russian so there's a large moneyed clientele for his work.

I have a few ideas for the dress, which could be adapted from his last show.

'Is it black tie?' he asks of the evening.

'Yes,' I answer, although I don't actually know. I haven't decided. 'Isn't it a bit of a bore having to wear black tie?'

'*Nooo!*' he shrieks, with joy. 'Black tie is super-chic, and you can wear long with a *train*.'

I say crisply that I will not be wearing long. That I have never had fun in my life in a full-length dress and I intend to enjoy the night.

'Well, just touching the floor? And would you wear a cape?' he suggests.

Again I say no. Not touching the floor either, please, and in late May a cape will be too hot. It's like snatching sweeties from a child. There is a black velvet dress, strapless and fitted tight to the body with enormous embroidered white calla lilies on it, that I like the look of, but I'm not sure I can get away with the exposure of strapless. He sketches how it would look if he added tulle above the body and covering the arms, which is a possibility. But I know it will take away the spectacle of it, the black velvet contrasting with bare skin.

'I think it must be very nipped in. Nipped. Nipped,' he says, sketching his ideas quickly. Handing the paper to me he suggests maybe we should be thinking about sequins and points to another dress from the show. There is a swatch of gunmetal sequins with black embroidery pinned up on a board against the bookshelves and he does another quick sketch of a very linear woman with long drop earrings, a heart-shaped face and short hair wearing an adaptation of that dress, calf length, with a deep V at the back. She couldn't look less like me. 'Earrings,' he says, 'and you could have a diamond tennis bracelet. Very subtle. But *sizeable*.' I have never heard of a tennis bracelet so we check it out on his computer and up come rows and rows of plain diamond bracelets. 'But now I'm thinking this might be super-chic.' He points to another swatch of devoré velvet shapes on what looks like black chiffon or tulle.

It's a massive privilege to have someone make a dress like this
but it's frightening, too, and really quite baffling. I can't decide
what I want. I didn't have a proper wedding dress since I got married at two days' notice in a register office with only a last-minute
buy of an embroidered Dries Van Noten shawl to drape round a
white Ghost dress. But I imagine this is a little like how people feel
about their wedding dress.

When I leave I check my emails and discover a message from my
beauty director, Nicola, saying we might have Kim Kardashian as a
speaker at the festival. This is fantastic news since so many of our
audience would be fascinated by her. Nicola has made the connection via Charlotte Tilbury, whose range has been a barn-storming
success, and whom we have asked to speak. It turns out she's done
Kim's make-up a few times and they've become friends.

3 March

I leave for Paris in time to catch the Dior show. There is still no announcement of an artistic director running the team there this season, along with rumours about who will take the job. There is even more chat about whether Hedi Slimane will be leaving Saint Laurent. Last night David asked if a star designer is really necessary to head up these houses. I think you do need one for two reasons. First, there must be a strong creative leader, with vision, and second, it's much easier for people to become involved with a fashion house if they can put a face to the designer heading it up. Listening to this, he makes a comparison with football managers and their teams, saying there's a lot of emotional stuff that the supporters feel about the relationship between the team and the manager, which often isn't entirely related to how well they're doing in the league table. That's often the case with fashion houses. There is a loyalty to the idea of a long-term leader.

The results of the Boston Consulting Report, commissioned by the Council of Fashion Designers of America to look into the question of fashion shows and selling timetables, is published. It further confirms my opinion that there is almost always no point in using teams of management consultants to look at problems. They charge a fortune and invariably interview hundreds of people to conclude what anyone with half a brain could work out for themselves. In this case they've taken months to announce that there is no single answer to what should happen and instead offer a 'menu' of options that cover all possibilities. Either people can show a collection that will go immediately into stores, or they can show a collection that sticks to a long lead delivery but put in a few pieces that will be on sale immediately, or they can remain with the traditional strategy of showing to press and buyers months in advance. This is not news. All it does is confirm that nobody can decide what the best strategy is.

The British papers and news programmes are swamped with Brexit stories, and if there's nothing new to say, they run a story on how the opposing camps are at loggerheads. I don't understand why there is radio silence from Labour and the Lib Dems on this subject. I have no idea what Jeremy Corbyn's line is. Presumably they think it best just to keep out of the frame and watch the Tories tear themselves apart. The flat landscape of northern France, with its whirling wind turbines and small villages each with its own church tower sticking out from the barren trees, is flashing past the Eurostar windows.

This season Dior is being held in the Cours Carrée du Louvre, a cobbled courtyard, which, like the Rodin Museum, is an establishment Parisian spot. The ready-to-wear collection is filled with beautiful clothes – butterfly-embroidered high-waisted skirts with the same off-the-shoulder silhouette as the couture, once again produced by what everyone imagines will be a place-holder design team.

I sit next to my German counterpart, Christiane Arp, who is a Valkyrie – very tall, very blonde and extremely good-looking, with a placid northern-European face. To pass the time as we wait for the show to start, we discuss designers and she says she loves Victoria Beckham's work. Since I have only ever seen Christiane dressed in mannish black trouser suits (broken by an occasional white tuxedo jacket), I assume that it's her trousers she admires. 'No,' she says. 'It's the gowns. I have at least nine of her gowns. All black.' I ask when she wears them, and it turns out that in Germany there are many white-tie occasions when she has to appear in full-length eveningwear. Thank heavens I don't edit German *Vogue*.

5 March

Yes. It's snowing – sort of – when I wake. A wet, sleety drop that doesn't stay on the ground for a second. David has joined me in Paris, which is lovely, and I take the morning off to visit the Fondation Louis Vuitton in the Bois de Boulogne. At first we're disappointed that the current exhibition is of contemporary Chinese art, which we don't know much about, and that because of the snow and general wet, the magnificent Frank Gehry-designed terraces, which I want David to see, are all closed. But there are some really terrific pieces on show. The monolithic ash paintings of Zhang Huan, made with ash gathered from Buddhist temples, show hundreds of tiny figures at work with a photographic realism, and remind me of Andreas Gursky's panoramas. There's also a fascinating video piece by Cao Fei, set in the Osram light-bulb factory in China. I don't think it has ever occurred to me to ponder how and where light-bulbs are made but this piece is about the workers, defining the gap between their real life and their dreams.

Ultimately our favourite is an Isaac Julien video installation based around the horrifying drowning of the Chinese cockle-pickers on Morecambe Bay one night in 2004. I wonder whether we like it most because Julien is not Chinese. Although the subject matter is China – a mix of the mythology, the world of anonymous, undocumented migrants, the glamour of old Shanghai, to put it at its most basic – it's still China through a Western eye, and we probably understand more of it than we do the work of the other artists.

We snatch a quick lunch in a café near the Trocadéro. At the next table there are three Irish women of about my age, I would guess. They're talking loudly and drinking gin and tonic and generally seem to be having a good time on a short trip to Paris. David is more interested in a gamine French girl at another table but I'm intrigued by them and wonder who they are, since from the smatterings of chat I can hear, they clearly have something to do with Fashion Week. Much of the conversation is about waiting for one of their sons to arrive; he's having trouble with his Uber and had been at a party until late last night. It's a wonderful moment when the prodigal son appears and it's Jonathan Anderson in dark glasses, clearly suffering from celebrating his previous day's Loewe show until the small hours. I would never have put this cheerful group of women together with one of fashion's biggest talents of the moment. I like him even more for pitching up to see his mum with a terrible hangover.

7 March

When I wake this morning I try to order wood stain for the proposed garden shed. Obsidian, Carolina Stone, Pea Green – the colour chart is hard to gauge from a computer screen in a hotel room off the Champs-Élysées. I have a vision that this shed will bring an order to my life quite out of proportion to its actual function.

The beat of the tom-toms is getting louder around the Saint Laurent show tonight.

I sit next door to someone at the Sacai show, who says, 'So he's not there, right?'

'What do you mean, he's not there?'

'He's gone already. That's why it's going to be so small.'

Like the rumours over who is going to head up Dior, this chatter is fuelled by an awful lot of time everyone has spent corralled together over the last month. They all have a different take on Hedi Slimane and Saint Laurent. He has provoked mixed emotions during his tenure, when he has managed to take a very mainstream teen street look of vintage car coats, leather jackets, miniskirts and ripped tights and made it part of one of Paris's most upmarket fashion houses. I clearly remember when I saw his first show in 2012, I was shocked by the models, who looked just like Saturday-afternoon shoppers in Topshop. But, despite that, the collection sold extremely well: on the runway the pieces looked tacky, but in reality they were wearable and cool. I bought a black Saint Laurent pea coat for myself a few weeks back to see me through the shows and it's well cut and beautifully made. Anyway, Hedi's arrogance has infuriated some people, while for others he has an almost messianic allure. When he arrived he quickly banned various people from shows and was very controlling over the way we were allowed to shoot his work so for some there is a certain pleasure in the speculation over whether his contract is being renewed. The business is doing so well I can't imagine that it won't be, but word is that he's asking for a huge amount of money.

At Stella McCartney's show, where, as usual, her dad and step-mother are seated front row to watch her parade of leggy, sporty girls, I'm sitting next to my boss, Jonathan, and we have the now mandatory Saint Laurent conversation. I ask him what he thinks and he says, 'Well, there are a lot of rumours.' Bit of a pause. 'Usually, rumours are true.'

Later I drop into the Chanel studio to see Karl Lagerfeld in advance of the show. It is quiet there at the moment and the girls are presented to him so that he can add the final styling touches. Each has a leather hat in the style of Coco's famous brimmed bowlers and they are all draped with chains of oversized pearls. I really want him to come to the festival or the gala dinner or both, but as yet he is the fish I'm failing to hook. I've asked him so many times now in person and in writing that I can't bring myself to ask him again, so instead I watch him watch his live video of Choupette playing on his bed. As Jo, the head of the British press team, escorts me out, she's relentlessly positive and brightly asks if I mentioned the dates of the festival again to him. She thinks the issue is that the advertising campaign is being shot at that time and if that's the case he'll need to be in Paris. But I'm not so sure. If Karl really wanted to come, he would make it work. He probably just doesn't want to. It's a real pity.

*

Every season Jonathan gives a big dinner in Paris for the *Vogue* and *Vanity Fair* teams, with photographers and designers as guests. It's an interesting mix of people from all over the globe and he always gives a welcome speech as if he were a character from *The Godfather*, taking care of family business. He's very good at making us feel as if we're united as a somewhat disparate family, but at the same time, as with Mafia families, some members have always disappeared from the picture in mysterious circumstances, while others are newly initiated. Nicholas Coleridge, Lucinda and I are among those who have been coming the longest.

8 March

The security at the Paris shows is higher than it was during the couture. Bags and bodies are scanned before each one, and outside the show tent in the Tuileries, policemen are carrying shotguns in a casual manner, as they dispassionately watch the parade of exotically dressed fashion-goers. Much of the general discussion is about the new proposals of when to show and when clothes go into the stores. I meet with Demna and Guram Gvasalia in a showroom on a grubby boulevard near the Gare du Nord. Nirvana is playing in the big black space filled with a few rails of both the mens- and womenswear Demna has created for Vetements. They are riding high on the success of his first collection for Balenciaga, which was shown yesterday. It was clever in the way it mixed a substantial dollop of Vetements street style into the play on proportion and shape that Cristóbal Balenciaga originally brought to fashion. A bit like mixing Banksy with Picasso, although way more successful than that sounds.

Demna and Guram are Georgian and were brought up during that country's civil war. Demna strikes me as the gentler of the brothers and Guram has the intensity of many a visionary. Wasn't Stalin Georgian? When I ask if they will talk at the festival Demna makes it clear that he doesn't want them to be sharing a platform with any other designer. I have to think how to make this work since, although they are absolutely the names *du jour* in the industry this month, I don't know how many people who are not industry insiders will pay to hear them. As always, the festival is a balancing act between involving people whom the business is interested in and those who reach a mass audience. We need to sell 600 tickets for the large auditorium and about 150 for the smaller. It's always a problem – the gap between perceptions of this kind. Gurum asks me if I'm aware of their plans to move their shows to June and January and that they have a completely different idea of what will make up their collection. I had thought that his pale skin, ginger hair and blue eyes were common to Georgians but he says that it's quite the reverse and he's most unusual.

Hurrah! David Beckham has finally been photographed at home by Jamie Hawkesworth this morning. The long to-do list is starting to get ticked off.

9 March

Paris is meant to be grounded by a huge strike today and gridlock is predicted. Last night I hit my wall in terms of having had enough of fashion weeks. I want to get home. I'm feeling bloated and my face is saggy. With no exercise and eating too much bread, I have gained five pounds, which is depressing. An email I get this morning gives me the impression that our *Ab Fab* shoot is going belly-up. So, I'm not happy. Although we made it clear from the outset that we wanted to shoot a tribute to the programme, supplemented by models and designers of our own choosing, at just a week away from the shoot, it appears that 'they', whoever 'they' are, won't agree to this. Yesterday I thought we had managed to get John Galliano to feature in it, and now it looks like I'll have to go back and say the whole thing won't be happening. Frankly, at this point, I don't care whether it happens or not.

I wait in a cavernous black geodome for the Louis Vuitton show to begin. Suzy Menkes is bending Lucinda's ear about whether or not the theme for the show is Atlantis, which she says would be crazy as McQueen did that ages ago. Lucinda is clearly not engaging in this discussion. I check my phone to avoid getting caught up in the conversation and to see if there is any more *Ab Fab* news. There's an email from Nicola, my beauty director, titled 'OK, we have a yes'. For a moment I don't want to scroll further in case it's not what I'm hoping it is. But it is. She has sent me confirmation from Kim Kardashian's agent that Kim will speak at the festival. Suddenly it's all-change and I'm soaring and all is good with the world.

11 March

Although it is chilly, spring has arrived in London by the time I return from the shows. It may have been snowing in the north a few days ago but the light has shifted and the sun when it shines has a new depth rather than the thin brightness it casts in winter. Audrey arrives for yoga and asks me how my body has been. I tell her that it's been fine, it's my mind that's all over the place. She thinks that Pisces is involved in something or other to do with a new moon and that it will give certain star signs the ability to engage in some kind of peaceful resignation. Clearly I am not one of those signs. Yoga offers me no mental calm but it definitely makes me feel less lumpy and helps ward off muscle ache when I've been running so I stick with it for that reason, and also because I really like her. She is lovely to look at and very practical as well as new-agey so I can pick her brains over things like the endless plumbing saga in the house.

Jaime Perlman arrives back from New York where she has been working with Josh on the cover and the pictures of the duchess. I wanted to make sure there was minimal retouching, and in something as important as this, I felt more confident to have my woman on the ground. She shows the final images to me on her laptop. I've seen them so often now I can't judge them, and now I have a kind of gauze over my reaction to them. I think they're really gorgeous, but I can't view them as objects in their own right because they're of her.

I call Nicholas Coleridge and say we have something to show him and he comes up to my office. Jaime reopens the laptop and pulls up the cover. Thank heavens he clearly loves the picture although he says he can't remember quite who it reminds him of. And then says it's James Bay, which is not exactly what we had in mind.

I still have to work out the text to go on the image. At the moment the words aren't quite right. They need to encapsulate the idea of 100 years, celebration, style and culture, and the specialness of this particular issue.

The return to the office post-shows is always difficult. The demands and travelling of the show timetable allow me to escape some of the more mundane chores in my life. I suppose it's like any job when you're on the road, which has its own impetus. The return to reality is a come-down.

I need to scrutinize the rolling budget for the costs of the magazine's content and see whether I have overspent. We have to decide on job titles and descriptions to replace people who are leaving, and my desk has two piles of paper on it which have not moved in months, save for being shifted from tray to tray. A couple of years ago Louisa McGillicuddy, my then assistant, put three stickers above the desk trays, 'To Do', 'Doing', 'Done', and they are still there, though the words no longer bear any resemblance to the content. I learn a lot from my assistants. She taught me the benefits of rigorous email filing and urged me to empty my inbox every day (another unfulfilled task). Many years previously my then helper, Kendra Wilson, tried to alleviate my fear of flying by saying I should think of myself as a stamp on an airmail letter. How often did letters not arrive? It's true that when she told me this in the late eighties the mail was substantially more reliable than it is now.

Charlotte Pearson, my current assistant, has collected piles of non-urgent emails to go through with me and a folder of invitations, most of which I decline – private views, parties hosted by small brands, launch dinners, press days. I have a rule that if I accept I can't change my mind later as I know how infuriating that is. It makes me think hard about whether, when the date arrives, I'll be able or indeed want to turn up. On her desk is a copy of the Rihanna issue with my note to Rihanna, and I snap at her about not having mailed it out days ago. She's always calm and cheerful and, as with almost all of my assistants, I constantly marvel at her ability to keep the torrent of information I fling at her under some kind of control. That's probably the most demanding aspect of her job – knowing how to prioritize. She triumphantly hands me a small Jiffy bag of metal parts. I'm delighted: it's the missing bolt for the kitchen clock, after months of waiting, and excites me even more than a pair of Erdem shoes that has also arrived.

On the wall in the art room are the first finished layouts for the Centenary issue. They are so important to me and I'm nervous that I won't find them as good as I hope they are, but I take a quick glance to see what's there and decide to look more intensely later. There is a dummy of the Front of Book pages stuck down that I find less frightening to go through, probably because they're easier to alter. There are some great things in there but it doesn't have the magic that I really want yet. It's hard to evaluate with so much still missing.

Jamie Hawkesworth's portrait of Beckham has arrived. He's a small figure shot in black and white on the steps of a house with a dog in the window and a child's scooter beside him – a picture that deliberately diminishes him. With Tim's ideas rejected and the shoot shifting to Hawkesworth, it would always have been a simpler portrait, but Beckham was meant to have brought something personal with him to the shoot. That doesn't seem to have happened. I find it a little weak for such a big character and I want to see if there are any others. Apparently Jamie found the location difficult – it was the garden of the Beckhams' rented house. It's becoming a fact that the things that take the most time to organize turn out unsatisfactory.

The afternoon is a car crash of meetings with everything colliding and not enough time to do anything properly. Nick and Catherine Roylance of Genesis, the publishers of *Vogue – Voice of a Century*, the limited-edition book I've planned, arrive with a big box of leather samples. There is a proposed cover for the box with the word *Vogue* in gold and a little oval window that can be pulled open and shut to reveal an image, along with a leather design for the actual cover. We have to decide what will be inside the window for the proposed 1,916 copies (one for each year of publication). Initially it seemed like a good idea to put a different cover inside each but I doubt we could manage that for all of 1916 and, anyway, as nice a concept as it is, not only would it be a huge amount of work but also *Vogue* covers are rectangular. The crop involved would mean it would get a partial logo and would look a mess. So we decide instead to use one image per decade and spread that throughout the print run. The actual cover of the book is to be a fashion image worked in leather. I want something that has the elegance and grandeur of a traditional vision of *Vogue*, and Nick (everyone seems to be called Nick in my world at the moment) presents three options of which one, the back view of a model in a long gown, could be beautiful.

He shows me the first layouts for inside and I'm very disappointed: they don't have the lush, expansive quality that seems important for a book that will cost more than five hundred pounds. There are too many big blocks of quotes from people they have interviewed and not enough original layouts from the magazine. Having seen how people are poring over the actual pages in the National Portrait Gallery, I'm more than ever convinced they should be the backbone of the book. I don't have time to spend on working this through with them so we agree to have another meeting.

When I get home Joseph has left five wooden panels with different-coloured stains for the shed. Where the shed was originally sited there is now a huge damp pile of old wood and next to it a crumpled green tarpaulin covering the contents that I will need to go through tomorrow. The thought of riffling through old weed killer, rusty trowels, bags of cat litter and such is not particularly appealing.

I sit at the kitchen table with an adult dot-to-dot book I've been sent, as I talk to David. As a child I loved dot-to-dot and it's rather an effective wind-down activity. When I get back from work I need at least twenty minutes to turn into the person I should be at home, ideally a mellower version of the office me. Sometimes I achieve it and sometimes I don't. When Sam was little, and that time was some of the few precious hours I could spend with him, I would throw myself into it the moment I saw him, but I didn't have much grace or patience left for his father or, indeed, years later, for David.

David has spent the day gathering reminiscences and anecdotes for the address he is giving next week at his friend the author Louise Rennison's funeral. I know he'll do it brilliantly and it will be clever and human and funny. David gave her the break years back that led her to become one of the most successful children's book authors in the world when he commissioned pieces from her at the *Evening Standard*. I cook some steaks and make a salad and Sam joins us. We get into a discussion about the difference between what is called a museum and what is called a gallery, and how museums contain galleries and where the word 'museum' came from, which is a nice way to end the day as it has nothing to do with *Vogue*.

12 March

Josh calls to say that he would like another image to be considered to be hung alongside the cover at the National Portrait Gallery in the *Vogue* 100 exhibition. Perhaps, he says, we could run a second cover as a special edition? He really loves a black-and-white headshot portrait that at the moment is not in the edit in the magazine. Something similar is, but not that exact gaze, that exact tilt of the head. And it's such details that we all care about so much. With a lot of different people involved in this story, I feel incredibly anxious at the idea of going back to Kensington Palace and the gallery with a different proposal. Equally, though, I know how important this is to Josh, and he should be able to have his say and know he has been listened to. I don't think we're going to be able to run two covers, but it's just possible that everyone will agree the more portrait-style black-and-white image he likes can be hung there.

He called as I was about to meet my friend Louise Chunn for tennis in the park opposite. We are usually fairly evenly matched although she is consistently the better player not least because she runs for the ball and I don't. It's my first game of the year but I can't concentrate on it as my mind is whirring around possible ramifications from the phone call. I'm all over the place and unable to remember the scores or even when I'm serving or not serving but, even so, I win the first three games. Every game of the set reaches deuce and finally I lose, 8–6. But it was good to play, and by the time I get home, I'm able to stop turning over the different scenarios in my mind and also feel able to wait till Monday to work out this next stage.

I further soothe myself by making a fruit salad for dinner. It's the blood orange season and I enjoy seeing the dark segments split as I chop.

15 March

I go to have my hair coloured by Josh Wood at his salon in Holland Park. As always the appointment was made weeks ago and now it's the last thing I want to be doing – more than two precious hours locked down when I have a million calls to make and conversations to have in the office. On the way the cab driver asks if I'm working and I say yes, as I jab at my phone, there's a lot going on. When he asks what I do, I tell him I edit *Vogue* magazine. He says, 'I have to admit I've never read it. Don't it have a model or something on the cover? Seen it in the doctor's waiting room. It's, like, take-your-mind-off-it kind of stuff.' I agree that, broadly speaking, that is what it is, although clearly not for me.

He knows that the magazine has a birthday, which I'm pleased about, and I tell him of the exhibition at the National Portrait Gallery, which is a big success. 'So can't you just sit back, then?' he asks.

'No, not really. You're only as good as your next success.' Which is true, if a bit glib. Whenever something works out, there is an incredibly short period of time to feel pleased about it before the only thing that really matters is whether or not the next project comes off. Surely psychologically this is not the kind of attitude self-help books would advocate. I remember reading somewhere that you're meant to wake up every morning congratulating yourself in one way or another.

Just as I'm about to go into the salon, I get another call from Josh Olins, asking for news on our last conversation, and I tell him I'm working on it. He's obviously quite concerned about whether his choice will be hung, so by the time I'm wrapped in a hideous gown having icy paste daubed on my head, I'm even more impatient than usual about being there and not being able to talk to anyone about it.

I have too much to do to be spending two hours having my hair done and I'm bad-tempered. The other Josh (Wood) ignores my snappiness and chats convivially. He has been doing the hair at the Paris shows and shows me his iPhone with the photo references for the hairstyles at Givenchy – 'Albino snakes,' he says. 'I've never had a reference like it.' They are the weirdest objects, like plaster sculptures with creamy, intricate scales, but I see how the style of the models' plaits was fed from them.

Nicholas Cullinan drops by the office and I show him the picture that Josh would like them to have. He loves it and thinks it's probably fine to have two images there.

Yesterday I stayed at home trying to write the piece to go with the June cover. The house during the week is a stranger to me and I sit in my study, freezing, as I feel I should suffer as David and Sam do, with the heating switched off until late afternoon. It's nice for me to have a day like this – going downstairs to make coffee every hour, talking to the carpenter who is working on the shed, making the odd unnecessary phone call. The only bad thing is the piece, which I don't feel I've got right yet. By the afternoon I have a first draft and walk to the local supermarket to find food for dinner. My mother is coming over and I want to cook a cauliflower dish with a capers, parsley, chilli and pine-nut sauce that I've never tried. However, I find myself walking in a dazed manner up and down the aisles of Sainsbury's, completely unclear as to which shelves will house the capers and pine nuts. Eventually I find the former but there are no pine nuts.

After such a quiet day I wake really early and fling myself into the office. There are about thirty pages of layouts for the Centenary issue for me to see and most of them look wonderful. There are the rewritten captions to go with Mario's shoot of ten decades of fashion, which have added some commentary on the style of each decade, and the small story called 'What the Intern Saw', which is the recollections of assistants over the years – it looks good and reads very well. For the first time I'm getting a real sense of the issue. Much of it will appear so simple in the magazine but I know how hard it has been to track down everyone and get interviews organized. Emily has been brilliant at doing this and searched out a fantastic range of people to write about their first experience of *Vogue*. The Richard Branson copy, on when he was first photographed as a student for *Vogue*, has arrived and is funny and self-deprecating, and there is a nice quote from Cheryl Cole about seeing herself on the cover of *Vogue* for the first time. Throughout the magazine there are endless references to Bailey, who of course is one of the great *Vogue* characters, even though it annoys him that people think that.

On which note the *Ab Fab* shoot finally took place yesterday. As far as I can tell Bailey and Lucinda, though far from in love with each other, managed to survive the day. Everyone turned up and Georgia May Jagger was in the end the model, as planned. I have no idea what the pictures are going to look like.

We have a huge meeting about the design concepts for the interiors of the festival tent and the gala dinner. Patrick Kinmonth has already suggested a black carpet that he used in the design for the exhibition but it's obvious that Richard at Timebased does not agree. He thinks it will look filthy. He shows us an alternative of black lino but the idea of black flooring has led him to an almost entirely black theme for everything, with bits of gold and white. The last thing I want is an expensive tent in beautiful Kensington Gardens kitted out to look like the Ghost Train in a theme park, which is the direction of travel I'm looking at on his boards. If we don't go with the black floor there is a pale grey and rose gold alternative.

Patrick and his creative partner Antonio arrive and I explain that the black floor seems to be generally affecting the whole design and how wedded is he to it? His design for the National Portrait Gallery has been so brilliant that I'm keen to take his lead on design ideas, and since I asked him to be involved, there's no point if we don't listen to him.

However, I'm not entirely seduced by the black floor, so I'm delighted when he says it's fine if we don't want it and picks out a kind of deep grey instead. Sacha is looking a bit green at the end of the table as we go through ideas for having twelve huge screens at the dinner, which will show a live feed of the evening (after it has gone, I hope, through a flattering grading, and black-and-white filter) as well as animated moving imagery. She is in charge of the budget, which is already stretched, and this is going to mean there is not a penny for anything else that could crop up in the next two months.

19 March

We're in Suffolk for the weekend, staying with our friends Dan Franklin and Lucy Hughes-Hallett. David and they have gone for a walk by the sea but I have stayed in the house to sort through the ideas that all the fashion editors have pitched for new-season fashion shoots. I have a folder of papers in front of me with their thoughts on a concept and a photographer. I like Lucinda's suggestion of 'A pretty modern army' by Mario Testino, which she says would be blanket coats, and military references softened with romantic dresses, and also one about the tweed tailoring shot through with Lurex and a distressed feel, which she calls 'I should Coco' in reference to the Chanel tropes throughout, like chains and bouclé tweed. Kate Phelan suggests the same army idea but calls it 'Uniforms' and pairs it with the photographer Alasdair McLellan, and also pitches two travel stories with Tim Walker, one to the Faroe Isles and one to Japan. We have been discussing the possibility of them travelling to Japan for a year and I love the idea but need to work out if we can afford it. Hardly any magazines shoot their fashion pages in interesting locations now, but some of my all-time favourites have been as much travel stories as fashion. There are three or four other editors' ideas, and as I study the pile of paper by my mug of coffee I know I'm looking at 200 pages of fashion pictures.

The mix of the photographers, the budgets and the advertising credits in the issues are an intricate pattern and I always find this moment tricky. This season I'm also reconsidering exactly what we're trying to achieve in these shoots. With all the talk about the immediacy of social media, particularly in the messaging from Instagram, it seems that, more than ever, the strength of what Vogue can offer has to be in the uniqueness of the image. Our ability to be the informers of which trends are the newest and strongest has obviously been diluted by the speed and reach of digital websites where so much information will already have been published, but none of them has, as yet, managed to create the memorable imagery that we can. So this season I feel less bound by the stories being trend-driven than I have at other times, and more by the originality of the photography.

En route to Dan and Lucy we went to look at the estuary where a Suffolk cottage might become available. It couldn't have been a less prepossessing day – heavy grey cloud and mizzle – but as we drove off the main road and down a track, then another track to the estuary where the cottage is sited, the landscape was magical: flat planes of dense colour even in the grey, the fields bordered by the spires of Scot pines, the naked trunks and broad flat canopies of cedars, and finally the silver sludge of the estuary at low tide. It was immensely bleak but I love that strange badland landscape, a kind of British bayou. Even so, it took us three hours to get there, which is simply not an option for weekends, and if I'm realistic, I'm just too busy to make use of a weekend house, no matter how special the spot. Curiously, as I pretty well conclude it's not going to happen, David, who up until now has been entirely negative about the idea, starts to say how lovely it is and how it would certainly be worth considering if it really does come up for rent.

By the end of next week the whole festival programme needs to be ready to put up on the ticketing site. This means that final times have to be agreed in stone along with most of the speakers. We still have a couple of unfilled slots and a number of the people I have asked have still not replied, either yes or no. I wake this morning to learn from Stella McCartney's office that I won't hear until next week if she can speak there, and from Isabel Marant's PR, with the same message. The thing is, I don't have time to wait now. Stella took part in our first festival and it would be lovely to have her representing British fashion. Once the programme is online there is very, very little room for change.

When we left the house yesterday the garden was filled with the rubbish that Joseph had failed to get removed from the shed build. Next weekend is Easter and Sam is having his twenty-first birthday party at home so I'm hoping that somehow the lone carpenter, who has not, like Joseph and the rest of his crew, gone home to Hungary for the Easter break, will magic the stuff away. Otherwise it will be Sam and me lugging bags of coal and concrete and garden tools and planks into a hidden corner of some kind. Should I be having to do this?

20 March

It's terrifying that March is almost at an end. The month seems to have existed without me being present. I always think it's vital to treasure the next couple of months when there is all the promise of summer ahead: July arrives before you know it and then it's down-hill to autumn. Today we woke to sunshine and Lucy suggested a walk to a beach called Covehithe. After staying in yesterday I feel I should join them but I never really see the point of walks. I am not clear what one is meant to do. The activity of putting one foot in

front of another has limited appeal to me, and if it's about chatting with a group I'd rather do it around a table with a glass of wine. Then there is the question of the view, which, if I'm not careful, I miss as I'm normally looking at the ground for most of the duration and forget to take in the surroundings. Lucy is a keen walker and explains that it's just uplifting to be in the fresh air and for her the activity is almost meditative. They also have an enormous dog, which makes a lot of walking necessary, although I wonder why, if you're lucky enough to have a huge garden, dogs also need to be taken for walks rather than just let out.

We walk along the coastal path, which they explain has suffered shocking erosion even in the last month or so. Massive trees have been torn from their roots and sprawl across the beach, and notices everywhere say how fragile and dangerous the path is. While the others stride ahead I try to write the editor's letter for June in my head.

21 March

When we come back to London it is as if a poltergeist has had a sleepover. We have only been away two days, and there have been so many mishaps. The kitchen ceiling has suddenly sprouted a big brown stain around one of the spotlights, which is darkening by the minute. While trying to investigate the source, we discover that water is dripping from the base of one of the towel rails on the floor above, but also the pressure in the boiler has dropped to zero, so that, once again, there is no hot water and no heat.

I start today, Monday, very fraught with this domestic mayhem. David has discovered Phil the plumber who, he has been assured, is a good guy, so I leave with the usual triumph of hope over experience in that department, late for my breakfast with Wil Harris, who is our head of digital. Wil is the only man I know who accompanies his greeting kisses with a verbal 'Mwah, mwah' – no doubt an ironic nod to the fashion world we're in. He comes from a successful digital background and is constantly juggling the frustrations of working in a publishing company that still sets such value on print. He bends over backwards to avoid including me in his list of culprits but we both know that the print magazine is still where my heart really lies. If I had a choice between allocating funds to sell more print copies or drive digital traffic, most often I would choose the former. I love the magazine and it still makes much more money than any digital initiative.

Tim Walker delivers his portrait of Naomi Campbell, who is sprawled limply on the floor in a tiny white dress with a huge black Afro. It's a great picture, and now it's here, I don't mind the problems there were getting it done. My colleague on *GQ*, Dylan Jones, quips that his modus operandi is 'Big Smile, Short Memory' but I often find it hard to move easily on when the process has been difficult.

Next week is week four, technically the last week of production, and a number of the pages will have to be done twice – fake and real – so that at the last minute the picture of the duchess can be added in and dummy pages, like my editor's letter and the contents page, will need to be replaced with ones that refer to that story.

22 March

When I wake I go into the garden to admire the nearly completed shed. This basic structure of clapboard and plywood is giving me a huge amount of pleasure and I spend some time planning where the interior shelves should be placed and estimating how much I will be able to store in there. It's brilliantly sunny and the spring flowers are at their peak, with the pots of narcissi and paperwhites now all in bloom. Back inside, I switch on the radio and there are reports of an explosion at Brussels airport. By the time I leave the house for work there are also unconfirmed reports of another at a Métro station.

As, once again, the casualty list grows throughout the day and the TV is filled with blurred pictures taken from people's phones of the smoke-filled airport and the evacuating crowd in the Métro tunnel, everything around me carries on as ever. It's a ghastly thought, but the general horror seems to weaken each time one of these attacks takes place so that it appears an immunity is taking hold. No one is speaking of it in the office.

I lunch with Daniel Marks, who is one of the best public-relations guys in London. When I say how awful the events in Brussels are, I can tell that, because it wasn't at the forefront of his mind, he doesn't hear me properly and thinks I'm talking about some initiative to do with the fashion calendar. It doesn't seem worthwhile to clarify, and instead we continue to discuss our views on the see-now, buy-now schemes and he tells me about plans for his husband's big fiftieth-birthday weekend.

Bailey has sent in pdfs of the *Ab Fab* story, including two images of Jennifer and Joanna with hugely distorted heads so they look as if they are caricatures. The other pictures are terrific, Georgia May posed between Jennifer and Joanna, serene and unperturbed by their crazy personas. But I'm troubled by the distorted pictures, which I find offensive and ugly. So, it appears, does everyone else in the office.

Kate Phelan says she's sure Bailey doesn't mean them to be run and he's just having us on. Jaime Perlman has rung him to talk about the layout he's sent through and has had him scream at her that he knew she wouldn't 'get it', along with a vomit of expletives. I call him and say how great most of the pictures are but not the distorted ones. He replies in his gravelly voice that they are the *best* pictures, and everybody thought Picasso's women were ugly when they first saw them. My response is that he is not Picasso to which he answers that I'm like every journalist who takes comments out of context. It's a relatively benign call and we have some jokes. But I don't really know what to do. I need to get the actual digital files out of him for the magazine and if I say I don't want to run his favourite pictures he won't hand them over.

23 March

I measure the seriousness of being awake at night by whether the birds have yet started to sing. When I hear them, I've broken the back of night and feel calmer about being awake in the dark. I'd been tossing the Bailey situation around in my head for hours last night before I heard the first birdsong and decided that Joanna and Jennifer have to approve the distorted images. If they're content with them, our best bet would be to run them in a way that makes it clear that it's Bailey choice, not ours. As I write, this sounds pretty dodgy, even to myself, but right now it appears it will either have to be that or, if he won't give us the pictures, drop the story altogether. After all the work in making it happen, that would be a real drag.

I got to sleep at about five, and two hours later the alarm hauls me out of a deep doze. I check my phone and read that Stella McCartney won't talk at the festival but has said she will come to the gala dinner. As a counterpoint, the positive news is that Isabel Marant is on board. Now I need to think how to maximize that – who would be good to pair with her on stage? Englishwomen are obsessed with Parisian style. The skinny black jeans, blazers, ankle boots, liquid hair and boyish shape have become a template for a kind of chic we envy and which Marant's designs play to, with an additional dose of hippie flow added in. Her clothes are hugely popular here, but she's relatively unknown as an individual so hopefully tickets will sell quickly. Someone like Lou Doillon or Caroline de Maigret would be perfect.

Breakfast is my favourite meal for meetings. You can be done within an hour, then have the day ahead without the interruption of lunch. Lauren Santo Domingo and I meet at the Connaught Hotel where she's staying. The breakfast room is crowded and the manager is dealing with a number of disgruntled people who have all booked and for whom there is no table. Lauren is co-founder of Moda Operandi, the e-commerce fashion site targeted at high-net-worth customers. Those women who, like Lauren herself, buzz around between Paris, Rio, New York, Wyoming, Portofino and LA. She looks just as I would imagine many of her shoppers would like to look, with long sleek blonde hair and the bony physique of a crane. As we breakfast (an ''erb omelette' for her and black coffee for me) she tells me about her site, and reckons an average spend on the much larger and more established Net-a-Porter is about four hundred pounds, while theirs comes in at around sixteen hundred dollars. When I roughly convert this figure into pounds, underestimating by about two hundred, she quickly corrects me. No financial flies on this one.

'There is absolutely no reason for these women to get dressed in the morning. None,' she shoots, in a rapid American accent, describing a clientele who, she continues, would be content to stay in leggings and ballerina pumps all day if they weren't persuaded into more chic outfits by her team of buyers and stylists. 'They've got the bag. They've got the rock.' She stretches out her long thin arms, one angled at 90 degrees to demonstrate an expensive bag in the crook of the elbow, the other showing off an imaginary but unmistakably huge ring on a finger.

She makes an interesting distinction about the need to show women not what to *buy* but what to *wear*. Her team get involved in planning details of how a whole look is put together top-to-toe if a client wants that. It's like a DIY kit, so that getting dressed requires no consideration. Or any personal imagination. Since many of the biggest major labels don't sell through her, the stock includes independent labels with an emphasis on designers who will collaborate on their trunk shows, dinners and pre-orders. 'It's like opera,' is how she dismisses her lack of the huge brands, while pulling a how-dull-can-it-get? face. 'You go to it once a year because it's the thing your mother did. But? Enough.' She shrugs dismissively. That is so New York, both talk and action. Turn the problem into an asset.

She's funny and quick, and I leave breakfast wanting to see if I can get her on stage with her friends Alexa Chung and Derek Blasberg for the festival's style clinic. Derek and Lauren have the same sassy wit, and Alexa, with her self-deprecating Brit humour, would be able to cook up a lively question-and-advice session. She seems keen on the idea, although she has to be in San Francisco the day after for the *Financial Times* Luxury Conference. That doesn't appear to faze her.

Tomorrow is Good Friday. We have to plan the running order of the pages of the Centenary magazine and get 90 per cent of those pages finalized before the four-day break. To my slight disappointment, but greater relief, Jennifer Saunders and Joanna Lumley have come back saying they're perfectly happy with Bailey's treatment in the pictures so I make the decision to run them, in spite of my own opinion that they're ugly. It's probably better for the reader to see the story and read Emily's funny article than for me to follow my taste.

We're struggling to find the right photo to lead Lucy Hughes-Hallett's excellent piece on how the weather in Britain has always been, and for ever will be, a chief determinant of our lifestyle. So often it's these tasks, which should be simple, that are left to the last minute and then there's a panic. There's a beautiful Gerhard Richter photograph of a hazy landscape in moody tones that I really want to run but the picture desk can't find out whether it definitely shows Britain. Ninety-nine per cent of the people looking at the page will pay no attention to what country is depicted, but I don't want even one clever clogs writing in and saying surely we knew it was Bavaria. After a lot of discussion we settle on a different picture of an endless sky above a Welsh valley by Alasdair McLellan.

Jaime, her deputy Felix and I are filmed as we stand in the art room looking at the layouts and planning the order in which they will run. At the end Richard Macer asks me whether I had always intended that Mario Testino's Decades shoot would start the magazine. I snap, 'No,' uncomfortable in the knowledge that this is a fake running order since the story on the duchess will open the magazine, and one whole story that we're using as a place holder, so that we're working with an accurate number of pages, won't run at all.

I find the duplicity very hard. He introduces me to the film's editor, who has been looking at all the footage for a month or so now, seems really nice, and is very complimentary about all of us. That makes me feel even worse. When I'm back in my own office I get in touch with Nicky Eaton, who organizes our communications, and ask what damage limitation we can do to mitigate their not having any pre-knowledge of what will be the most talked-about item in the issue. There is a plan for filming the installation of the picture at the National Portrait Gallery the night before the images are released, and I ask her to see if they could be allowed into this, which would give them about four hours' prior knowledge. At least then they would be geared up to film the coverage the next day.

Below my office window there is a massive depot for the teams working on Crossrail. At about three thirty there's a big noise outside, and I walk over to see a queue of orange hi-vis workers, like so many Oompa-Loompas (all men), laughing and talking as they wait to file through a turnstile. I suppose they're knocking off for

Easter and I kind of envy them for a moment. In my fantasy they're clocking out for four days with families or girlfriends, totally unbothered by thoughts of work, entirely free of anxieties about things like whether we'll fill the talks at the festival or whether we're going to go over-budget on the gala dinner, or the frankly disappointing sales figures I've just been sent from the Rihanna cover. I know that this is not remotely the reality and they will have an equal number of problems, maybe about more serious things, and quite possibly many more personal difficulties, but all the same, that is what I'm thinking, as I gaze down from my fifth floor window above Hanover Square.

25 March

Good Friday. There's a vicious wind outside, and as I play tennis with Louise, I can hardly clinch a game in the whole first set. Then, in the second, there is a total reversal and she has the same experience so we reach a contented 6–1, 2–6. This time I don't even have the excuse of being thrown off by a phone call as today all I have to do is organize the house for Sam's party tonight.

I'm a little sad that David and I won't see any of it but he didn't invite us, and I knew there wouldn't be a possibility of sleep anyway, so we've invited ourselves to our next-door neighbours Charles and Virginia Brand's house in Devon to escape. Before we catch the train I move furniture, unpack a big delivery of wine and beer, and remove my most precious glasses and bowls from the kitchen, where he's planning to have dancing to the eighties playlist he has compiled. He seems pretty happy with everything by the time we leave, and I ask him to take photos. I can't believe he's nearly twenty-one when it seems only a few years back that I was buying *Thomas the Tank Engine* cakes and filling party bags. In fact, I'm thrilled not to be doing *that* any longer. I always found working out how to entertain a class of four-year-olds far more stressful than the seating plan at any *Vogue* dinner.

29 March

Easter has been uncommonly early this year and, as if to make the most of it, the weather has done its worst, with hail and gales, high winds and, very occasionally, just enough bright blue sky and sun to woo you outside, only to dump on you moments later. There are primroses on the slope outside the Brands' beautiful converted barn, and a stream rushes past, fuelled by all the winter rain. There is an Easter-egg hunt for adults and copious amounts of wine and gossip. I forget all about the things I've spent the past months obsessed by, like the festival timetable, and the content of the June issue, so that when we return home on Monday evening I'm overcome with a fizzy dread. I fear that by letting go of those particular reins for a few days I've now condemned myself to some catastrophe. Sam, though, has pulled off an amazing clearing-up job and shows me a picture he'd taken of the floor before he and his friends had done an industrial-style swab. All that remains are bin bags of bottles to be disposed of and the lingering smell of a thousand fags.

At about two in the morning I'm convinced my premonition of catastrophe has come true. My phone is suddenly making strange pinging sounds and the electric blanket that was off suddenly turns itself on, just as Coco runs into the bedroom and jumps on top of us. I wonder whether the evil spirits that caused our last daily, Merilyn, to leave after twenty years are, in fact, not the figment of her imagination that I stressed they were when she tried to resign.

That is the kind of crazy thought that takes hold in the middle of the night, and I'm able to take a more pragmatic approach when I wake in the morning, although after the spontaneous combustion of the rubbish, I don't rule out something nasty.

Today is a day of meetings. Now that most of the work has been finished on the June issue, I know I have to rev everyone up for the next. As well as myself. It feels relentless. As I am trying to finalize a working plan for July, Sam calls.

'I just wanted to tell you . . .' he begins, which often presages something I would rather not hear 'I just wanted to tell you . . . that last night something went wrong in my bathroom. There was a terrible noise with the loo, which stopped and then started again, and then the fuses blew all over the house.' Frankly, I'm highly relieved that it's Sam and his loo rather than evil spirits. But this is relatively short-lived as David immediately calls to inform me that there is no hot water, once again, in the house.

The only pages that are still outstanding are the ones that have mentions of the duchess that will replace the fakes and will be parachuted in under cover of darkness by Jaime and Clare Murray, our chief sub, just before we finally go to print.

Time takes on different shapes. If you're used to inhabiting a certain kind, change is unsettling. Yesterday I had a day without meetings and, in that unfamiliar situation, the space was discomforting rather than pleasant. Although there are a million things I need to be doing just in terms of basic maintenance of the magazine and myself, actually having time to do them is something I've almost forgotten. I want to plot the big autumn issues ahead and, in particular, focus on my idea for November's Real Issue.

This morning the choice of images to be shown at the National Portrait Gallery was finalized. Every time I look at them I can see them a little less clearly. I've seen them too often.

HRH has agreed that Josh can display his favourite head-shot picture and the one of her leaning over a gate in a striped jumper, which is Nick Cullinan's favourite. This makes two, which do not include our cover picture. I don't particularly mind as the cover will be seen everywhere but I had thought initially both Kensington Palace and the gallery had wanted to run with it. As so often in negotiation, everyone has moved their position a little from where they started and now we're all happy with the final decision. A decision is a great thing.

My assistant Charlotte is going through things with me this morning and says there is a rumour going around, starting in the advertising department, that there is a secret cover. With the amount of time Jaime and I have spent closeted in my office staring at her laptop, on which she's been working on the story, I'm not surprised. Also there are clear inconsistencies, not least that we have made so little fuss of the fake cover and have it lying around everywhere. I tell Charlotte to stamp heavily on the rumour, if she has an opportunity, and to say that of course she would know if something was going on. She says she has already done this. 'I said, "Alex is so busy she couldn't possibly have time to have another cover happening in secret." '

The pictures arrive from our cover shoot with Renée Zellweger by Patrick Demarchelier, and our fashion editor Verity Parker and I are really happy. She is completely recognizable as Bridget, who is, after all, the character she is loved for. And she doesn't have the strange plastic face that appeared in the papers a couple of years back.

It's not always the case that pictures arrive as I imagine them in advance, no I'm over the moon that here she looks pretty in the Prada dress I chose for the cover and just as I'd hoped. It's for our Ageless Style issue and it's important she has reality and accessibility about her. Patrick Demarchelier is always so amenable and will work with almost any editor I ask him to, which is not true of several of our photographers. They like to pair with someone they have built a relationship with or occasionally agree to work with anyone currently regarded as new and fashionable.

Creating outstanding fashion images is complicated and the chemistry between all the contributors makes a huge difference. They are often trying to shoot a story of fourteen pictures in one or two days, and it's understandable that people feel happiest with others they know and trust, but that often makes commissioning very difficult: trying to get the dates to coincide between a busy editor, photographer and subject, all in different parts of the globe, can be mind-numbingly complex. Luckily I don't have to do that work – Rosie Vogel does it in the fashion room, moving the pieces around until we get the fit. Patrick has the confidence to work with a range of people, which means that he's a great asset. He was shooting for the same issue with Lucinda in London yesterday and they did sixteen pictures in one day – almost unheard-of. I ring to thank him for both stories and he sounds more excited by the Lucinda story because he loves her and has worked with her for years, and also because her pictures are more extreme and high fashion.

She comes into my office with paper printouts of these pictures and some are really great and inspiring in terms of showing new proportions (a combination of oversized and shrunk) and clever use of colour. But she has put thick rubber chin straps under hats in several of them and I had specifically asked her to not style too many that way when we did the run-through. I guess it comes down to how many is *too many*. I find the straps ugly and they make the model look as if she has a broken jaw. Lucinda knows this is my view but, as often, she doesn't share it and has ignored it! Not for the first time I despair a little at not being listened to while also being not 100 per cent sure that my opinion is right. This is a minuet we have been dancing for twenty-four years and there's not much point in getting worked up about it this afternoon.

Sacha shouts into my office from her desk just outside. 'What do you want to do about the Tramp guest list?' She's referring to the big party we're hosting after the gala dinner.

'Nothing,' I shout back unhelpfully. But another guest list right now is beyond me.

'No. It'll be fine,' she replies.

'It'll be fine' is our mantra of the moment, when one or other of us thinks that, maybe, it won't be. She is concerned that we're inviting too many people to the dinner where there is a finite number of possible tables. The invitations have arrived from the printer and look beautiful, with their soft-focus Clifford Coffin ballgown image – a glamorous smudge.

Zaha Hadid has died of a heart attack. I didn't know her at all well but I remember her at the National Portrait Gallery patrons' dinner in February, swathed in her ostrich feathers, and how I was always surprised and pleased to receive one of her smiles, which were unexpected and warm.

APRIL

1 April

I wake from a dream in which the gala dinner has been transplanted to India. I have forgotten to get my hair done and have no evening bag to carry my phone and such. When I arrive late, dressed in something that resembles a tablecloth, the whole party is evacuated because of a huge fire. A vast black plume of smoke is racing across the city towards us, and appears to have started in our hotel.

Last night when I got back from work, I found a large plastic laundry bin containing water on an armchair in our bedroom where a seat cushion should be. None of us remembered to alert Ana, who is now our cleaner, to the fact that the pipes in Sam's bathroom aren't working and it shouldn't be used, so the loo has leaked through yet another light in the ceiling. I feel as if the house is an alter-ego, erupting with my stress. Never before has so much gone wrong so often. Every day there is a new leak or short circuit or crack emerging in the building, which, I suppose, is preferable to the same appearing in my body.

It's April Fool's Day and a slow Friday, apart from confirmation that Hedi Slimane has indeed left Saint Laurent, as so widely speculated. There's also a story in one newspaper about the Wendi Deng and Putin rumour that David and I had been told months back at dinner, and I wonder if it's the paper's April Fool. But it isn't.

Today we have almost finalized the festival programme, and I'm really pleased by the mixture of the talks: Kim Kardashian, Christopher Kane, Laura Bates of Everyday Sexism, Juergen Teller and Alessandro Michele.

3 April

I've made an error on the festival timetable: although I knew that Lauren Santo Domingo could only make the Saturday, I scheduled her for Sunday. It's now the weekend but we need to move around three talks involving eight people before tomorrow afternoon if we're to keep that panel together. With several of the speakers flying in for the talks, I don't know how possible this will be, and I'm furious with myself for not having spotted the mistake earlier.

To cheer myself up I go shopping. What an error. Who in their right mind cheers themselves up bikini shopping in April with a body that has been nowhere near the sun for months? The best time to buy swimwear is when you're on holiday and used to seeing yourself half naked.

The shops are filled with smock tops and floating midi dresses. These are exactly what my twenty-year-old self would have loved, but they look frightful on me now. The black versions are just possible in an Italian-widow way but white cheesecloth veers worryingly into *Shirley Valentine* territory. I try on a lot of Isabel Marant pieces and several from the Spanish label Masscob, but without success. In the end I buy two incredibly pretty silk tea dresses by Edina Ronay. I know they risk making me look like an ancient geography teacher and they're not in the slightest bit fashionable but I also know that I'll feel happy when I wear them. So much of clothes shopping is an act of imagination. When I leave the Cross boutique, with my dresses wrapped in tissue, I have a vision of myself and a summer ahead of gardens and parties, Pimm's and the scent of mown grass.

Today is Sunday. I tried to see the Paul Strand show at the V&A but it was sold out when I arrived late afternoon. Instead I wandered around the glass collection and the metalwork gallery, partly because I want to buy a gate for the front garden and partly because I realized that I never look at the permanent collection. I was sent a book called

Cooking for Artists and for supper decided to break ranks with my repetitive meals. I plumped for a Persian chicken stew (yes, it's chicken again), and spent the early evening preparing it. When I placed the casserole on the table Sam peered into the dish suspiciously and asked, 'What's this? It's weird,' which he knew was caricaturing his unadventurous taste in food. 'It's not roast chicken. Or steak. Or pasta.'

I explained to him and David that it was Persian chicken stew, with tomatoes and chicken and green beans, and there was also a bowl of couscous with chickpeas and pine nuts. 'There's nothing in here you don't like,' I conclude, hoping I brook no argument and helping myself to a large portion.

David attempted loyalty, saying, 'I suppose this is very healthy,' but after a few minutes added that, actually, he didn't really like tomatoes. Not when they were *cooked*.

'I agree with David. I always think it's kind of weird when you get, like, meat and tomatoes,' Sam contributed, warming to the theme. There was then another ten minutes of analysis, which included David saying that he never really *liked* stews, and how they often had fat in them, pointing to a scrap of chicken skin he had discovered in the deep orange sauce. I consider leaving them to make their own food from now on.

4 April

Sophie Dahl is interested in returning to writing now that her two girls are a little older and she suggests we meet up since a few years ago she was a regular contributor. She's a real beauty, and it's hard not to keep staring at her face, which has the slight strangeness essential to beauty. Certainly most of the men in Cecconi's, where we lunch, followed her with their eyes as she walked by, in grey high heels under her jeans, even though she is naturally so tall. And when we're leaving, the male attendants at the coat check ignore the pair of dumpy middle-aged women in front of her, eagerly scrambling to fetch her coat. Does she realize that her looks mean she inhabits a different sphere of existence?

She's like a delicious ice cream – with her heart-shaped face, huge blue eyes painted with bruise-coloured shadow and pink-lipsticked mouth. She is also very driven, and really quite determined about what she wants and does not want. She has wonderful stories of generations of her large and complicated family, and when I suggest she writes a book about the complexities, it turns out she's already working on one. Sophie suggests a piece about what to wear to the White House – her husband, Jamie Cullum, will be playing there at the end of the month with Aretha Franklin and Herbie Hancock. Two years ago that would have been a good story for us, but now I can't decide whether it will be too long after the event by the time we can publish and the story will have been everywhere the next day.

In the office we have our weekly digital meeting and everyone is pleased that for March we are three million views over our target.

The figures are so huge that they're hard to consider, and it's never entirely clear what they mean in terms of revenue or real interest in the content, but on any level 38,813,597 page impressions is a massive number.

The news has just broken that designer Anthony Vaccarello has been handed the Saint Laurent job, vacated by Hedi Slimane last week, and we discuss how to cover this. I don't know him personally but he has a smaller footprint than Hedi in every way. That doesn't mean he won't do a good job, but powerful personalities are often hard to follow. Sometimes the next incumbents of these roles are appointed speedily on the rebound, just like a replacement boyfriend or girlfriend. Sometimes they fit the vacated role perfectly and other times they end up as an unsatisfactory stop-gap. I have no idea which this will be. But we must involve him with the magazine.

Our early-access offer of festival tickets for magazine subscribers is going live tomorrow, but just as I walk through the front door at home I realize I have absolutely no idea how this will work. I probably don't *need* to know but I would prefer to. How will the ticketing site know that someone is a subscriber? I call the office to check. 'Actually, that's something we're looking at right now. There's a slight problem,' Anna Cryer says, sounding fraught. 'You put in your personal subscriber code. But the system can't verify whether the code is actually yours.'

'So you mean anyone could type in any old number and be able to buy tickets two days before they go on sale?'

'That's correct. It seems Richard imagined that our ticketing would be more sophisticated than it actually is.'

In the way of all offices, the beginning and end of the tale is not particularly clear. Richard Kingerlee, who runs our circulation department, had always said that the use of a code was for 'data capture rather than verification purposes', and none of us had grasped what this jargon really meant but no one admitted it. Now, as we're about to go live, it's clear that this special offer can be breached by someone simply typing in a random number. From my bedroom, looking out over the park as I talk on the phone, I decide to procrastinate and make the decision as to whether to stick to this plan in the morning, when my irritation over it has calmed down. It would be good to get those early-bird tickets up tomorrow, but it annoys me that we have such a flawed system that a five-year-old could hack into it. Richard obviously thinks I'm making a fuss about nothing, and that we should work on the premise that most people are honest and if they're asked for their code will not make one up. I have less faith in people's behaviour, obviously.

Tonight the Stones exhibition opens at the Saatchi Gallery, and the private view is a real case of all the old dudes – Jagger in his soft shoes and Mount Rushmore face, Charlie Watts paper thin with white hair, our friend Christopher Sykes in his Mr Toad tweeds, beaming with pleasure at the pictures he took back in the seventies of the Stones on tour. Carinthia West, a doppelgänger for Carly Simon and friend of Jagger's, alerts us to a platoon of Winnebagos outside the gallery where the Stones and friends are hanging out. There are very few young people and many who look like record-company execs of the vinyl years, now grandparents. It's a brilliant exhibition with a mixture of original art from record covers, to posters and photographs and excellent moving footage, including a Martin Scorsese-narrated overview of the Stones on film. At one point we troop downstairs to the basement to be welcomed to the show, where everyone is handed a pair of 3D glasses to watch them perform 'Satisfaction' in Hyde Park. And then you see the total genius of the music and of them belting it out. A bevy of old blokes enchanting hundreds of thousands with their performance, style, charisma, sound.

The May issue is released today with the Kate Moss/Stones T-shirt cover and it's perfect timing – so much better than the previous month it was planned for. At the exhibition curiously it was the display of clothes that was the weakest link. What looked wonderful on stage and, indeed, in our fashion shoot, appeared tawdry and a little sad on the mannequins. Exhibiting clothes is always very difficult and disappointing. It's why I didn't want to have any at the *Vogue* exhibition. Once you take the human away – the movement and the moment – the fabric very rarely sings out on its own. So, a collection of velvet trousers, dandy coats and skinny T-shirts had none of the glory that they would have had when worn by the band on stage.

I made a bet with Ben Goldsmith, who was at the party with Jemima, his pregnant wife, that his brother Zac wouldn't win the mayoral election. He has to buy me dinner if Sadiq wins, and vice versa. I told him that the latter had said how much he and his daughters had enjoyed seeing the National Portrait Gallery show when he had taken them, and how, of course, that had captured my vote. 'Smug little fucker,' he replied, laughing, with the zealot eyes he shares with his late father.

5 April

In the end I okay the tickets to go on sale this morning, with the flawed system, and we announce our programme line-up. It's not Glastonbury, but now at least forty participants are involved during the two days. I have a code to track the sales, and it's fantastically exciting the first time I log in – within twenty minutes of the tickets going up – to see that everything is getting take-up, including our new initiative of very expensive gold tickets, which give access to all the talks and some extras. From previous years I know that watching the sales becomes completely obsessive and mood-altering. If they aren't moving, it's very lowering, while a good day gives me a real lift. Perhaps I should give myself a limit of checking no more than twice a day. In two days they will be on sale to the general public, which will be even more exciting as that's when we get the real activity.

Fitting number one for my party dress at Erdem's shop on South Audley Street. I explain to him that I'm feeling anxious about it, and he says there's no need and it will be 'super-chic'. He has made a toile in dark blue sequins and I can see immediately that the shape will be a disaster on me, no matter how much 'nipping' he does. I stand in the pale sea of the carpeted dressing room, and the mirror reflects me in what looks like a bulky sequin tunic. We cut off the arms, fold in a tight waist and decide that the skirt must be narrow with maybe 'a kick'. As the craftsman he is, Erdem begins to shape the dress in front of me so that my appearance as a sequin sausage lessens and I can start to see how it could be beautiful. Erdem himself is rather beautiful. He has smooth pale skin and dark almond eyes, and he's so charming about the dress that I begin to gain more confidence. He isn't easy to read and I suspect that what he says is probably far from what he's thinking much of the time, but for a couturier who is trying to make women feel good about themselves, this approach probably stands him in good stead. Of course, it is not the dress that's the issue but me, and if I were three inches smaller all round and three inches taller, there would be less to fix.

9 April

Today is David's birthday. It's also the weekend, which is extremely welcome. I had been urging him to have a party but he didn't want one, and now I'm very grateful as it's a relief not to be holding that tonight. We sent the Centenary magazine off to repro yesterday so, from now on, it is what it is. I turned the pages of the black binder file holding the dummy paper layouts to see it all in order and felt very proud of all the work everyone has done. Anyone who buys it will have something filled with originality and creativity, not just the rehash of red-carpet pictures and PR pack shots of so many magazines.

Now the focus is on the festival and the gala. I have put on a lot of weight, which I know is stress. Not the kind of stress that people have with difficult lives or health problems but first-world stress induced by rushing from one thought to another with the questions whirling in your brain and an overload of self-imposed ambitions. My diary has appointments on the half-hour every hour. That sounds as if it would make one thinner but not in my case.

David says, 'You have to go on a selfish programme,' which is apparently a Narcotics and Alcoholics Anonymous term meaning that, however inconvenient it is for others around you, you need to do what you need to do. In their case this would be recovery from addiction. In my case it would mean ceasing to cook meals at night for the next month. That way I would eat less and even give myself a bit more time to breathe. But it sounds bleak and depressing, and with Sam living at home, I would feel terrible if I stopped feeding him, even though much of the time he's self-providing. I would also miss that gathering round the dinner table to discuss the day, and sign off with a plate of food and a glass of wine.

The film crew have practically disappeared from the office and my staff keep asking me what I think the documentary will be like. They are suspicious of what Fiona Golfar calls Richard's 'hapless' approach. His apparent naivety in the questions he asks makes them feel they're being tricked in some way. I trust him about 70 per cent, but in the end I have no idea what will emerge. I know that any documentary-maker is likely to be searching for stories, and that not all of us will come across well. I also know that documentary-makers, like journalists, can be confusing personalities. Their drive to get to the bottom of their subject often makes them behave in either wildly dramatic or emotionally neutered ways. What on earth made me think it was a good idea to do it all those months back, other than a belief that this year was important enough to do everything to commemorate it?

Now that the festival programme is finalized, the new terror is of people pulling out, as Chloé's designer Clare Waight Keller did this week. We need to find a replacement for her, difficult at this late stage. It has to be someone who will make sense in the specific talk and work with the other speakers. I need a woman. Luckily it's the only time anyone has ever done this.

I meet up with my friend Janice Blackburn for lunch on the day that the release of the Panama papers is all over the news. She tells me that she went to the Cayman Islands once, years ago, with her husband in its earliest days as a financial haven, that it was the most horrible place she has ever been to, and so infested with mosquitoes that you had to run from the club where you stayed (there were no hotels) through a thick swarm to the next-door restaurant.

11 April

Ben Elliot barrels into the office in the afternoon. I adore Ben, who is the founder of the concierge service Quintessentially and the nephew of the Duchess of Cornwall. In another life I wish I were married to him – I don't think you could ever be bored. Before he has even sat down he is taking me to task because I've been quoted as saying I'd be voting for Sadiq Khan, whom he thinks is totally dodgy. Ben is Zac Goldsmith's close friend and unofficial campaigner in the mayoral race and he rattles on about how he was furious when he read in the *Standard* that I was voting for Khan. I say I was surprised, too, since that information had not come from me, and I didn't think much about it being made public when it was an off-the-record comment to him. I tell him I've already had Zac's brother Ben bending my ear, and my personal vote won't affect anything *Vogue* might do. On the subject of mayor, I have every intention of being even-handed. On the question of the Referendum I feel no such compunction.

Coincidentally this afternoon our online site has just been told that, after days of asking, Zac won't answer the questions we had given both contenders on what they would do for fashion and retail. Sadiq has, though, so we'll be able to release only the latter's answers. I tell Ben this and he immediately pulls out his phone to put in a call to Zac's office, saying it's important they give us the answers, especially as 'Alexandra is such a *committed* Zac supporter.' He has a booming toff voice, littered with 'cunts' and 'fucks', speeding from one subject to another. Ben is one of the few men who can get away with wearing a three-piece suit with a kerchief in his pocket. He leaves me with Zac propaganda and a promise we'll have dinner, with his wife, Mary Clare, and David, which I intend to hold him to. No matter who wins.

13 April

The ticket sales have slowed after a racing start, which I remember from previous years but that doesn't stop it being nerve-racking. We need to promote all the extra activities on offer, like our trend talks for the season ahead, and Lucinda's styling tips for this summer. It's often easy to think that everyone knows as much as we do about how the festival works but I realize that a lot of people think they're buying tickets to hear a speaker and don't appreciate the amount of other activity included in the price. The tickets are expensive, though, and the date in late May this year will hit any students who have exams.

I've just done another whole hour's interview in the boardroom for the documentary. Richard surprises me by saying Mum had said I was the most upset of her children about her always being in an office. I don't think she's ever told me that.

My levels of existence right now are confusing. There is the reality of every day, the world that is being filmed, this diary in which I'm recording both, and then, at the moment, the secrecy of the royal cover. Sometimes I can't remember what I've said to whom. When Richard asks how I've felt about the filming, I'm also thinking of writing about him asking about it. How do I feel? A mixture of apprehension and interest, I suppose. I was the person who decided to do this yet all my staff have had to take part, so I feel very responsible. Richard is put out when I say that in general there is mistrust in the office about him. As always, it's hard to know whether his response (he's hurt that people feel that way) is genuine or not. While I'm sure that the intention is not to do a hatchet job I also know that at the end of the day entertainment is about confrontation and surprises and broad-sweep portrayals rather than detailed personality analysis. His questioning often sounds pretty dim, but those questions aren't going to be heard in the film so perhaps that doesn't matter.

My shoulder is hurting and yesterday's yoga hasn't helped it. I was moaning to Audrey about feeling fat as she was trying to perfect my warrior pose, and she said that coffee grounds were good for cellulite. I don't really have cellulite, just fat – but she said they were probably good for that, too, if you rubbed them on in the shower. I had thought they were meant to be effective at keeping snails and slugs off plants but have never tried this other use, and probably won't.

Anna brings in some of the things we are producing for our pop-up shop at the festival. There is the biggest beach towel ever known in cobalt blue with a *Vogue – This summer's beach goddess* printed in white, which I definitely want to buy for my goddaughters. Patrick Foillcret, who works in our subscription department, has made it his business to hand-make tote bags to give to anyone who buys a subscription. This worked very well indeed in a previous year, when he produced a gold bag with *Vogue* lettering, but he says he couldn't bring himself to make it again since it was sold last year as a limited offer. He also says he couldn't really *live* with himself if he produced the same thing again as it would seem like cheating. In his French accent, this sounds very emotional. Instead he has proposed a clear plastic bag, which neither Anna nor I think looks as glamorous, but we have to finalize the idea today and, as she says, we're 'facing a mutiny'.

The papers are a combination of speculation over Corbyn's first endorsement of staying in the EU, and Alexa Chung's M&S range going on sale. Her reviews are broadly very positive, stressing that she'll appeal to the younger audience that the store is missing. Although there are pictures of eighteen-year-olds wearing a few mini-dresses adapted from the archive, I would still wager that young girls are unlikely to shop at M&S. The range might include things Alexa is quoted as saying are perfect 'festival' wear, but I think it will be mums wearing the fluffy pink sweater or that mini-dress over leggings. No matter what the product, the brand's values are unlikely to be those that attract really young shoppers. And nor should they be. There are countless other stores out there for them.

In the end, however, it surely doesn't matter who buys it so long as it sells, and I'm sure it will do so, in large quantities. I'm not surprised she has plans for her own line, although one of the big advantages of working as a designer for a known label is that there is already a huge team behind you and the all-important distribution.

One of my colleagues, who is on maternity leave, comes to visit. Her Instagram is filled with pictures of a beautiful baby and comments about a blissful life, but she says she spent the second month mostly in tears, with her husband saying, 'Call your mother.' That's what drives me mad about Instagram. The pictures feed a version of a perfect life that is designed to induce envy and admiration. Of course, everything we put out about ourselves is edited – this diary a shining example – but there's something about Instagram that particularly lends itself to transmitting unreality in the guise of reality.

The other day, I posted a picture of my first commissioning note from a magazine. It was from Beatrix Miller, editor of *Vogue*, in

1977, and she asked me to write a 'letter' from university about who was wearing what, talking about what, watching what. I didn't say on the post that the reason she asked me to write the piece was that at the time my mother was features editor of *Vogue* and had suggested me. In the office I was discussing how it had had more likes than anything else I have ever posted and many more than pictures from any catwalk show. Sacha said, 'You have to learn what people want from you.' Her popular posts are all of landscapes, she added, never of people. I wonder if that means people want nostalgia from me and *Vogue* memories. I hope not. It would be depressing to become simply a depository for the past.

Erdem's shop is a clever blue-grey that is a perfect foil to his lace and florals as well as his pale wood mid-century furniture and pieces of art. I arrive a little late for my second fitting, feeling sorry for myself because the cold that everyone has already had has caught up with me. My head is thick and my eyes feel and look red – not ideal for scrutinizing yourself in a mirror while being pinned into a gown. To counteract this I have made more of an effort for this fitting, putting on more make-up and wearing high heels, both of which achieve some damage limitation.

The dress is now a recognizable semblance of itself hanging in the dressing room. The blue sequins have thankfully been replaced by the far more fluttering gunmetal silver, and the boat neck I asked for is in place, trimmed, along with the armholes and deep V back, in black grosgrain. Although it's not right yet – the skirt is too wide and the grosgrain stripes on the front that are part of the catwalk look don't work on me – this time I feel happy wearing it. Once the thick embroidery is stitched on and we've managed some superhuman Erdem 'nipping', I think it will look really lovely.

'Chandelier earrings,' Erdem says, looking at me in the dressing-room mirror. 'You must wear chandelier earrings.'

'Yes,' I say, adding, as a tease, 'and a tennis bracelet.'

'Yes, of course. A tennis bracelet,' he repeats excitedly, as if it were the first time he had heard the notion discussed, in such a deadpan way that I can't tell if he's forgotten we've spent quite a lot of time on the subject and he had been the person to suggest this hitherto unknown (to me) piece of jewellery. 'We need to focus on the underpinnings. Would you wear something structured?' he asks, narrowing his eyes but discreetly not looking straight at my bosom, which could do with some help in that department.

I ask him what he thinks of Alexa's M&S collection since I know they're friends. He doesn't really answer. 'I used to work at M&S,' he says brightly. 'I used to work in frozen food. With big mitts. I loaded the fridge . . . And, if you want long . . .' he adds, looking at me in the dress and imagining it full length ' . . . and a train? That's not a problem.' I tell him again that I'm sorry, I know that would be his ideal, but it won't be long or with a train. 'I'm wearing a slub silk tux from Lanvin,' he tells me, as he takes some pictures on his phone. 'I love black tie.'

He shows me a picture of the dress he is making for Emilia Clarke from *Game of Thrones*, who is his date for this year's Met Ball in a few weeks. Although she is the tiniest pocket Venus, she looks wonderful in this confection, very long and with the most beautiful feathery train.

Zac Goldsmith's responses to our questionnaire arrive at the end of the day so we can post both sides online tomorrow. Neither say much I wouldn't have expected. Sadiq's answers are more engaged with the names involved in British fashion while I get the feeling that Zac doesn't want to be seen to be too well acquainted with them and is more comfortable being quoted in terms of workplace rental and banging the gong for British product. That would not be unusual. Zac, whom I regard as more of the Establishment candidate, would have natural suspicion of endorsing something that might be seen as frivolous or privileged whereas

Sadiq would be likely to think he'd get Brownie points for being in the know.

15 April

I have succumbed to bed, with hot lemon and ginger. I can feel the cold working its well-trodden route from throat to nose. Luckily it was kept at bay for a day so that Jo Ellison of the *Financial Times* and I were able to conduct a discussion in the National Portrait Gallery's theatre last night. It was focused on changes in the fashion world from 1992, when I first started my editorship, to now. I wonder if in film, or theatre, or publishing, the changes have been so varied – probably. For me, the biggest difference is in the way so many people know about and are interested in fashion – the labels, the shops, the designers. In 1992 it was still relatively rare, and *Vogue* was one of the only sources of information. Then came a huge increase in fashion coverage, especially from newspapers, whose accountants clocked that fashion was a substantial revenue source, then digital, which allowed everybody to have a say.

The audience asked good questions. One young woman had spotted that the cover line on my first issue, April 1992, had read, 'Do we still need feminism?', and asked me if I felt we did, and did I consider myself a feminist? I always find that difficult to answer since I know I should unhesitatingly say yes. But, if I'm honest, feminism is something I have rarely considered in a personal sense as opposed to the theoretical. I know I should feel more passionate on the subject and transcend the personal, but if you've been brought up in a household of journalists, where it was always expected that as a woman you would work and be as successful as a man, it doesn't have the kind of emotional resonance it might for women coming from a different background or working in a different world.

But then my father often shouted at me that no man would

marry me if I didn't lose weight, or if I continued to argue so much. It didn't matter, though, since his love for me was never in doubt. Last night, for the first time in years, I woke in the night and really wanted to see him walk through the door of the flat where we lived, put his trilby hat down on the hall table and come into the study where we ate dinner, with all the bustle and purpose and, it has to be said, self-absorption he carried with him. I'd be able to smell the sweet scent of his skin that had always been the same from when we were tiny and crawled into our parents' bed in the morning, and he would make a tent of the sheets with his legs in the air, which we could huddle under.

Stephen Quinn sends me an email, asking whether we have a video we can use to go with what he calls the NDA cover, and also to say that he doesn't like the July issue cover pictures he has just seen: 'She seems to be sort of spread out all over it.' We don't have a video of the Duchess of Cambridge, no, and he's wrong about the Renée picture, which I find particularly engaging.

I've been following the coverage of the duke and duchess's tour of India and Bhutan to see what is being said. Broadly speaking, it looks as if they've pulled it off, with none of the 'lazy duke' stuff being regurgitated. I can already write the headlines that will accompany our story, which, no doubt, will range from 'She has time for a *Vogue* cover shoot but no time to fulfil her duties' to 'Does it take a whole *Vogue* team to make the most photographed woman in the world look like the girl next door?' There's the potential for every sector to stick a dirty oar in. But as I look at photo-ops on the tour, and the huge number of changes of clothes, I feel, more than ever, we have a set of pictures that really capture Catherine Cambridge rather than 'the duchess'. I know we'll get criticism for not shooting her as a more fairy-tale princess but it would be the wrong thing to do at this moment. I think people are more interested in seeing something 'real' and, to some extent, the gowns and lady-like dress are more of a uniform than the jeans and T-shirts.

As David and I drive to Vogue House I listen to Nick Ferrari's white-van-man phone-in on LBC. They are discussing whether short skirts and tight trousers should be banned as school uniform and replaced with looser clothes so that 'hefty' girls (their word, not mine) don't feel undermined. The eating disorder 'expert' on air suggests that it's important to help teenagers feel good about their bodies since schooldays are a time when one is very aware of all the physical changes and many have a vulnerable sense of identity. David, who is trying to read the *Guardian* in the passenger seat, grunts when I say I was aware from the age of three that I was 'hefty': I had to be the thundercloud in dancing class rather than one of the raindrops.

Last day at work before I head to Tenerife with Sam for a long weekend break. We have a meeting to write the cover lines for August. There is a long discussion about what to call a piece about three women who go on different spa-breaks and come back having decided to change their lives – have a baby, lose a husband, move job. If we use the word 'spa', does it sound too flat? If we say 'go on holiday', does it sound interesting enough? In the end we settle for 'Transformation Trip. The get-away that changed my life.' If you wrangle over cover lines for long enough, none of them makes sense or has much appeal.

I ask whether we should shout out the interview we have with Federico Marchetti on the cover, along the lines of 'Fashion's king of e-commerce', whereupon Emily begins a rant. 'That's another man. Just another man,' she says. 'It's not an inspiring story for our readers. A brilliant woman gets replaced by another man in a suit. I don't feel that's a particularly good thing. Natalie [Massenet] was very popular here.'

Yet again I'm surprised by how her and my reactions are so

different. I don't care so much whether a man or a woman does a job so long as they have something to say and are doing something interesting. And Federico is now a major player on the scene. She clearly feels we should always be rooting for a woman.

22 April

I am in room 136 in the Tagor Villa section of the Ritz Carlton Hotel on Tenerife, deciding what to wear for a day to be spent lying by a pool, when I hear the ping of an email from the laptop. It's only nine in the morning, the second day of Sam's and my trip, and I'm trying to tread a path between cutting out of work for a few days and making sure I deal with anything vital. The act of reading emails minimizes the chill-out effect and I argue with myself about it. If I don't want to engage in whatever they might be telling me, I should simply not read them. But I can't stop myself. It occurs to me that I'm in danger of becoming a crisis junkie, only feeling that I exist properly if I'm involved in some drama or another. So I don't read the email for about ten minutes, and when I do, my stomach does a little jig of excitement as Sacha is telling me that, unexpectedly, Kim Kardashian and Kanye West are coming to the gala dinner.

I'm pleased because, although I've never watched an episode of *Keeping Up with the Kardashians*, even I am not immune to the Kardashian force field and, in a room where there are already going to be a large number of famous people, the halo effect is important. With each recognizable face, the others in possession of them will feel that they're in the right place at the right time that night. And indisputably K and K are recognizable faces. It follows on from learning yesterday that Emily had heard her brother-in-law David Cameron is considering accepting our invitation. He's thinking of coming for the drinks reception, giving a speech about the creative industries in

Britain, then leaving – though Samantha would stay on. I'm hoping for another Kerry-and-Victoria moment this time with Cameron and Kim. It's the amazing mix that makes my whole job such fun.

So far our mother-and-son holiday is heavenly, and while I read and lie in the sun, Sam is revising for his theory driving test and we meet up for meals. We don't spend much time alone together now, and this is probably the only holiday we'll share all year, so I'm treasuring the moment. I tell him about Kim and Kanye. He's politely interested but if I wanted to get a more enthusiastic reaction I should probably have waited till he'd had some breakfast. Once we're seated in the restaurant overlooking the Atlantic Ocean, with black coffee for me, orange juice and a croissant for him, I see that Sacha has sent another email saying that Tom Cruise might come to the dinner, too. I tell Sam. 'Tom Cruise? That's *really* creepy,' is his response. I decide to keep the gala dinner guest list to myself for the rest of the day. He's looking at his own phone and tells me that Prince has died. I'm interested, of course, but (unlike the David Bowie news earlier this year) feel nothing. News, but somebody else's news.

I've brought a ridiculous amount of clothes with me for five nights and make this list in order to remember not to do the same next time:

5 T-shirts
5 loose tops
2 sweaters
5 trousers
2 skirts
1 swimsuit
2 bikinis
3 dresses
2 cardigans
2 jackets
5 pairs of shoes

That doesn't include the computer, iPad, iPod nano, Rescue Remedy, Sisley suntan lotion, four books, five magazines, Kindle, make-up and general bathroom paraphernalia. My father used to travel with a bag of in-case medication, like throat tablets, aspirins, indigestion pills – and I have unquestionably inherited this habit. If you're prepared for all circumstances, you're less likely to have to use the kit, is how the thinking goes.

I refer myself back to Patti Smith's packing list in *M Train* and the similar list Joan Didion tabled in her essay 'The White Album' that she kept 'taped inside my closet', which includes 'stockings, cigarettes, 2 jerseys or leotards, bourbon, typewriter' – a snapshot of a different era. Here, I am reading her novel *The Last Thing He Wanted*, a tale of arms-running and dirty dealing on a sleazy Caribbean island. Today's *Guardian* reports the British gang found guilty of smuggling the largest-known haul of automatic weapons from Eastern Europe, including Kalashnikov-style rifles and submachine guns. Fact and fiction so easily merge. Now it's almost impossible to enter a large international hotel like this one without thoughts scudding around of (a) Tom Hiddleston and Hugh Laurie in their shades stalking around hotel lobbies in the TV adaptation of Le Carré's *The Night Manager*, and (b) the Isis attacks on resort hotels in Tunisia and Ghana.

Another email is pinging through. What is our position on 'glam and security services' for KK? Will we provide them? No such thing as a free celeb.

24 April

A single black bantam parades around the pool, following Oscar the pool boy, who continually and cheerfully offers drinks and help with the parasols. Eavesdropping on my lounger neighbour's conversation with another guest, I gather many of the visitors would previously have gone to the Middle East at this time of year – Dubai, Oman, Ras al-Khaimah but they've come to Tenerife because they think it's safer. Alvaro the tennis coach tells me he thinks there's a bit of a *calima*, a dry, dusty, sand-laden wind from North Africa. On the hill above the courts, ranks of palm trees are gathered like an army battalion waiting to invade. You can hear them rustle in the wind as Alvaro tries to reconfigure my unsatisfactory backhand.

Despite the industrial amounts of medication in my suitcase, I neglected to include anything for the upset stomach that has hit me on the last night. My neighbours around the pool offer Imodium, which I gratefully receive. Everyone here is reading the *Daily Mail*. I imagine what they will think of the pictures of the duchess when they see them in the paper in a few days' time and can't decide whether they'll like them or not. But I know they'll be interested.

27 April

The final countdown begins. We have the June issue PR meeting to discuss what we'll release to whom and when, and I feel guilty that most people in the room still don't know the really big news story. But it's too soon to risk. Lauren Milligan and Lucy Hutchings, from the digital team, take their work incredibly seriously, and as we talked, I knew all their careful plans were going to be thrown up in the air once they knew about the pictures of the duchess, which they would then have to scramble crazily around.

I want to have the pictures released with the intention of their first sighting being in print or, at least, digital versions of the print newspaper. *Vogue* is so much about the object, and although I know that they will probably be leaked online before papers hit the Sunday breakfast table, I still want to get the excitement of seeing them first on a front page rather than on my Instagram feed. I can't go through this with them, though – only with Nicky Eaton, who is masterminding the release. It's a miracle that we've kept it under cover for so long but there are still about eighty-four hours to go.

In Tenerife I told myself not to check ticket sales to the festival, but as soon as I was back at my office desk I logged straight into the ticketing site. Strangely, yesterday we had a spike after a very flat weekend. Live events are nerve-racking since so many people don't commit till the last minute. I've warned Stephen Quinn and Nicholas Coleridge that, due to the cost of building a huge marquee, this year's festival will make less money than last. In true supportive form, Stephen sent me the nicest email to say don't worry, outlining all the great things that we've put together this year. Nicholas is a bit sharper, and said that he 'broadly' agreed with Stephen but, surely, next year we won't have a marquee and we'll be able to do better. Next year is a concept that I'm vacuum-packing in my brain to examine in a few months' time. Right now, 'next year' sounds like something I don't want to happen.

Philip Green has hit the headlines over his role in the collapse of Bhs. It doesn't look good that he's about to take ownership of a massive boat when the pension fund is in meltdown. But I've always got on well with Philip, and I'm going to give him a call today to see how he is.

Tomorrow is the launch of the paperback of my most recent book, *The Parrots*. Poor parrots – they feel neglected in all of this, when they were so central to me for almost three years in their writing. The parrots in the book are a pair of exotic and corrupted Italian siblings and are based on the gold, emerald and turquoise parakeets that swooped into the garden at home and sat sparkling on the branches of the trees. Last July I had a launch party in the garden, and although I missed it, several people told me that a flock flew overhead during the evening. That was the last time they've been seen there. In previous years, by April they were flashing in and making all the little birds dash away. I know their absence can't possibly be because I wrote the book about them, but even so . . .

We have the meeting to approve the Renée Zellweger cover. I tell everyone at the start that Stephen doesn't like it but he's good as gold and doesn't elaborate on his opinion. Nicholas thinks she looks a bit uncertain – she's hunched forward resting her chin on her hands in the image I now like best – but I feel she looks as if she's settling in for a good gossip. All in all everyone in the room is relatively keen and we all agree on the choice of a patterned pink Prada dress as opposed to a green one. The paler dress is clearer against the background than the green and, thinking of a browsing buyer at the newsstand, this gives it the edge.

28 April

Today is the publication of *The Parrots* in paperback. While we were away in Tenerife the garden has come completely alive with tubs of parrot tulips standing sentry alongside some more successful pots of hyacinths and the *Clematis montana* just about to burst. I post an Instagram arrow made up of the paperbacks on the garden table to draw attention to this achievement, but my pleasure in this is diluted by knowing that I must call Mario Testino today to tell him about Josh Olins shooting the June cover. It's a call I've been dreading for months. He's on location with Lucinda in Seville. I would always rather be talking to someone about something difficult face to face – on the phone it's so hard to gauge reaction. Mario has been the unofficial royal photographer for us and, indeed, for them for many years, and we had discussed a cover of Catherine Cambridge so often it seems a betrayal now that he is not involved in this big moment. I don't know why I've got myself into quite the state about it that I have.

The next few days are going to be dense with excitement. I can't wait for it all now. Late morning I tell Lucy and Lauren from online the news about the cover. They said all the right things about how it was the most amazing scoop and all anyone would want to see and read about on a bank-holiday weekend. They'll need to post the story on Saturday night and be on hand to upload everything, but Lauren said cheerfully they were in the perfect position to stay in on Saturday – she's eight months pregnant and Lucy's boyfriend is injured from a cycling accident. Buoyed up by their response, I make the call I've been dreading to Mario in Seville.

He answers the phone immediately and, above the clatter of plates and voices, he tells me he's having lunch with the team.

'I've got something I need to talk to you about. Can you move from your crew?'

'Of course,' he says obligingly.

I feel rank, as if I'm about to punch him. 'I don't know how to say this but we've shot Catherine Cambridge for the Centenary issue, and I'm really sorry that we weren't able to do this with you. I'm sure you understand why. That the comparisons with Diana would have become the whole story?' I gubble.

He replies immediately, 'I understand. Don't worry. I had a gift from Diana. I understand.' He says it so simply and genuinely that I'm nearly crying, especially when he says that it's good for someone else to have the opportunity and that we're family. I should know by now that the things you think are going to be the most troubling often aren't, and it's the unexpected that bites you on the bottom. But even so I'm poleaxed by the generosity of his response. I realize how much I'd been dreading hurting him and now it's all over. What a wonderful relief.

29 April

My head is fizzing. I was awake at four thirty and managed only a thin veneer of sleep for the next three hours, watching the day break through the crack in the curtains. My brother, Jason, has an exhibition of his work at the Cob Gallery in a couple of weeks. It consists of huge photographs of film – the whole length of a film compressed into one beautiful image that is abstract but has traces of the subject matter discernible, so *Deep Throat* is in pinkish, fleshy hues, and *The Wizard of Oz* is a chiaroscuro of Disney shades. I start a mental list of people who would be good to invite and might be interested in them. Even when I don't have to, my brain is obviously hard-wired to construct guest lists. I would prefer that it was finding a cure for cancer or, at any rate, having interesting thoughts about literature but I fear that is not the case.

It's twenty-eight hours now till the news of the cover is released. I remember when we first agreed the shoot with the duchess thinking that, with so many months till the pictures would be seen, so many things might go wrong in the interim. And now that period of time, the unknowable future, is the past.

The Philip Green story is getting worse. He was one of the first people I invited to speak at this year's festival and now it is clear why he called a month or so back to say he couldn't. All the vultures are circling, and today I heard Paul Myners, who was chair of M&S when Philip was trying to take it over, alleging that his actions at the company were probably ethically dodgy and those of the trustees of the fund possibly negligent. I'm surprised that Myners isn't regarded as too partisan to be in this position, given what a public face-off they had some years ago.

I didn't get round to calling him the other day and must today: he has been a friend to the magazine over the past years and a supporter of the British fashion industry in many ways, funding various enterprises through Topshop. He's also always been the first to agree to help with any charitable fundraising we've done.

In all the preparation I had almost forgotten that a physical issue of the magazine would appear at some stage, so I was completely unprepared for the arrival of five advance copies in white plastic wrappers, brought up to my office from production. I felt sick with nerves as I sliced one open, then teary when I saw the cover. The production team have done an incredible job with the gold foil logo that Jaime was so insistent on, and the picture of the duchess looking straight out at the viewer in a way she has never been seen before is really, really strong. All previous pictures of her have her looking slightly away from the lens as if it connects only glancingly with her. In this you feel you have really got her involvement.

I go into Stephen's office to remind him that there are twenty-four hours still to go and that nobody must know since he has copied me in on an email referring to a non-disclosure agreement (NDA) cover. The person he sent it to is going to wonder what on earth he's talking about. I find myself shouting at him that I haven't worked for the past six months to have the story leak today and, amazingly, he doesn't scream back. He is trying to organize an ad campaign for the issue to go on billboards and in the press and, of course, not having access to the cover is making it very hard to hit his deadline in a few days. But even so. This matters hugely to me.

I call Philip Green and leave a message but he doesn't ring back today.

30 April

Ninety-two minutes to go until the news of the cover is released to the press at 11 a.m. My plan is to email all of the *Vogue* staff half an hour in advance to let them know about the duchess shoot and apologize for the subterfuge and the substantial unnecessary work on fake pages for some. I hope they'll be as excited as I am. I know that several are convinced there *is* a secret cover, and I can only imagine they also presume it is of the Duchess of Cambridge, since who else would warrant such secrecy? But there's a large space between suspicion and confirmation.

I don't know what to do with myself. I've gone for a very unsatisfactory run, forcing myself through 4.5 kilometres as if the ground were marsh and each step a huge effort, but it was a way to pass the time that didn't require concentration. So now I am searching for *Cobaea scandens* on plant websites as a distraction. It's one of my favourite climbers, with huge purple flowers, but it's hard to track down. Now that this *Vogue* issue is about to be born I can start to think about the garden. Although it's icy cold and there is snow in the north, the sun is bright outside and the trees and climbers are heavy with buds all about to open. It's my favourite time in the garden – in fact, in the year. The point when you have the whole summer ahead to look forward to.

I felt like I was going nuclear as I sat alone in the kitchen, apart from Coco beside me on the table, and pressed the send button on my computer. Eight minutes have passed and so far radio silence, apart from a reply from Nicholas Coleridge, who has loyally sent congratulations although he, of course, already knew. Talk about anti-climax. I check my laptop and phone again and again, then decide that if I stop looking somebody will more likely reply.

Instead I consider what to feed the friends who will be coming for lunch on Monday (a bank holiday). It's good for me to think about something other than how the pictures will be received. I know the degree of self-obsession I'm displaying at the moment must be intolerable. I decide on asparagus and mint risotto, and maybe some kind of kale dish: I read in today's *Times* that kale is meant to help you lose weight. The rich chicken stock, Parmesan, butter, rice – all of which I'll be using for the risotto – is highly unlikely to be mitigated by the kale effect but it can't harm. I still have to drop that pesky five pounds before I wear my party dress.

MAY

1 May

The last twenty-four hours have been so intense that I find it impossible to separate one thought from another as they whirl around in
my brain. If I wait, perhaps they'll arrange themselves into neat
layers. I'm reading a book called *How to Read Water*, and have discovered that as water becomes deeper so the blue, one of the
rainbow colours present in the ambient white light that surrounds
us, separates to become dominant. The reds and oranges that are
also present don't register as the depth increases. Perhaps as the
week of coverage of our royal pictures continues, I will get similar
clarity of thought as the experience deepens, because at the moment
I have no focus at all.

After alerting my office to the impending cover, there was no comment back for at least an hour. No danger of the *Vogue* staff being
glued to their emails on a bank-holiday weekend. And then the
responses started to come, congratulations in the main but, because
the senders hadn't seen the images, the comments were sort of theoretical. Geordie Greig left a message asking me to call just as I was
rushing out to play tennis, and I knew I couldn't add anything at that
point to the press release. The day was curious – a fuzzy space waiting for something to happen in it. The pictures themselves weren't
being released till the evening so it was just the news of them.

At about six thirty David and I went to the National Portrait Gallery to watch the two portraits being installed in the exhibition. The
gallery was closed for the occasion apart from all of us interested

parties, a Sky camera crew and our BBC documentary crew. It felt odd being in the exhibition without the usual crowd of viewers, and the pictures looked a little abandoned in their solitary state. The two portraits were being positioned side by side on a wall of relatively recent portraiture, so that on the right they were aligned directly with Mario's portrait of Prince Charles feeding his chickens in a Kashmiri dressing-gown, and above them, Sofia Coppola crouching in her knickers. Boris Johnson, who had previously occupied that slot, had been moved to the top of the neighbouring wall. Although he just happened to be positioned where the gallery wanted the new pictures to sit, today I think it's entirely appropriate that somebody who seems to have gone rogue in terms of Brexit, with his ludicrous, puffy comments, should be moved out of the way.

Everyone was talking *sotto voce* as the crews filmed the hang. Rebecca Deacon and Jason Knauf arrived to watch, then join us for the celebration dinner we had planned afterwards. The portrait of the duchess in the red-and-black-striped T-shirt looked very golden and glorious in the finished print, rather than on a screen, and I think Josh was right that the head shot had a thoughtful quality that captured a side we rarely see. None of us could quite believe that the story had been kept under wraps and that there we were, finally, at 7 p.m. on the night of the launch with what looked like my dream of print-paper release coming true. The early newspaper editions would be arriving in a couple of hours. Richard Macer, of the documentary, seemed a bit stunned but generally extremely kind about being left out in the cold on this scoop. He says it will just add to the story, which I can see that it will.

The original plan had been for us all to dine in the rooftop Portrait restaurant looking over Trafalgar Square, but in the afternoon there had been a flood from the downstairs loos just as Nicholas Cullinan was showing a foreign grandee around the gallery, and the restaurant had to be closed. I couldn't make out why downstairs loos affected rooftop tables but didn't pursue the point. Apparently pickpockets are known to flush purses and wallets down the loos after taking the cards and money, thereby causing blockages. So we all walked through Soho to Blacks Club in Dean Street, to the dining room in panelled dark grey with a long table laid for eight. After we sat down I remembered to bring out the copies I had brought and everyone tore at the plastic wrappers so that the others could see the story for the first time in the magazine. Nicholas ordered champagne. For about an hour we managed a fairly civil conversation – what plans everyone had for the rest of the bank-holiday weekend, that kind of thing. Jason was leaving for Toronto with Prince Harry the next afternoon for the launch of the Invictus Games.

When the storm broke at 9 p.m. as our website posted the cover picture online, it was curtains for discussion of anything other than what was coming through our phones. It's fascinating how immediate the online response is. So exciting. I found myself very lacking in the Twitter department and had to keep leaning into Jason's phone to read comments. Practically all the coverage we could see was positive. The *Sunday Telegraph* was one of the first through with a piece that ended, 'When we look back we will find that the Duchess's clothes and make-up, the setting and the mood perfectly capture something of Britain in the spring of 2016.' Job done, I could hardly hope for more.

I should have known things don't all pan out like that, and moments later the *Mail on Sunday*'s front page emerged with the line 'Is Kate auditioning to be catalogue Queen? Liz Jones's deliciously waspish verdict on Duchess's *Vogue* debut'. I couldn't believe that Geordie, whom I regard as a friend and supporter, would deliberately let his rabid Rottweiler columnist Liz Jones loose on the pictures, and I was furious, sending him a text to that effect. He compounded the injury by texting the whole piece to me, which generally took the view that we had made her look more pedestrian than she is, as well as frumpy. At least the writer managed, for once, not to include several hundred words on how damaging the pictures were to her own body image and how we, in fashion magazines, are all corrupted by free handbags anyway. Everything else was positive, though, and Nicky and Richard, in our communications department, heroically spent the evening in the office, sending out the released images and the cover, then sending us links to the coverage. Geordie and I continued to trade increasingly bad-tempered texts until I went to bed at twelve thirty, his last saying that he would leave me to 'decide what is up to free press'.

I crashed out as soon as I hit the bed, and this morning I forced myself to keep my eyes closed till eight when I leaped out of bed most uncharacteristically to read emails and see the TV coverage. Clutching a hot water and lemon (slightly worse for wear after all the champagne), I channel-surfed with David, and stared

delightedly as we made the lead story on Sky. All the newspapers had one or other of the pictures on the front pages sitting next to stories on Philip and Tina Green being called to address a parliamentary committee about the Bhs debacle, the new BBC charter and updates on the anti-Semitism in Labour row. I tried, unsuccessfully, to engage myself in these other stories but in the end I kept reading the texts, emails and Instagram comments that were coming in now everyone could see the pictures. Christopher Bailey, whose Burberry trench featured on the cover, sent a lovely email, saying, 'This has put the grinniest grin on my face.'

This morning's trip to the local farmers' market felt strange, as if I were inhabiting someone else's life, buying the asparagus for lunch tomorrow, and loading my shopping trolley with new-season carrots and cherry tomatoes. I deliberately left my phone at home to try to be a normal person rather than someone fizzing with this news feed and a big dose of self-importance. Thankfully, there is still the actual issue to come out in a few days, with all the stories aside from this one. What am I going to do with myself after all this?

3 May

Joseph the builder is back. This time to build a new wall to the front garden and install a wooden gate. It will be the first time since we moved here ten years ago that we have had a gate, and certainly the first time I have ever considered what decisions gates involve – height, posts, distance from ground, solid, picket, handles, hinges? And pillars: should there be pillars either side? Our conversation, which involves walking up and down the road looking at neighbours' gates, means that I'm much later than I wish to be arriving in the office where the June issues have now landed in large glossy piles. It's oddly morgue-like when I walk in. No conversation and a lot of empty desks. I feel cheated of bustle, but the reality is that nowadays everyone is staring at screens and last night was the Met Ball so many people are checking on the pictures to see who was wearing what.

Hardly anybody on the staff mentions our cover unless I bring it up, which I find very strange. In fact, they don't mention the issue at all. I don't understand this disconnect and it worries me. I ask Fran Bentley, who manages the magazine and who is my trusted sounding board in so much at *Vogue*, why she thinks this is, and she says maybe they didn't like not being included in what was happening. Or possibly they don't like the cover as it's so non-fashion. But I don't think that is the case and, anyway, there's everything in the whole issue that they could be talking about. I'm tempted to ask some people what they think but I've learned that as editor it's best to keep my own feelings about reactions in the office to myself and not to poke at people. On the plus side I'm getting a steady stream of nice emails. Is it always necessary to have the endorsement of others to feel achievement? I'm also surprised by how few of my friends or even my family have said anything. Apart from my mum, who said she'd suspected that the HRH cover was happening. This has been such a massive enterprise for me but, then, for many others I guess it isn't such a big deal.

I write notes to the many people who have contributed to the issue, from Keira Knightley and David Hockney in Tim Walker's portfolio to Joan Collins and Richard Branson, who gave us their anecdotes about the first time they appeared in *Vogue*, and all the designers who provided such intimate and enchanting pictures of themselves as children. I want to have a day of luxuriating in the issue and how good I think it is but now the need to sell three thousand more tickets to the *Vogue* festival squashes that. We have vaulted one of the huge hurdles but I see a course of them stretching in a line ahead.

4 May

Every time I'm interviewed I start with the fear that there is nothing of interest I can say. This is followed by suspicion of the interviewer. as a journalist myself, I know they're waiting for the nugget that will make the story sing. Perfectly nice answers to perfectly nice questions do not really cut it, and we're all encouraged to do as much media as possible to promote the magazines. I smile as I lead Rachel Sylvester and Alice Thompson from *The Times* into my office but I'm feeling vulnerable and guarded. Rightly, as it happens, since there's a distinct feeling of good cop/bad cop about the duo as they quiz me on the cover shoot. I hadn't anticipated the direction of questioning, that it would so quickly, immediately, veer into whether the duchess is too thin, whether she is too much of a voiceless mannequin, whether young people are damaged by our image-led culture and social media. Rachel smiles benevolently in her blue-and-white shirt-dress while Alice, face often furrowed with enquiry, hits harder. Once they finish I'm hugely apprehensive about what will appear in the paper at the weekend.

Sacha and I head off to an industrial zone in deepest south-west London for a tasting with the festival and dinner caterers By Word of Mouth, who have won the commission for the food in the *Vogue* café at the festival and the gala dinner. First, we look at the place settings on tables laid up in the tasting room, which has a large plate-glass window onto the kitchen and is lined with samples of tableware. Half of a round table is covered with a pale blue, or dove grey, cloth, the other in dark charcoal, with two hideous china fish, mouths gaping, suggested as water jugs. Each place setting is in different cutlery so the whole table looks extremely unattractive, like a stand at a car-boot sale. Decisions have to be made – napkins, white, charcoal or dove grey? Classic thin-stemmed water glasses or thicker Venetian (our choice) to go with the coloured Venetian striped tumblers being shipped in from Marcantonio Brandolini.

Then there are flowers to consider. Vic Bretherton from the florist Scarlet and Violet was standing beside her four approaches: strands of scarlet sweet peas in short, narrow-necked vases that slightly resembled specimen bottles, white peonies in frosted glass, a large bunch of pale and deep red peonies in a square glass vase ('That's what I've done for every corporate dinner for years,' commented their managing director Justin Tinne disparagingly) and, our final choice, a huge stem bowl of multi-hued flowers – thick purple hydrangeas, orange ranunculus, crimson peonies, violet sweet peas. Then tea lights? Or were they too dinky? Which style of cutlery? The fluted handles or something more modern? Napkins folded so that a menu could be slotted in? We discuss how to display the names of photographers I want for each table rather than numbers.

I worry that white napkins look too glaring on the grey cloth, and will the grey work if the sun is shining through the clear roof of the marquee? But a measure of Justin's scrupulous expertise is that he has immediate answers. 'We're sitting down at eight thirty that night and I can tell you sunset is at . . . eight twenty-nine,' he rattles off. 'So that won't be a problem.'

We taste the canapés we have chosen. They are all delicious – with names as long as directions to Land's End: Inverawe smoked salmon, horseradish and potato galette with quail's egg, crème fraîche and caviar; chilli crab tostada with dill, brown crabmeat and smoked aubergine purée and dried chilli. For the first choice there are two different kinds of smoked mozzarella to ponder versus a plate of burrata, with shaved courgettes and asparagus and truffle dressing. Truffle: how did that get there? I don't think the smell of truffle is good for a party. And then a confusion as the chef explains there is a Parmesan and black olive 'soil', as edible decoration: it seems an oddly inedible word.

As in all things the attention to detail is fascinating and the concerns of these professionals are over the smallest elements that I might not even notice. The way the lamb is carved and displayed on the plate – is it to be separate from the chunks of aubergine, each component in its own island of white china, or are they to nestle up close together?

The puddings appear – a choice between two miniature glasses of a red champagne Bellini jelly with a white froth atop it or a mound of pistachio and apricot. We go for the apricot option but I ask if we can lose the dabs of white froth, saying heartlessly, 'I don't really want these blobs.' The pudding chef is brought through to explain that if we lose the foam we'll need some other liquid so that the dish is correct. I suggest we could add some mint leaves for a different colour and texture, and he says, 'Perhaps a few micro herbs,' which I fear will have the same quality as the soil I found tricky in the first course. I like food to look simple, but I can tell this is very unrewarding for these chefs. Justin says diplomatically that it will be sorted out but, through the glass, I can see the chef returning to the far end of the kitchen, looking most unhappy as he appears to recount the verdict to his co-workers.

Mid-afternoon I get my return call from Philip Green. I say I was just ringing to see how he was. He answers he's tired and there's no let-up and that he's calling me about coming to the dinner. Or, to be more accurate, about whether it would be right for him to come. He tells me he hadn't gone to the Met Ball the other day even though he'd bought a table, and I try to explain that this dinner isn't about paying and therefore showing he has money to spend. It's a different thing entirely and this is a straightforward invitation to someone who has worked with the magazine for years. But he barks that I'm not listening. I have it wrong. That I don't understand. That he doesn't want to embarrass me.

5 May

There's a soft pinky sunrise this morning. I make some coffee and just watch as the light travels across the houses opposite and washes over the garden. Last night was the Duchess of Cambridge's viewing of *Vogue* 100 and her portraits at the National Portrait Gallery. The deputy director, Pim Baxter, was clutching a piece of paper detailing the progression that was planned and who was going to be introduced to her, and when I arrived it was clear that to get everybody into position, and to prevent people from what would effectively be photobombing this progression, was like herding sheep. From my position, just inside the gallery's front hall, I could see Nicholas standing outside to greet her as the cavalcade of outriders arrived, lights flashing before her car sped up, stopped and she swiftly got out, a delicate figure in a flesh-coloured dress with a peplum. I imagine with the crowds on the pavement, and the volley of flashing lights, security must be a nightmare.

We talked for a few minutes about how here, finally, it all was and how she had been back to the site of the shoot the other day and had remembered what fun it had been. Robin Muir and Patrick Kinmonth had been detailed to meet her in the middle of the illuminated Toblerones – our royal cover girl surrounded by glittering covers of a hundred years. Robin is very smart in his royal-blue velvet suit, and Patrick, who had arrived just seconds before, sports two-tone brogues and the theatrical grey beard of a music-hall entrepreneur.

Josh had flown in from New York, looking slim and happy in a blue suit as the duchess greeted him in the room where the photographs had been installed. 'Do you often look at your work in exhibitions?' she asked.

'Well, no, this is the first time there has been any,' he answered wryly. 'So I've started at the top. Where to go from here?'

I had forgotten how tall she is and how her face is more interesting than it can sometimes appear – mobile and expressive, though I suspect she has been taught how to contain expression and to keep still. We moved towards the pictures to examine them and she asked Josh questions about the printing process. I realized that she asks questions without offering opinions so when, later in the evening, David said, 'Did she say whether she liked the pictures?' I realized that at no point had she said so. As I watched the walk-through later on the news, I compared myself, looking beyond hideous with swivelling eyes and hands waving all over the place, with her: her hands still, her feet rooted until she moves purposefully – no jiggling around.

The reception was in the room where the seventies images were hung – Snowdon portraits such as a black-and-white one of Martin Amis, a Helmut Newton fashion image. The *Vogue* team were lined up to be introduced, first Jaime who, as an American, is the most dedicated monarchist of us all and had worked hard on getting the cover to look so gorgeous. We explained about the memory stick she'd had to carry around with her of the images, and Nicholas Cullinan recollected how, the first time I had come to his office to show them to him, neither of us could open the stick or even get his borrowed laptop to function. She asked Jonathan Newhouse about whether the business had changed and he said it had in some ways but not in others. How for *Vogue* it was still important to commission the most wonderful work and we never considered what it would cost to produce. Several raised eyebrows about that and chuckles. 'Well, I don't,' he said, laughing. I'm going to bring him into one of our budget meetings as work experience.

She greeted Lucinda warmly – on the day, she and Rebecca had clearly trusted her – and then Rosie Vogel explained that, in her role as *Vogue* shoot producer, the team of twelve we had been on that day was the smallest we have ever had on a cover shoot. The duchess gave everyone more time than she had to, always adding another question or two after the point where you felt she would move on, a gesture that I'm sure wins her fans wherever she goes.

It's odd. Kate Middleton, Marlborough girl of pleasant appearance, now the wife of our future king, with us all in thrall. One part of the brain says she's just another nice woman, but when you come face to face with her you can't help but feel she's something more. It's so powerful, the mantle of royalty she has now assumed and owns, intangible but so very pervasive in the flesh. Is that to do with the way people react in her presence – the hushed tones, the waiting to speak, the eagerness to please, the utterly different experience of meeting her from meeting another person? I don't think it is. Film stars and politicians can have similar degrees of fame and be as interesting to meet, but they don't have the same force field that keeps a degree of separation and also reinforces their otherness.

This morning I opened a slim black box that Josh had given me last night and inside was a beautiful print of the black-and-white portrait and a sweet note of thanks. That will be a truly historic memento and lovely to have.

Off to vote in the mayoral elections. I don't care that much about who wins. I've backed Sadiq but I'm sure Zac would be fine. All my caring is on Brexit. When I get into the office I have an apology on two postcards from Geordie, which is kind.

6 May

David and I go to the launch of our friend John Preston's book, *A Very English Scandal*, on the Jeremy Thorpe saga. Michael Gove gives a long and clever speech about the general brilliance of the book. Sarah Vine charges up to me with a big smile, saying something along the lines that she sort of owes me an apology for writing in her *Mail* column that *Vogue* and the Duchess of Cambridge have together embarked on a concerted attempt to kill off style. 'But it's a game, isn't it?' she says cheerfully.

No. Not for us. It's not a game at all. That's one of the things newspaper commentators don't get. For the people they write about, it's not a game. I love hacks and journalism and the spinning of a story, but it's not the way we work on *Vogue*, where everything is taken really very seriously. I remember when I worked on the *Sunday Telegraph* back in the eighties that so much of what was written had that element of game – the idea of wanting to cause controversy by taking a point of view rather than necessarily believing in it. Throwing out words, like stones into a puddle, to see how far the ripples go. It's not like that in the fashion world. Sometimes I would prefer a bit more humour but I admire the sincerity of so much of it. The genuine passion.

7 May

Far from a feeling of ease and satisfaction after the launch of the Centenary issue, the past week has been crazily busy, fascinating and intense. I crave a moment that says, 'We did it,' which I hope I will achieve after the festival and the party, but I know myself better than that, and it's not the kind of thought I ever have. There will always be another goal that immediately pre-empts the current one.

The office is filled with flowers sent not only from companies featured in the issue but from some who simply sent them as a birthday present. I briefly wonder when it became the norm for bunches to be sent wrapped with a bubble of water. Not so long ago bouquets arrived covered with cellophane, no water, so that a sink or vase had to be immediately found.

Now we are all heads down in the final details of the festival. After a lot of angst I have the programme filled. The speakers (all sixty-five of them, finally) are hopefully in place but they all need to be talked through their participation, call sheets organized with addresses, times and departures, and the many activities in our *Vogue* World need to be fixed in stone. Venetia, who makes a lot of our online moving imagery, sends me the scripts for each talk's introduction, which will be read out to the large audience just as the lights dim and before the speakers arrive on stage. I find them a little too discursive and not quite proclamatory enough. They are there to induce a sense of anticipation rather than to be read as a biography, so I scribble all over them and send them back. She also sends me links to voice actors' demos to read them as I don't think anyone on our team has the right voice. It's fascinating to listen to them as I sit in the back of a taxi stuck in a long jam from Liverpool Street to Hanover Square this evening. Should it be the cheery classless voice of a relatively (or so he sounds) young man, or someone a bit gruffer and time-worn? Is the right note patrician or Everyman? I have a gut feeling that the announcer should be male not female, which is reinforced by recordings of the three women I'm sent who either sound as if they're selling lacy knickers or are auditioning as a *Downton* housemaid.

It's now the time that we fix the shoots for the autumn issues and I'm going through all the rails of suggested clothes with the editors. Although there is the current big discussion about whether the fashion shows should be showing clothes that are about to be on sale rather than a season in advance, the stores and the press are still operating in the opposite direction. It turns out that many of the looks we want to shoot for our August and September issues are being photographed for even earlier issues elsewhere. I'm standing firm on this, though. We already have an August issue full of coats and sweaters, which hits the newsstand before most people in the UK are taking a summer holiday, and to move our coverage further forward is just insane. But it's clear that other publications are more concerned with racing to have the looks first and less so with relevance to the readers. I know my point of view makes sense but it's frustrating for the fashion editors not to have clothes first for their images. We need to make the brands agree to hold back the things we want to shoot, which in some cases we manage and others we don't.

On top of this is the celebrity dressing issue. The stylists employed by stars all want their clients in clothes straight off the catwalk. So, the Louis Vuitton dress on the cover of our August issue on Alicia Vikander has already been seen everywhere on actress Jennifer Connelly at last week's Met Ball. This kind of event has become huge PR business for fashion houses. It's why they'll pay more than a hundred thousand dollars for a table at the Met, then also pay names to wear their clothes and all the expenses involved in getting everyone out there.

8 May

A perfect May weekend. Temperatures in the eighties with small white clouds in the brilliant blue sky and everywhere in bloom. We head out of London for lunch with Sophie Dahl and Jamie Cullum at their home, which was originally owned by her grandfather Roald Dahl and is the perfect distance from London, just over an hour. Sophie appears at the gate in a floral dress that wraps around her curves and emphasizes her loping walk, and guides us through the series of beautifully landscaped garden rooms – a maze with paving stones engraved with Dahl's words, an avenue of trees lined with scarlet tulips, a gypsy caravan and trampoline, and a meadow for wigwams and long grass to the terrace outside the house, where the actor Tom Hollander is standing with his girlfriend Eleanor.

The party is completed when Charlotte Tilbury and her husband, George, arrive, with their children and a nanny – Charlotte wafting in maxi florals, with make-up kits for everyone and her creamy breasts pushed up so high that they nearly meet her serious eye make-up. She's more *Ab Fab* than Jennifer's Edina, but under the speedy delivery there is a very shrewd business brain.

Charlotte clocked that many women wander around beauty halls knowing they want to buy *something*, but with no idea of what would work with what, so she has devised whole kits around different looks. It's simple, painting by numbers, and it's a big success. At lunch (Sophie had made a delicious Coronation Chicken and there are countless salads), I sit next to Charlotte, who has no off button when it comes to her brand, and she tells me the average buy at a counter is 1.7 items and at hers is four. I *love* that kind of figure. 'I thought you were my Dolce Vita look,' she says, as she hands me a cotton bag filled with the kit of that name, adding that I must use her Miracle Night Cream because of all the peptides. I hate going to bed with cream on but I give it a whirl that evening, utterly sold by her conviction that it will make me look better.

Tom Hollander is clever and funny and, of course, like Jamie with Sophie, he is a short man who always has a beautiful tall girl with him. I got the impression he was bored of talking about *The Night Manager*, in which his corrupt, bitter 'Corky' was a star turn and a brilliant foil to the other Tom H, as every time I ask him something about it he simply changes the subject. I invite him to the gala dinner, as he is always a good addition to a party.

9 May

The First Monday in May is a documentary about the organization of the Met Ball and a few of us from the office go along to an early screening. It's impossible not to make comparisons between it and our forthcoming documentary as I watch the preparations for the evening. The film is co-produced by Condé Nast in the States so it's hardly warts and all, but even so it gives a sense of insider access. I fear that ours is going to be a good deal more *cinéma-vérité*. As I watch Anna Wintour and her team dealing with the ball's seating plan, I feel a surge of panic: Sacha and I will be doing precisely that in a week's time. The number of people American *Vogue* employs to do everything in comparison to our resources was one of the most striking elements for my team, but for the general audience, the tensions between the Asian department at the Met and the Costume Institute are a terrific narrative trail. As the former voices concern that the general hullabaloo and styling of the evening was going to overshadow their historical treasures, Anna coldly responds that that was not the point of the evening. Interesting how no one ever seems to answer back.

Before the screening I go to George Northwood for a trial run on a hairstyle for the dinner. Looking at myself in hairdressers' mirrors is one of my least favourite activities, followed only by being asked questions about what I want to do with said hair. I would like George to make me look like a cross between his clients Alexa Chung and Alicia Vikander but I imagine that is beyond even his considerable powers. I explain what my dress is like, and he suggests something quite severe, prompted, he says, by my description of gunmetal sequins. Although I want my hair up, a Mrs Danvers-style bun is not what I have in mind at all. Eventually we settle on a kind of double chignon, which looks pretty and possibly, if pulled tight enough, might even give me a kind of Essex face lift. He pulls out some strands and stands back to look at his work. 'If you want to pull it out you can be like that Timotei lady,' he suggests. My only memory of Timotei advertising is of a girl wafting around with long blonde hair so the allusion is lost on me. 'I'm tempted to say it's better on the jaw,' he adds, tilting his head to look at my profile. I agree. And better on the jaw is what I'm looking for.

The Lord Chamberlain is commanded by Her Majesty to invite Ms Alexandra Shulman and Mr. David Jenkins to a Garden Party at Buckingham Palace on Tuesday, 10th May, 2016 from 4 to 6 p

Buckingham Palace Garden Party on a May afternoon, a place that is for ever England. The heat of the weekend broke last night, and today dawned damp and determinedly grey, which deepened to wet steel, then travelled through the whole national vocabulary for rain as the afternoon approached – showers, drizzle, light rain and eventually downpour. David and I took a cab with Charlotte, my assistant, who had also been invited, and her mother to join a queue lined up against the walls of the gardens at Hyde Park Corner. Although the invitation comes from the Lord Chamberlain, we were there as guests of Kensington Palace. The length of the queue was daunting but it moved surprisingly quickly – UK Border Control could do worse than get some advice from the palace on this. Within about ten minutes we were strolling around the lawns with their long grass borders, admiring the lake and, nestled in a dip, a very lovely tennis court. Hats and nude tights, pastel colours, floral prints and waisted jackets were the order of the day, punctuated by a scattering of military and clerical uniforms, saris and turbans among the mix of dress. I was thrown by the predicted rain and opted for a blue wool dress I'd worn at the opening of the exhibition and a loose check coat by Erdem in a kind of rubber texture that I hoped would act as a smart raincoat.

It was bliss from start to finish. Such a treat to see the immaculate gardens and imagine the Queen sitting out there under a willow on a bench, perhaps from time to time throwing a ball for a corgi. And fascinating to watch the other guests in the downpour, mainly walking in pairs or occasionally in family groups, like so many animals heading for the Ark.

Shelter in the form of the Main Tea Tent as opposed to the Diplomatic Tea Tent or the Royal Tea Tent was luring all of us in its direction, but just before reaching it, despite the near monsoon, two long lines of guests were forming on either side of a broad grass pass, which we joined. Men in morning suits and top hats were corralling everyone into the closest thing to a neat line they could produce. Holding their umbrellas across their bodies like cordons they prevented anyone moving too far forward, keeping back what they all referred to as 'the bulge', the somewhat unflattering term for any member of the crowd moving too far into the area where Her Majesty would be walking.

Across this invisible but unassailable line small groups waited to be presented. Each was accompanied by these Establishment equerries, who had clearly had an education in seemingly safe conversational topics, such as the shame about the weather, bending towards their small party in the slightly condescending manner that they must be taught at prep school – or maybe it's Sandhurst.

One jolly fellow asked David and me if we had come far. David got in first with a 'Not far. NW6.'

'Ah, NW6?' His brow furrowed in a brief attempt to work out where that might be, then cleared as his mental scan came up with an answer. 'Isn't that Lord's?' he suggested happily. It was indeed near the cricket ground, we agreed, and I asked him about the provenance of the tie so many of them wore – deep blue-and-maroon stripes decorated with gold crowns and in his case worn with a diamond tiepin. 'Ah. This tie has been the subject of much controversy. We used not to have any tie and then we had a perfectly nice red one. But we had to swap it as everyone said we looked too like the Royal Engineers.'

This somewhat opaque answer continued to bug me until I got home where my Google search showed it to be the tie of the Grenadier Guards. David thought the Royal Engineers were not so high up the military ranking, which might account for the comment.

We were a happy crowd, sharing the dripping umbrellas and enjoying every second of the display, craning our necks for the first sight of the Queen, who appeared as a bright pink dot at the start of the grassy avenue. As she progressed through the groups, a slow-paced retinue of ladies-in-waiting and others followed in her wake. She eventually arrived in front of our section, head to toe in pink, right to the plastic tip of her clear umbrella. I had forgotten how small she is in person, her pretty face covered with a darker foundation or powder and a pink lipstick to match the coat and hat. For the first time I noticed that long upper lip and her bright white curls. I remarked to David about the lip, claiming it (cleverly, I thought) to be a trait of Hanoverian physiognomy, but he put me back in my box with the comment that the Queen is a Windsor. I don't think he's right there as they're all descended from the same line anyway.

The next day the news broke of the comments the Queen made about the Chinese being rude during the last presidential visit. Having watched her that day and seeing how far away a camera was, it seemed odd that her remarks were picked up. But it made her more human in my opinion. In all, royal occasions may not have changed that much from the days of Wolf Hall – similarly militaristic and courtier-laden.

12 May

The countdown to the festival is getting extremely tense. I'm snippy with everyone, I know; Anna Cryer, whose default stress activity – twirling her curls round her finger – is nearly Afro; and Sacha is tap-tapping at her computer much of the day with a don't-bother-me look. She has been told about a party-seating computer program, which she is trying out today and which might improve our usual paper-and-sticky routine. There are many details, most of which Anna is juggling, meeting me every day with a long list to 'sign off': the choice of *Vogue* photographs, which will become huge decorative blow-ups, the price list of the items in the shop – should a *Vogue/* Levi's jacket bust the hundred-pound mark? How much is too much for a specially embossed Smythson diary or a box of Bella Freud matches? The BBC crew want to film Kim Kardashian in the Green Room – is that okay with me? Yes, if it's okay with her – and we still have to knock a thousand pounds off the catering budget in there.

I speak at the PPA conference, an industry event, and notice that the catering in their Green Room extends to two flasks of tea and coffee and some bottles of water, but at *Vogue* people expect rather more. I've nixed most of the alcohol, though, which mainly gets drunk by retinues rather than the speakers.

We gather around Venetia's computer to look at her video introductions to the speakers, and for the first time in weeks there is a sense that this is all going to work. She's done a great job. The voiceovers we've worked on with the rewritten script give the speakers a proper launch onto the stage.

13 May

A man is seated on the pavement by the ATM outside Vogue House, surrounded by plastic bags, his long grey hair under a baseball cap. 'Have you any spare change? I'm intending to get a job,' he says, to each passer-by. I hand him some, noticing that he has a collection of business cards sitting in a hat beside him. 'I used to work at *Vogue*,' he says. 'I knew them all. Peter Lindbergh, Naomi Campbell, Martin Brading.' He's reeling off names of photographers and models not specifically to me but to anyone who is passing by. 'They paid me a hundred pounds a week. No health insurance or anything.' I ask what he did. Had he been a photographer's assistant? He doesn't answer, repeating again that he had 'worked with them all', the words on an unstoppable loop. I believe him. He would have been a good-looking man. I wasn't sure I didn't recognize him from somewhere. How did he get from that eighties fashion world to the street? 'I went to Australia to get married and it didn't work out. They deported me and I've been on the road now for fifteen years. I intend to get a job,' he says again, as another person passes. I take my money out of the machine and go into Vogue House, separated by revolving doors from the poor guy who's worked with them all. And then it all went wrong. It's really just a flip of the card. He could be any of us when the safety nets of family, friends and mental health fail.

It's been a few days of things going wrong. Earlier this week I got a text from my friend Kari Allen: 'Sally walked into the sea today and died.' I was writing this diary at the time and it was a sober moment to think that Sally Brampton, who had been slightly my senior when she was made the first editor of British *Elle*, had finally lost her battle with the cruellest depression, while there I was, sitting at my nice desk, writing about problems with budgets and seating plans and fashion shoots. She had been offered the job of editing *Vogue* before I was: had she not turned it down, my life would have been completely different. I gave up writing and went into the kitchen and poured a large vodka and tonic.

15 May

So much of working life is not about what one has to achieve but about how one psychologically manages the ups and downs in the process. I've always been blessed with an ability to separate work and home, and these last months have been one of the relatively rare periods in which there is a constant seep of work worries into evenings and weekends. Exercise is definitely a good idea although trying to building it into the schedule is stressful in itself.

David and I head across the road to the park to the tennis courts for a singles match this morning, which isn't nearly as enjoyable as playing with Louise, who is away. He's very competitive and takes every game deadly seriously. And he's so much better than I am that I have to rely on his double faults and his volleys going wrong. But I manage to get two games in each set and I head into work pleased that we did it.

When I arrive in the office I'm told that we've lost Gucci's Alessandro Michele from the dinner. He has to return to Rome after his festival talk. I had always said that, given a choice, I would prefer him at the festival rather than the dinner, but it's a blow and puts me into a new panic about who else might pull out with two more weeks to go. Until bottoms are on seats I don't take anyone for granted. Sacha and I are going to make the first stab at the seating with her bells-and-whistles computer program on Monday, although there are still seventy-eight unconfirmed guests. I often wonder whether their parents never told them that they should reply to invitations, like mine did! On a much better note, Fiona called last night to tell me that Kanye may now come with Kim to her festival talk and they also might do a tour of the *Vogue* tent. What is our security situation?

We have made a video of *Vogue* editors talking about the festival to drive the last week of sales, which are slower than I would like. Increasingly my team are being asked to perform on film and it's becoming a whole other skill. The most successful are able to sound knowledgeable, but wear it lightly and humorously, look attractive and have a democratic voice. Too posh (like me) is fatal, a slight foreign accent ideal. Being serious is a no-no. It's becoming part of the culture that we watch as much as we read, even if we work in magazine editorial. Some love the performance and, I guess, the attention; others would rather go on the rack than be filmed again. Why ever did I agree to the TV documentary, since I can't even bear to watch my own split-second contribution to this latest video?

16 May

Dog Poo Park is a much more benevolent spot this morning than it was after Christmas. There's a fledgling orchard on the west side – Cox's Orange Pippin apples, Montmorency cherries, Invincible pears. I hope I'm still living here when they're established enough to bear fruit. The distance I can currently run has wildly decreased since last summer and, once all the festivities are over, I need to catch up with my fitness as well as get the house tidied up – there are at least twenty pictures and photographs waiting to be hung and every table is filled with books needing to be shelved.

Next week I'm trying to find a morning when I can run in Kensington Gardens to see how the marquee is going up, but today I go for a walk there and look at the empty space. The trees, which had been bare when we looked at the site back in the winter, have thick canopies and I make a note to call the event producer Richard Dodgson tomorrow to check out the leaf-drip situation, even though I'm not quite sure what it is. Because of the leaves, the space that the tent can inhabit looks a lot smaller than I'd thought. I hope it's big enough.

A heavenly morning in the garden. I'd quite forgotten how pleasurable it is to potter around weeding and planting, and with the new shed, currently the only organized space we have, it is additionally satisfying. The *Cobaea scandens* has arrived and I have placed the seedlings in three spots, hoping at least one will take. The first outside space I owned myself was the smallest roof terrace on the fourth floor: to get there I had to crawl through a window, and below, without any barrier, there was a sheer drop of about seventy feet. I grew *Cobaea scandens* successfully there but have never succeeded again, so I'm hoping this will be the year. There is a ladybird crawling up the climbing rose, which I have to rescue from the toxic pest control I've sprayed over it. The last thing I want at the moment is to skew my luck by killing a ladybird.

I have a very long phone conversation with my best friend, Jane, who is now a Lib Dem peer and is involved in the Remain campaign. To me she is still the seven-year-old curly-haired girl who wore pretty pointed-toe Clarks sandals with diamond cut-out shapes at school rather than the ugly round-toed ones I had because of my E-width feet. We gossip about mutual friends, then get onto the subject of Brexit. She is, as always, positive about a Remain outcome (you don't survive as a passionate Lib Dem without being an optimist) and says that, in her opinion, it is generally the women who are 'being sensible' and likely to vote to stay while the men are less sure-fire. Once the festival weekend is over I want to get a bit more involved in helping the campaign, if I can. It makes me feel really quite panicked to think that we might revert to small-island status. But I wish Remain were putting out more positive reasons to stay in Europe, rather than so much information warning of plague and pestilence if we don't.

I'm thinking of putting a reference about it into my speech at the dinner if I can find a way to do it that doesn't sound crass. After all, we'll be standing shoulder to shoulder with all the international designers, who are making an effort to be there.

17 May

Richard Dodgson laughs when I tell him about visiting the site and my leaf-drip concerns, and defines the drip line: if it is raining, the water will fall from the trees but we will be safely inside it. He sends me a photo of the bare bones of the marquee structure with the Albert Memorial just visible at the back.

I'm now awake for much of each night with seating plans on repeat in my brain, and when I do sleep I have dreams like last night's, where I stand to give the speech at the dinner and discover that the orange wig I'm wearing is slipping off my head, and when I speak I have no voice. It's sad that my subconscious is so clichéd.

On Monday Sacha and I had the first stab at the seating plan for the dinner, with Richard Macer looming over us with his camera, like a praying mantis. Although we have the computer program that is meant to simplify this task, we still seem to be compiling a first draft manually with paper, pens and Post-its. We had a very rough plan sorted but just then an email came through from Daniel Marks that Donatella Versace was now 'sadly unable to join us due to unforeseen circumstances'. That is another big blow to me as I really wanted her there and had thought she was one of the big designers who was definitely coming. She had accepted the invitation ages ago. I ring him furiously as I don't have Donatella's number and ask why. He says he doesn't know. I add, would he please tell them not to send flowers. I know I'm overly sensitive and irrational in my reaction but such cancellations make me feel so impotent, and for the next hour I fret horribly over who else might fall out – we've now lost her and Alessandro.

Tea is booked in with David Lauren. He's in town with his father, Ralph, for Prince William's formal opening of the Ralph Lauren Centre for Cancer Research at the Royal Marsden Hospital. We meet at Claridge's and he asks whether I've seen the centre yet. I say, 'No, they haven't been in touch.' He had asked if I would be there tomorrow at the opening and was told I wouldn't since I was 'press', and only the royal press rota could be included. Well, I wasn't 'press' when I made the introduction and helped put the fundraiser together and I'm disappointed and annoyed that I wasn't even told the opening was happening this week.

David proudly produces pictures of his baby son, saying that he is now on the ninety-eighth percentile in both weight and height, the latter of which he is surprised by since height is not one of the good-looking Lauren family's usual physical traits.

I have my final dress fitting this evening and run into Erdem's store with a variety of bras and knickers to try with it. The dress is again hanging in the dressing room, a little like a child waiting to be collected from school, wanting someone to listen and pay attention to them alone. I try it on with a pair of fine-gauge Lycra cycling-style knickers and a new bra and it fits perfectly, though the shorts make me feel horrible. The lace embroidery now snakes across the sequins and the boat neck is wide enough. Erdem stands back to survey his work and says, 'It's great. Really nipped and . . . wicked,' as he looks at me with those sloe eyes, adjusting the neckline a fraction to lie flat across my collarbone. I'm tempted to ask if it can be taken in a fraction around my waist but then I discover I can't sit down comfortably if we do that. He leaves the dressing room for a moment and I remove the shorts, which are clinging to my hips. As usual I can't bear to wear such hideous underwear, even if it does give me a better shape. Standing in front of him in the shop we look at me again together in the mirror and he photographs me from the back and the front. I ask him if he can see any difference from moments before, and he says perhaps the waistband is sitting a little better now the neckline is adjusted. I tell him about the removal of the shorts and he's polite enough to say that it looks better without, though I immediately feel I've loaded him with too much information on the underpinnings situation of a fifty-eight-year-old woman.

19 May

Clearly I'm undergoing some kind of trauma. I bought a brown trouser suit yesterday. Trouser suits of any colour have never featured in my wardrobe. But brown. I think a desire for order of some kind led me in the direction of the matching jacket and trousers. I'm very pleased with it.

Unfortunately, I can't wear it today as this morning I've been stained my own shade of brown for the weekend ahead and I don't want the colour coming off all over new clothes, even if it is nearly identical. I hardly ever do fake tans but it's really helpful if you're going to be filmed under lights and have endless pictures taken. We have sold five thousand festival tickets, which is great news, but because of the massive costs of putting up the marquee and all the activities inside, our profits will be negligible this year, as I'd thought some weeks ago. Stephen is being very understanding, but as the estimated figure slips ever downwards I start to worry, even though I've told everyone else not to. We're three days away.

The weather forecast is currently dire and we have to think about not leaf but umbrella drip. As if there are not enough drips in my world. Last night while we were eating supper there was the rat-a-tat-tat of dripping in the kitchen and we discovered the stone floor and counter were covered with water, as was the kettle. David and I peered at the overhead lights where the skylight guttering lies, imagining another leak had sprung there, but we couldn't spot anything. This morning it is clear that the kettle is leaking and there is a new pool of water on the floor. I didn't know it was possible for kettles to leak. Into the bin it goes.

This morning more people are changing their plans for the dinner. Ed Vaizey and his wife, and Tory Burch and her boyfriend, LVMH's Pierre-Yves Roussel, have dropped out. Bill Nighy has dropped in. And Tom Hollander has dropped in, then out, all within an hour.

At the end of the afternoon, Anna Cryer and I visit the marquee accompanied by Richard Macer and his trusty, silent aide George carrying the boom. The very long wall of *Vogue* covers is lying on the floor at the entrance, in the space that for dinner will become the red carpet. The early build looks fantastic and my immediate reaction on being inside the tent is massive relief and, as always, a thrill at how good the *Vogue* fashion pictures look blown up huge. In particular the Mario Testino shoots always have a real sense of theatre about them. The huge tent looks bright, polished and very appealing. Richard Dodgson walks us through, pointing out where walls will be built and the *Vogue* Café will be installed. Once we have gone through it as the festival space, I want to do another walk-through imagining it as the dinner scene. We spend some time pacing out where the tables will be. It's a big space and some people will probably feel they are not in prime position, but I don't see how we can avoid that.

When we leave I walk through Kensington Gardens to Lancaster Gate to try to wind down. It's a murky green evening with heavy cloud cover so there are only a few people in the park. I pass a man with two parrots perched one on either hand, just like the ones in *The Parrots*, and as I pass the Serpentine, covered with a layer of bright green algae, and a helicopter flies low above me, the scene almost duplicates the opening of my novel, which is really odd.

20 May

People keep calling the office to ask who they're sitting next to at dinner. Not, obviously, *them*, but somebody who works for them. I find this odd and infuriating and Sacha, whose eyes are now permanently glued to a computer screen, says tersely that she thinks it's *very rude* to ask. I tell everyone to say to anyone who asks that we're unable 'give out details of the seating' but that we are, of course, placing them with people we think they will enjoy. Even if I wanted to give them the information it would be pointless since the plan will continue to change till we're all seated. Joan Collins wants to know what the menu is as well as who she's sitting with.

At ten this morning we get the news that David Cameron *is* coming to the reception and wants to give a speech about the creative industries. I'm really pleased about this, particularly since I know that Nicholas very much wanted him to be there. It's only a month before the Referendum so we always knew it was a big ask. Emily veers between being pleased she has managed to get him there, and not wanting the responsibility of our disappointment if he doesn't come at the last minute. I tell her we're all fully prepared for that as I bash out an email request to the British Fashion Council for statistics he can use in the speech. They get them back to me within minutes.

23 May

Saturday morning: George Northwood comes to do my hair at six thirty and we sit in the kitchen and talk the kind of nonsense you talk when you're having your hair done. Good hairdressers are the masters of inconsequential conversation, just keeping the chat going while demanding no particular train of thought. A vast Range Rover nearly the size of a small private jet arrives to collect us both as George is going to help with my hair all day, and we pile in with my clothes (three changes) and George's huge suitcase of equipment to drive to the Royal Geographical Society, over the road from the marquee, where the big talks are and where I have a dressing room. In the car George shows me his Snapchat feed and the footage of Kim Kardashian she has posted during the night of her in bed with cartoon ears and insomnia.

We have a makeshift Green Room at the RGS. It's the council room with three giant, precious antique globes (one made for the Great Exhibition of 1851). When we arrive Sacha has prepped it with the morning's newspapers and an open wicker basket of things like plasters and mints and ibuprofen, displayed under a portrait of HM The Queen, which I thought lacked a certain chic. Across the road queues were forming outside the tent and suddenly there it was. It was for real. The festival was live after all these months of planning.

Lucinda is on stage first with Grace Coddington, who on arrival had been shown the display of her perfume in the *Vogue* shop and had insisted on removing any other products from the bottle's vicinity so that it sat on a plinth alone, unsullied (in her opinion) by anyone else's merchandise. The audience loved her and there were long queues for her to sign the perfume and her books. I watched most of the talk and admired Lucinda's tenacity as an interviewer in refusing to allow Grace *not* to answer questions and pinning her down on the fact that, despite her persona as the reluctant celebrity (created via *The September Issue* film), she now rather enjoys it. Lucinda had planned to wear a dark green tunic but Grace, who was as always in total black, had said she looked better in a white shirt and black trousers so that was what she wore. The assistant/ boss relationship never fades. 'She who must be obeyed,' was Lucinda's observation. But she looked really good in it, so perhaps Grace was right on that one.

I'm anxious about my talk with Juergen Teller, which is next. I'd hoped to plan it around specific photographs – Juergen naked with Charlotte Rampling, Victoria Beckham in a carrier bag for Marc Jacobs advertising, a variety of his images for *Vogue* fashion – but his office say he is adamant that he doesn't want to talk about these and has requested one long, moving slide show as background. He's determined that all the different aspects of his work should be shown as one whole, rather than segmented. By last night we still hadn't reached a clear agreement on this and I'm fearful that he'll simply refuse to answer some of my questions.

He arrives looking really fit in bomber jacket and trainers, and we're joined in the Green Room by the ICA's Gregor Muir, whom I've roped in as back-up. I hadn't felt I was an appropriate person to interview Juergen when I first approached him as I don't feel I'm strong enough on contemporary art photography but he seemed to want me to do it. So Gregor, who mounted a huge Juergen show at the ICA, is my security blanket.

The first moments when you walk on stage are always disorienting, and although I'm no longer as frightened as I used to be, each talk is nerve-racking to some degree. It's easiest not to focus on the faces in the audience and, in my case, not to examine whether the auditorium is full enough. As interviewer, I fear disappointing the audience with pandering or dull questions but, as *Vogue*'s editor and festival organizer, I also feel obliged to make it all right for the subject so that they come away feeling pleased to have been part of it. If they're nervous and feel uncomfortable it's much less likely to be interesting, and I've learned over the past years that it takes about fifteen minutes before anyone says anything unexpected or personal.

Juergen is intensely interesting and I'm so absorbed in his replies that for some time, after all the fuss about the slides, I forget to click into the slide show at all. He describes how as a teenager his first job had been as an apprentice to a bow-maker for instruments but he suffered from asthma caused by the wood in the workshop. It was on a weekend camping trip with a friend that he looked through the viewfinder of a camera for the first time: a life-changing epiphany. He knew instantly he wanted to take photographs, to see the world framed in that way. We end on an emotional note, when he talks about his difficult relationship with his father, who eventually committed suicide, the effect of that on his mother, then of the pictures he took of himself naked on his father's grave, when he was trying to make sense of his father and himself.

Waiting for Kim Kardashian is the next activity. In the general scheme of things she has been extremely low maintenance, compared to some previous speakers. No dietary requirements, no specific scented candles or flowers in a private dressing room, no pre-passed list of questions, so a bit of a wait seems like a small price. A constant relay of information comes through phones and the team's walkie-talkies – 'We don't know where she is'; 'She's left the Dorchester'; 'She's on her way'; 'Kanye *is* with her in the car.'

And finally, 'They're being told they're in the wrong place!' Surely we can't have managed to let her get lost! I look out of the window of the Green Room at the crowd gathered below as a tour bus slows to a standstill so its travellers can stare at the ever-increasing horde on the pavement outside the RGS. It's an extraordinary level of fame for someone who has done nothing but be themselves. Even though I've not watched *The Kardashians* I was intrigued to meet Kim and Kanye, and fascinated by what a draw she has been for the event.

She is, of course, tinier than I'd expected and much prettier, with tawny skin like silk and her hair in loose waves. Both she and Kanye are extremely personable and well mannered, greeting everyone they're introduced to and not surrounded by a retinue and bulky guards. She explains that they'd been in Cannes for the film festival earlier in the week and flown back to LA for a day to take their daughter to Disneyland, then flown back here. She says, 'It was worth it not to have the babies on the plane for thirteen hours.'

Charlotte Tilbury is fizzing alongside her, like Stevie Nicks on speed, spattering 'darling's' and looming over her diminutive friend as everyone gets mic'd up while Kanye stands apart talking to Emily, his lower teeth covered with a glistening gold grid. There are huge cheers when Kim and Charlotte take to the stage and Kim is a real pro answering Fiona's questions. Fiona keeps the talk bouncy and fun especially since the arrangement was that it would centre on the subject of make-up. She does a much better job than I would have done, weaving around the subject of foundations and blushers and contouring. Charlotte sounds wonderfully bonkers when she says that her husband never sees her in bed without make-up because *she* doesn't like the way she looks without it. While Kim, looking sweetly down at Kanye in the front row (he was gazing at his phone throughout most of the talk), says she's trying to use less but he's happy with her *au naturel*. That's probably true of most couples. The men aren't the ones who appreciate the hours women spend putting on their face. Women do it for themselves.

The rest of the day sped by. Alexa compèred the live Q&A style clinic, with Derek Blasberg and Lauren Santo Domingo, who looked so up-town New York as she calmly read the *Financial Times* in the noisy Green Room before going on stage. There was a great moment when someone asked a question from the floor and she didn't quite understand and asked, 'What's the high street?'

'The mall,' interpreted Derek, although it wasn't clear whether her ignorance of this point was entirely linguistic or because she wasn't acquainted with cheap clothes. When, a little later, he had to translate 'dungarees' ('She means overalls'), I thought it would be fun to do a US/UK fashion glossary in the magazine. Lauren was en route, via private plane, to the party in Rome that Valentino were hosting that night and taking Derek with her. But Alexa was grounded with us, loyally staying in London for dinner. Isabel Marant and the sickeningly good-looking Caroline de Maigret closed the day.

When I got home I was completely exhausted and unable to keep my eyes open.

25 May

So much has happened in the last couple of days that there has been no time to write. Memories, like bubbles of conversations and meetings, float into my mind and I've been desperate to hold on to them, fearing they will disappear, irretrievable.

The second day of the *Vogue* Festival, there was brilliant sunshine and the *Vogue* World tent was like a greenhouse so extra water supplies were rushed in for the crews manning the hair and beauty stands, which were positioned right under the glare.

Stefano and Domenico, Dolce & Gabbana, were my first inter-
viewees of the day and arrived all smiles – Domenico very chic in
his pinstripe trousers and immaculate black wool jacket, which he
had bought in their store in New York. He said they always pay, but
they get a discount. Their English is way better than it was at the
first festival five years back when they'd wanted a translator with
them on stage. Good enough now for Stefano to offer his usual
non-PC views, such as not caring whether we stayed in or out of
the EU.

The Green Room was overcrowded as Christopher Kane, Peter
Dundas and Jenny Packham arrived for the next talk, and Stefano
and Domenico were unmic'd to go and do a walkabout in the tent.
It's one of my favourite moments when the designers wander among
the crowds and these two are brilliant at working it – posing for endless selfies and agreeing to sign the special Dolce & Gabbana tote
bags that a long queue of people have lined up for.

By the time of the last talk of the festival I was cruising on a high,
so pleased that there weren't any emergencies. Anna had done an
amazing job in keeping everything on course in the tent, with all
the smaller talks, demonstrations and general hang-out. I wasn't
sure how comfortable Alessandro Michele would be in front of the
audience, as I had him down as more of a shaman (incidentally, a
description he applied to his father who died when Alessandro was
young) than a showman, but he was every bit the performer, and
thrilling to look at, with his baroque rings, snakes of black hair,
Gucci sandals worn over white socks with a red-and-green strip
and a gorgeous embroidered bomber jacket. We waited together to
go on stage, peering at the huge globes, as we tried to work out
what the criteria had been for demarcation of territories on each.

It was clear from all the designers that their work is their lives,
twenty-four hours a day and seven days a week. The rewards are
huge but personal lives become a big second, magnified now by all

the travel involved – they're continually hurtling around one of those globes with store launches, fashion shows and personal appearances. It's the same with the most successful photographers, stylists, hairdressers and make-up people, whose diaries are at the mercy of their agents so they can never commit to anything until a day or so in advance. It also probably accounts for the insecurity and neuroses of so many players. If you can't own a personal existence, then the control over small aspects of life becomes important – the same room in the same hotel, the restaurant you dine in, who collects you at the airport.

There was a curious nothingness about the end of that day because, although the festival was over, the gala had still to take place. It's hard to celebrate when you're still in the middle of the job so I packed my clothes, unplugged the charger and went home. Even after these last forty-eight intense hours it felt just like the Sunday night that it was. The Royal Geographical Society was already being un-*Vogue*d as I left – temporary carpets dismantled, white china teacups being packed into crates, the many *Vogue* photographs being ripped off the walls. George Northwood, Hannah Martin from Bobbi Brown, who had been doing my make-up over the past two days, and I posed for a valedictory picture – confirming times to meet the next afternoon for the same 'glam team' prep.

Tonight, to pass the time, I cooked some steaks for us. Sam asked, as we ate, what I thought I'd be like 'when you don't have all this to do'. I replied that perhaps I'd be calmer, to which he replied, emphatically, 'You're the most unchilled person I've ever met.' David infuriatingly piped up in agreement, and there then started a diatribe from them both about the demands I placed on them by being me. Although I *thought* I was doing things that would make *their* lives better, they announced, they didn't need me to do them. If I was following this correctly, they were saying I was doing all these things for myself, not them, although what these activities are wasn't clear. Maybe cooking dinner is one of them. This was not at all how I'd imagined spending the evening and I was quite hurt by the attack. The truth is that I'm sure I can't be the relaxed and easy-going person that it would be pleasant for them to live with all the time, but there's not much I can do about it, especially with the huge *Vogue* 100th birthday party to host the next night. I retired upstairs to smoke a cigarette and play Spite and Malice on my iPad.

26 May

The next morning I wake and immediately check the emails to see that, as expected, last-minute requests for extra guests and cancellations have already begun. I decide for reasons of sanity preservation not to look again until I get to work. As I'm in the bath David brings in his laptop and sits on the bathroom chair to read me the diet sent to him by a friend who has recently had a heart attack and suffers with Type 2 diabetes. David has neither. It's not what I really want to hear this morning but is a distraction from the mounting anxiety. I try to convince him that he does not need to go on a plant-based diet and, no, I don't know what chia seeds are.

Driving into work I'm aware that I can't find the sweet spot between terror about the evening ahead and a post-festival low. I have a sense of real melancholy waiting just over the horizon. Stuck in a traffic jam around Maida Vale, I give in and glance at my emails to see one saying that Stella McCartney has cancelled. I'm furious because there had been so much toing and froing about whether she could speak at the festival and whether she would be at the dinner. I pull up to the kerb and send a text saying I find it rude and hurtful, and immediately one pings back to say that her husband Alasdhair's father has just died. Of course now I feel like the most terrible heel and apologize, again by text, which I realize is insufficient. How incredibly sad for them.

The office is buzzing with post-festival relief, apart from my little corner, which is a tight knot of concentration and controlled panic. Within seconds of my walking in we have lost the prime minister (I suspect that with Brexit he didn't feel it was appropriate, given the massive amount of press coverage of Kim Kardashian and *Vogue*), immediately followed by Bill Nighy. A message arrives that Anna Friel (whom I had invited because I so loved her performance in the cop series *Marcella*) can't come after all as she has to go to Borneo tomorrow. Surely no one has to travel unexpectedly to Borneo.

Sacha, Charlotte and I sit around my desk staring at the table plan on the screen. There are thirty tables and 292 people to allocate. The tables have to be positioned – which will be placed next to which – and the precise seating at each one. Every time we think we've got one sorted, something happens that means it has to be changed. 'Can I just say?' we shout to each other constantly, as Charlotte, who is manning the mouse, drags the little pink and blue names from table to table. 'Can I just say? Would Tom Ford be good with Joan Collins and Natalie Massenet?'; 'Can I just say that I don't think Laura Bailey is right next to Sadiq Khan as she's thick with Jemima and so there's the Zac [Goldsmith] thing?'; 'Can I just say? Should we swap the Norman Parkinson table with the Cecil Beaton?' And so it goes, hour upon hour, until at four o'clock we finally have everyone's bottom on a seat. Just then Simona Baroni texts to say that Stefano and Domenico can only come for drinks, not stay for dinner. There are no late landing slots tonight at Linate airport, so that whole table has to be reworked from scratch.

When I arrive for a last-minute recce of the marquee, there is bright sunshine and, frankly, the place looks frightful. There's nothing tackier than a build at this stage in the proceedings, with bits of gold cardboard lying around a floor covered with masking-tape crosses. What is meant to be a glamorous curved bar simply looks cheap. The brightness of the daylight has turned the planned black-and-white live feed of the dinner on huge screens to a kind of toxic and unflattering green, and the brilliant purples, reds and blues of the flowers for the tables look vulgar. I know that when the light changes and the room is filled and candlelight is glinting on the striped Brandolini Venetian glass tumblers, it will look much, much better, but this is not at all a good moment.

Timebased's plan, which I approved, is for three triangular sections of tables, with walkways between them, but standing there I see how some of those tables are marooned at the furthest edges of civilization while the walkways look unnecessarily bare. Richard Dodgson reminds me that this is the design I agreed, and that it will help with the service and let people move around the room easily. I spit back at him, 'I promise you that in four hours nobody, *nobody*, will be looking at that design. They will only care about who they're seated near and that they haven't been placed way out in the boondocks. Please, please close up the gaps and move the tables closer together.'

He looks at the room again and resignedly says, 'Whatever you want.' The army of black-T-shirted workers starts lifting the painstakingly laid-up tables into different positions.

In the taxi home I call David and ask if he could just put on a bath for me as I'm now running very late. When I walk through the front door I see him looking worried outside the cupboard under the stairs where the heating controls are. 'I'm afraid there doesn't seem to be any hot water,' he says, clearly concerned that this is going to provoke total meltdown on my part. I find it hard to believe that this can happen now, when I'm getting ready to host the biggest party of my life, yet given the activity or non-activity of our boiler over the past six months, in some way it makes complete sense. He has deputed our neighbour Charles to boil a kettle of water for me (as we haven't had one of our own since the leaking kettle a week back) and he has a huge pan on the hob that shows no sign of reaching a simmer. Anyway I kitty-wash perfectly satisfactorily and run down to meet George Northwood in the kitchen for my hairdo, wearing a dressing-gown and ninety-thousand pounds' worth of vintage diamond earrings loaned by S. J. Phillips.

Richard Macer has asked to travel with me in the car to the dinner, and sits beside me in a smart black suit with his camera. I'm finally in the numb limbo that occurs when I'm about to do something I'm very nervous about. In this space I give a probably ill-advised interview about my feelings, which I hope he doesn't use. I look out of the window at the people queuing for the bus home and the early-evening joggers. I'm in a world of my own.

The marquee is still relatively empty when I arrive but I can see my co-hosts Nicholas, Jonathan and Stephen in their black tie, jaunty and joking in a way that I don't feel capable of joining in with.

As hosts we're positioned in a vague receiving line just inside the entrance, and have a clear view of who is arriving, alerted to their fame quotient by the number of flashes and yells from the television crews and paparazzi who line the entrance. Giorgio Armani and his always smiling niece Roberta arrive first, then Stefano and Domenico in jazzy evening jackets, apologizing for the jet situation, as British designers, such as Erdem, Christopher Kane, Simone Rocha, Roksanda Ilincic, appear almost simultaneously. From then on it's like watching a slide show as guests pour in. The artist knights, Sir Antony Gormley (limping with his foot in a cast) and Sir Peter Blake, who was shot for the Centenary issue, Penelope Tree, with a man I don't recognize and then realize is Lucinda's husband, Simon, Twiggy and her husband – Twiggy explaining that she won't make Tramp as she has early filming the next morning.

As I watch Sadiq Khan and his wife, Sadiya, process along the red carpet, constantly stopping to be interviewed by news crews, Kanye and Kim arrive, she in a transparent lace Cavalli, and I have a blissful sensation of knowing we are now quorate: the party is going to work. I grab Sadiq to introduce him to Armani, who, I think, might like to meet London's new mayor. Sadiq launches unselfconsciously into how honoured he is to meet the Italian designer and how he cried when he lost his treasured pair of Armani sunglasses. I'm not entirely sure Giorgio quite got the whole narrative, but he couldn't have failed to register the admiration.

By the time we're sitting for dinner only Kate Moss has not shown and the sky is darkening so that the jewel colours of the flowers and glasses look dramatic and the live feed of the party on the huge screens has lost its green tint. I have a slight panic when I see Helen McCrory arrive, but not her husband, Damian Lewis, who is meant to be with her at my table. He is at the school play, she says, and is coming on. Within minutes he's there, thickly

bearded. I remind him I always think of him emerging from a tiny tent in a garden in Wiltshire, which he was sharing with his then girlfriend about twelve years ago. 'I've been in a lot more tents since then,' was his reply. I was going to seat him next to me since I'm a real fan, but thought he might be bored so have given him Alexa instead.

Miuccia Prada is in a gold damask trouser suit and looks, with her tiny legs, like a bejewelled figurine. She has, as always, a pair of incredible earrings, chandeliers of gold with green gems, and at dinner she removes them, spreads them on the table, and says they once belonged to the Queen of Bulgaria.

Nicholas silences the room to give his speech, and as I stand beside the dais listening to him, I see Kate Moss at the end of the tent, with Charlotte Tilbury and Sam McKnight, who have been getting her ready, posing for pictures in the reception area. I'm trying to wave to Mike Trow, our picture editor, to get them into the room so I don't hear all that Nicholas is saying but I do hear him pay tribute to Stephen and the amazing job he has done. Then I hear my name and the applause when he introduces me as the editor for twenty-four years. It's a wonderful moment, and although I don't cry, I feel I ought to, as I replace him on the dais and thank him for what he said (which, annoyingly, I now can't remember). In a weird way I'm beyond feeling, and even when I give my own speech, squeezing in a gratuitous no-Brexit mention, it's as if I'm watching rather than being myself.

Once I am seated I keep scanning the room to see if the tables are working and am surprised that Tom Ford, who I know I put with Joan Collins, is with neither her nor Natalie Massenet and instead is sitting alongside Lucinda. Someone swapped their seats somewhere but I can't work out who. I have no idea where Joan has ended up. Emily's table beside me has haemorrhaged and is only half full as neither Aidan Turner, the *Poldark* heartthrob, nor young actor Max Irons have shown. But in general it looks wonderful and everyone is talking rather than glancing around to see who else is there.

Around eleven, David and I leave for Tramp, which is already full when we arrive. A waterfall of guests from the dinner is pouring down the small staircase and it's impossible for me to do more than say hello to each. At a banquette sits Condé Nast's daughter Leslie Bonham Carter, with her four daughters and her granddaughter, including my best friend, Jane. They have been my second family since I was seven – and this is bizarre, as if my whole life has been crunched into the sight in front of me.

The rest of the evening is a blurred series of impressions. But what a party. I had signed over and out and abdicated all responsibility from then on. Fat Tony, the DJ, kept the dance floor rammed all night with hordes of *Vogue* girls and guests. There were no VIP corners or sad also-ran spaces filled with onlookers – it was a proper party with everyone mixed in together. At one point I went downstairs to the decks and was given headphones to put on, like a child playing at being a DJ. I remember pointing at 'Ride on Time' again and again to get it played but it was Madonna's 'Vogue' that came on. Just at that moment Kate Moss decided to do a Kate and treated everyone to a burlesque dance above the decks to the delight of all on the dance floor, captured on a hundred smartphones. It was, of course, a high point of the whole evening.

Later I saw Dominic West with very short hair surrounded by a gang of girls and I wanted to go up and gush about *The Affair* but was too shy to do so (my big regret of the evening). Sacha said she'd asked him about his philandering role in the series and he said, 'The guy's a complete dick. Why would anybody want to be with him?' Demi Moore sat wedged on a sofa with her friend Debbie von Bismarck, who had brought her to the dinner, while next door in the smoking room, Debbie's youngest son, Sascha, was with Sam and their posse of friends crammed round a table. At one point I was lolling in the bar with Tim Walker, and Kate appeared, with her arm draped around Sam, looking like a cat with a baby mouse – a mouse it has to be said who appeared determined to scarper. (The next day Sam says he has her hair extensions in his jacket pocket.)

Understandably David wanted to depart when it was close to two, and I was about to follow him when I looked back and thought: This is the party of my life! Why leave? I want it to go on for ever. So I headed back onto the dance floor and stayed for another two hours.

The taxi ride home is a complete blur. But I did wake up in my own bed the next morning and that day had the worst hangover and the best memories of my life.

27 May

Today was Sally Brampton's funeral down on the south coast. On the train from London more and more fellow mourners kept emerging in the carriage, journalists from many fields – social commentator Peter York, Rosie Boycott, food writer Henrietta Green, my old colleague on *Tatler* in the eighties Lesley White, my tennis partner Louise Chunn. I felt drained of conversation after the past few days and listened to them chatting as I looked out of the window at a very green Kent speeding by. When I saw the first sliver of silver sea on the horizon, I had a sudden memory of being on a similar train when I was about three and going to the seaside at Westgate for a holiday, and how that first sight of the sea was so exciting. It's now fifty-five years later and I'm going to the funeral of a contemporary, who has died too young.

29 May

I'm on the roof of Soho House in Berlin, where David and I are staying for our friend Joe Boyd's wedding. It's Sunday morning after a day of celebrations, first on a boat travelling slowly along the canals, then mooring for the actual ceremony, and later a dinner in a vast dilapidated Berlin ballroom. All around me are skinny German women in swimming costumes and sunglasses, their toddlers wrapped in towels after the pool. It's heaven to be here, far from the *Vogue* world, with somebody else doing the organizing after the past few months. Joe and Andrea look very happy and I love Berlin, strangely quiet with its wide streets and enormous buildings but, compared to London, so few people. The trip is a fashion-world free zone as Joe is a world-music pioneer and Andrea works in Albanian water (I haven't yet discovered what that means).

30 May

Berlin is emerald at this time of year with vast terraces of box hedges and trees in full, brilliant fig. There was a moment at the post-party brunch yesterday, as we sat outside under a canopy of plane trees, when I thought I would change my life and come and live here. I would write poems and stories, paint, take photographs and be the person I thought I was going to be when I was a teenager. But, of course, if I did that, I wouldn't be able to stay in an incredible room in Soho House, contemplating the purchase of a Balenciaga coat. And, anyway, who knows if we'll be able to do any such thing after the Referendum? This whole weekend has made me more pro staying in the EU than ever.

31 May

Back in London the heavens have opened and there is a deluge. I type in the back seat of a car that is taking me to Blenheim Palace where Dior are holding their Cruise show. They can't possibly have imagined they were going to encounter weather like this in late May with visibility about twenty feet and the M40 more like a stream than a road.

I get an email from Sarah Harris, who is already at Blenheim, asking if I've I heard 'the rumour about Maria Grazia Chiuri leaving Valentino to take the helm at Dior. Apparently an announcement is being made next week.' I think back to the couture show in January where she was speaking of the rumour, current then, of Sarah Burton leaving McQueen where she still is, and who, when I saw her at our dinner, looked very happy and relaxed. What would we do without the rumours that provide such entertainment? Maria Grazia Chiuri would be an interesting idea, and she and her colleague Pierpaolo Piccioli have been a very successful double act for

Valentino for years. I wonder, though. She has children and they would be at school in Italy, and she and he seem to come as a package. Gilbert without George?

We reach Blenheim in record time and, despite the rain, the huge palace is glowing and monumental. A regimental band is on the terrace between the pillars on the left flank of the building, playing to a row of damp photographers and a collection of black-coated attendants holding umbrellas in preparation to escort guests inside. I am shown in through a side door, where I have been invited to a small reception with Dior's owner, Bernard Arnault, and the current Duke of Marlborough, who, before inheriting the dukedom, was once notorious as Jamie Blandford. However, neither is in evidence, although many very friendly and somewhat bemused members of the Spencer-Churchill family are gathered in a sitting room with family portraits, big armchairs and several types of salted caramel chocolate on the countless side tables.

Outside, in the distance, there is an endless slow crawl of black limos, like a funeral cortège, across the parkland, while news keeps arriving of trains delayed and helicopters cancelled. As always, in this country, the weather rules the day, untamed by enormous amounts of money or pre-planning. We wait for about an hour and a half before eventually the audience is gathered in the long library, with a carpeted runway of a hunting scene, as a long line of girls appears, beautiful robots in their intricately crafted modern Dior garb.

JUNE

2 June

There is a very real danger that the Brexiteers will pull it off. Yesterday a poll was published, showing them pulling ahead for the first time. It makes me realize how Nazi Germany evolved – so many watching a nation sleepwalking into catastrophe. This, combined with the bleakest grey skies, is a grim start to June. It was Graduation Day at the Condé Nast College and I went to look at the foundation-year students' final projects, with Suzy Menkes, and came away feeling impressed and utterly underqualified. They were all able to design and create print pages, make videos, understand digital communications, and draw up marketing plans – none of which I'm the slightest bit capable of. There are several foreign students among them who, I imagine, will find it more difficult to come to the college if the country votes Leave. How much poorer we will be not to have them with us.

7 June

There are so many beautiful places on the earth and it's easy to forget that when I'm immersed in day-to-day life. I'm in Évian, and my hotel room has a spectacular terrace with the vast Lac Léman below, so calm that in places it's like a mirror, and over to the east the mountains. The massed bands of Condé Nast International are gathered here for a conference – delegates from twenty-five countries. I remember the first ever CNI conference was in Berlin in

1998, and we were a small enough group to sit around one horse-shoe table with little national flags in front of us. Berlin then was one huge building site. The view outside my hotel room was a sky-scape of endless cranes, and I wept all the time I wasn't in a meeting because my marriage had just broken up after only three years.

Jonathan kicks off the proceedings with a very good state-of-the-nation address – honest and inspiring. The talk is all of the publishing business in the light of digital. China looms as a big beast, one that nobody quite understands, and Angelica Cheung, who is the editor of and launched *Vogue* China, stalks the rooms in her white trouser suit and razor-sharp bob. Our last session is about what magazine brands look like without print, and there is a lot of discussion in my break-out group about what *Vogue* would be if it had none of the traditional attributes but the name *Vogue* was applied, say, to a cruise ship or a shopping mall. I always feel sym-pathetic to the majority of the others for whom English is not their first language and have to struggle through these days when that is all that is spoken.

The newspapers are filled with Philip Green, and every day another picture of him and Tina in postures of careless hedonism is dug out. People have started to say 'your friend Philip Green' in that sneeringly amused way, and it's amazing how quick they are to put a distance between themselves and someone who is now the big bad wolf. As more emerges of the back story at Bhs it's harder to find the space between loyalty and condemnation.

Part of me feels I should be utterly condemning of what looks like such lack of concern about his staff's welfare and another part keeps remembering the likeable moments. When Sam was about seven we were in New York and had a Chinese dinner with him and Tina, who taught Sam a game you play with corks. Philip had offered us a lift back on his plane but I was too scared of flying to accept it. It is always so baffling how people can make such monumental errors of judgement, as he seems to have done and keeps doing. He just doesn't see how it plays out in the general public – and possibly he doesn't care. Philip is a bulldog and the more he's backed into a corner the more noise he'll make. He's probably been like that all his life.

8 June

Damn. No discipline at all. I gave in to the minibar Toblerone when I got back to my room last night after an evening on a paddle steamer that moved slowly along the lake with vertiginous and wooded green hills, which sat above small chalets, as a backdrop to our corporate outing. Now that the company has grown so big, the differences between the groups from each country are much less pronounced. Before, the Russians were always talking on mobile phones, the Greeks were always late for the first session, the Italians gossiped among themselves through many of the talks, and we Brits played the good guys – always raising our hands first should questions from the floor be required, eager to avoid the embarrassing silence. This time it's much less clear where anyone comes from. The guys from Thailand and India look incredibly chic with their pointed brown brogues and well-tailored lightweight suits, while the women are generally in non-label-specific clothes, save Danielle from Video, who had on a stonking pair of Vetements boots last night on the steamer with sharp heels that would pierce the heart of any proper seaman.

We were given a presentation today by the chief digital officer in the States on the subject of data collection. Not something I've thought a great deal about but now I will, although it is terrifying. The ability of websites to collect information about users' behaviour on that site is an incredible breach of personal privacy in many ways. What in the digital universe is called 'personalization' – the ability to feed us the kind of things we might be interested in (a.k.a. want to buy) – is also an algorithm that edits the information we are actually fed, with which I am immensely uncomfortable. Although I like listening to sad American singer-songwriters, I don't only want to be alerted to yet another, and never want to be told anything about, for example, a new stadium rock band. In some ways the digital shopping universe appears to encourage us to stay in our conservative silos, constantly feeding us what it knows we already like, rather than throwing random ideas and product at us.

Everyone is incredibly nice about the Centenary issue, and although I'm something of a grand old lady of *Vogue* here, as one of the few who have been working on it since the early nineties, I'm not made to feel like a member of the *ancien régime*. In all, the two days have made me determined to think of a really good new project for *Vogue*. The festival is five years old, and that was my last real new idea, so it's time for me to come up with something else.

11 June

Yesterday Richard Macer filmed me for the last time. He had wanted me to think of something that had some personal relevance to me so I suggested we visit a huge old horse-chestnut tree in Hyde Park, which I remembered playing under when I was very young. Then I was so small that the crevices in the thick trunk were caves. With the festival being in the park this year it had a sort of relevance, or so I thought.

After the filming he travelled with me in a car to the office and we joked a bit about this being the last time he would be filming me in a car. Then he leaned forward to fiddle with his camera and said, 'There's something I want to tell you about the documentary. Kind of what we're doing?'

'Aha. What's that?'

'Well, you know I said I didn't want to use a voiceover narrator, that it was a bit tacky and overdone?' 'Yes. I remember.' I'd always thought what a relief it would be not to have that clichéd narrator.

'Well, we've had to change it a bit. And now, well, there is one. Or a kind of one. You know how usually they're narrated by an actor? Well, we aren't doing that.' At this point I was becoming concerned by what he was about to say. 'Um . . . It's going to be me. You know, not a huge amount of it. But it's kind of about how a man who knows nothing about any of it goes into *Vogue*.'

My mind went into split screen – one half thinking: Keep calm, there's nothing you can do about this and maybe it'll be okay; the other thinking, I've made a massive error here and this film is simply going to be incredibly trashy and simplistic. I couldn't believe I'd allowed it to happen. Our one shot after so many years of refusing to let cameras into *Vogue* – and I'd blown it. This was now going to be a mocking Ladybird guide to the fashion world.

'What do you think?' he asked.

'I don't know that it matters what I think,' I said, staring out of the car window as we turned into Park Lane. 'The point is that you've done this and there's nothing I can do about it. So what I think is irrelevant.'

'Hmm. I suppose so. I don't know why, but I want you to like what we're doing.'

I didn't know what to say but I knew that if he'd wanted me to like what he was doing it would have helped if he hadn't misled me. 'If you'd come to me in the first place and said you wanted to make a documentary about *Vogue* where a man who knew nothing about our work comes in and narrates the story from his viewpoint as an ordinary bloke in this "crazy fashion world", would I have agreed? No, I wouldn't. Is that the film I thought you were making? No, it isn't. But you have. And there's nothing I can do,' I replied, just as we arrived at Vogue House where he had come to collect some equipment.

He said again that he hoped I'd like it, and I said that would become clearer when I saw what he'd done in two weeks' time.

I have a real intimation of both doom and embarrassment. When I tell Fran, she says it accounts for how he seemed to ask such trivial and basic questions, and that the team had been right that something not straightforward was going on. That makes it worse. Had he planned it like this all along? Was the 'hapless' approach a device that would allow him to be the simple fellow in our madcap world of expensive clothes and trivia? Have I led the whole staff into an enterprise that was not worthy of the magazine?

I'm back from a lovely short break in the South of France. Tonight is the summer solstice, the turning of the year. It will also be full moon. How the months have rushed past from the earliest hints of spring to now, when the days start to shorten. Not that the scene outside the window as I type is remotely summery. There is a downpour and the rain is streaming off the leaves of the trees and the grapevine that climbs outside the kitchen window. I hope it stops by tomorrow as I'm giving a party in the garden for my ex-husband, Paul, for the reissue of his book *Photographs of My Father*, about his dad, who was a pioneer of the civil-rights movement in America and murdered in 1966.

This is a really important week – the last week, really, for me of the Centenary celebrations. I will see the early edit of the two-hour *Vogue* film, the exhibition will reopen to have another life in Manchester and, of course, the Referendum takes place. I would never term myself a particularly political person but the Referendum is something different and I have never felt a vote to be more important. I got a couple of 'In' window posters from a bloke outside the farmers' market yesterday but I can't work out how you're meant to stick them to the glass. Good old Sellotape, I suppose. As a magazine editor, I'm incredibly privileged to be able to air my views in the magazine and I find it really hard to understand how anyone can*not* share my thoughts on this vote. While the EU is a very flawed construct, I simply cannot see how on any level in the world we live in now, the idea of being an economic entity that acts completely independently is a viable path for the future. Coincidentally this is a similar conversation to one we have often in my company – the advantages of each country's *Vogue* being entirely independent (as they are now) and where it might be useful to join forces. Sam is used to being a citizen of the EU, able to travel and work where he wishes throughout a wonderful treasure trove of cultures.

Anything that jeopardizes what is surely a fantastic freedom, shared by his generation and mine, seems sheer lunacy.

I've been having nightmares about the documentary but nightmares, like guilt, are a waste of time and I must try to relax until at least I've seen what has been done.

21 June

Just after I finished typing the last entry I telephoned my first magazine boss, Shirley Lowe, as her stepdaughter, Molly, had called a few weeks back to let me know she was very ill. I had missed her. She had died the previous day. Why, oh why had I not made that call sooner? I sat in the car parked outside the house feeling sorry for myself, then thought that kind of behaviour would have attracted very short shrift indeed from her. I was her secretary in 1980 when she edited *Over 21* magazine. We sat at adjoining desks, her deputy, Penny Perrick, Shirley and I, at the end of a big open-plan office space in Upper St Martin's Lane. Shirley had eyes like sapphires, short blonde curls, and a long nose that she would powder before leaving for lunch.

She was one of the funniest people I've ever met, and I loved sitting beside her, listening to her tales of her large family and many friends. She was mercilessly critical but always with fantastic humour as she edited the contributors' copy by cutting it up and sticking it back together in better configurations before bashing it out again on her typewriter. She was entirely no-nonsense and certainly would not have thought in terms of role models and mentors, but if anyone was a working role model to me when I was young, it was she.

I thought of her all day and especially as I looked at Charlotte and her colleague Lizzie White outside my office, fielding my calls and doing endless dull bits and pieces to help me. When I was

Shirley's assistant I had two files, called 'Boring' and 'Not Boring', and that was my system. It seemed to work at the time, but Charlotte has to organize so much more nowadays.

Today Audrey arrives for yoga and battles with the cough I've contracted and my distraction. She tells me that there are two full moons in Sagittarius this period, which, she says, is, broadly speaking, a good thing, although neither of us knows what it means. She also says that Donald Trump is apparently Gemini with Sagittarius rising, which makes him a kind of *über*-entrepreneur, a fact that no one could doubt. We do a lot of poses on the floor and I try to avert my eye from the dark rings of damp around the light fitting where water leaked and clear my head of thoughts of the *Vogue* Talent Contest lunch I am hosting today.

At work everything is hustle and bustle to get the September issue finished. I came back from holiday to look at the fashion shoots printed out on the wall and was fascinated by the images – several of which I hadn't seen. I can't claim they gave me a clue about what to wear this autumn but so many were utterly memorable and curious. I loved an opening spread from the young photographer Colin Dodgson of the red-haired model Natalie Westling standing beside an incredible pink salt flat in France, which put me in mind of something from the seventies. My mum always says there is no such thing as a new idea, and if that's true (which I'm not sure it is), fashion is certainly the best exemplar. Everything comes round and round in terms of style of clothes and photography but, still, in each iteration they do have something different.

I look at Kate Phelan's clothes for her trip to Japan with Tim Walker. The fashion room is filled with rails of them – pink and cherry-blossom gowns, more graphic cartoon colours in bomber jackets and shirts, monochrome polka dots – fit for a glamorous circus. At one end there is an utterly incredible cape, like a double-sized quilted duvet, embroidered with figures and scenes, from a fashion school graduate. Kate has an extraordinary calm. She is flying to New York tomorrow to shoot Victoria Beckham for our October cover, then back for about twenty-four hours, and then on to Tokyo. I simply couldn't do that. She has an understated beauty and always appears to listen to what I'm saying, as in 'Please don't shoot Victoria in too many heavy coats,' while I know that she's thinking she'll do what she feels she needs to do at the time.

I leave a little early to host the party for Paul. Sam greets me by saying the glasses have arrived and been delivered dirty and he's had to wash half of them again, and Paul is looking unusually sanguine as he tears up chicory leaves to dip in hummus. I had promised myself that, however they had organized things, I would not try to micro-manage, and I discovered that attitude worked very well. Undoubtedly it works better now Paul and I are long divorced than it would have when we were still married: things would have been a great deal more fraught.

It's a lovely evening. Heart-warming for me to have Sam and his dad there and lots of our joint friends.

22 June

Tensions are now really high about Brexit – everywhere. As I was getting my hair done this morning, I ask my stylist, Louis, who is covered completely with tattoos, whether he will be voting. 'Nah,' he says, as he wildly sprays huge amounts of Elnett into my hair for what is called a 'messy updo'. 'Nah. I've never voted.'

A colleague standing by says, 'See if you can make him,' and I answer that it depends which way he would vote. Louis doesn't say but I guess it would be Remain. In a small attempt at Project Fear I tell him that the Hershesons salon is likely to be a lot less full if we leave the EU, but that's probably not true as most of the clientele seem pretty home-grown, rather than the more international passers-by in other Mayfair places.

Last night at the party several people squared up against each other on the subject, and my neighbour Virginia said, in a wonderfully recherché way, that it reminded her of how a friend of her parents 'had to leave his own dining table one evening over Eden'. Whatever happens, it's clear that a huge number of people are going to be disappointed. How David Cameron must be regretting he ever suggested this thing. Such a Pandora's box.

There's a ghastly feeling of impotence, and as someone so used to being able to affect things, I find this difficult. But, more personally, the apprehension is amplified by knowing I'll see the screening of the documentary tomorrow.

23 June

The contrast between the mundanity of polling stations and the momentousness of what occurs inside them always amazes me. Ours is at our local school and I put my cross in the Remain box, standing beneath an array of paintings by Year Five. It is a day of near-tropical humidity, and the on and off downpours would certainly lead one to think that whoever controls the weather up there is in favour of Leave, since rain usually results in a smaller turnout and a smaller turnout in London would lead in that direction. I woke at five thirty, fretting about the screening and the Referendum, so I was one of the first voters, but even at 7.05 a.m. there was a steady supply of people in and out.

Last night Nicholas Coleridge had organized an enormous summer party at the V&A. The same person up there who controls the weather is certainly a friend of his since the heavy cloud cleared at about 7 p.m. so there was late-evening sun and the prettiest of skies over the Madejski courtyard, filled with women in their colourful summer dresses and men in pale suits.

I spoke to Stuart Rose, positioned as one of the business cheerleaders for Remain, and told him of a conversation I'd had earlier that evening with Hong Kong entrepreneur David Tang at a Michael Kors shop opening. He had said he was for leaving, in his beyond-pukka accent. 'But I'm not voting,' he boomed, appearing more interested in the arrival of Gwyneth Paltrow than the Referendum. Thank God, I thought. Stuart was wearing a navy-and-red In badge and talks so speedily out of the side of his mouth that it often sounds as if he's hoping you won't quite hear what he's saying. He was sure Remain would win – all the figures were pointing that way.

I asked if he had spoken to Philip Green and reminded him that he had told me a story, which always makes me laugh, of how in some competitive Alpha Male bantering between the two friends, Philip had been utterly disparaging of Stuart's financial prospects (and this a man who was then chairman and CEO of M&S), saying, 'And you don't even know how to *spell* jet.'

Stuart corrected me. 'No. It was "You don't know how to spell *yacht* and the only jet you'll ever know is easyJet." ' That kind of joshing now feels like it came from a different era. In fact, the evening had the aura of the famous Duchess of Richmond's ball on the eve of the Battle of Waterloo – a wonderful hedonistic glamour just before devastation. When I returned home, there was a huge lightning flash and the thunder began to crash.

I had been using the voting as a distraction from worrying about the documentary, but as I took my seat in a small room in Soho to view the two programmes along with a few others from Condé Nast and the production company, the nerves took hold. Watching yourself in something like this is the most curious activity. I kept wondering what I was going to say, rather as if it hadn't been me who had been sitting there, in far too many car shots, staring crossly out of a rainy window. Richard, behind me, was still and serious as we watched his vision of *Vogue* for two hours. His nine months of intense filming had been distilled dramatically, so that in the end there were relatively few characters and few stories. But that made it a much more emotional film than I had expected, and my fear that he was going to produce a silly film about a neophyte man in the wacky world of fashion was unfounded.

Through telling the story of a number of our shoots and the plans for the Centenary issue, he certainly succeeded in getting across how much we all cared about what we did and, also, showed the hard work that goes into each issue. Was it the film that I would love to have made about *Vogue*? No. I don't think it conveys how wide *Vogue* is nowadays, the influence it bears, the number of areas we are involved with, the fantastic journalism we include. Am I happy with how I'm portrayed? Not particularly – I seem very depressed through much of it, and prefer to think of myself as a funnier, lighter person than I seem on screen. I also dislike how I look most of the time, and can't understand why I'm wearing the same blue top throughout most of the first programme. People are going to say, 'There she is, editor of *Vogue* and all. You'd think she could change her shirt.' Are there moments I really hate? Yes. The whole saga of the swapping of the Rihanna cover with the previous issue because of American *Vogue* jumping ahead of us is given a ludicrous weight, and when Richard says to camera that I rang threatening to pull the whole film if he talked to Anna Wintour about it, I felt misrepresented. It was the one really devious thing he did. Of course, in the documentary when Anna is filmed she is hugely complimentary, which makes me look even sillier.

I don't know what the rest of the office will think.

I'm on a train now from Manchester back to Euston, and the day is whirling around my head. Fragments return from the film.

Everything is made larger than whatever it represented in real time, because so much has been compressed into two hours.

Nick Cullinan and I arrived in Manchester this afternoon for the opening of the show at Manchester Art Gallery. The emotion of watching the documentary has seeped into me like a heavy liquid and I feel thoroughly leaden, even though it was lovely to see the exhibition rise again in a new space in a new configuration. As I walked around the same pictures and volumes of *Vogue* displayed quite differently, it was like visiting my child somewhere and noticing how they behave differently with people who are not their family. Perhaps this tiredness is the melancholy I was expecting, now that I have finally seen the film, which I had been so nervous about, now that the exhibition is on its last journey. It's a beautiful evening flashing past the windows and I rather regret my decision to head back to London rather than stay in Manchester, especially as I've just learned the Referendum result is being announced

formally from there at 7 a.m. It would have been a historic place to be. Perhaps the tiredness is also my very real anxiety that this vote is not going to go the way I want.

When I get back to the house at 11 p.m., Sam and his friend Henry are ensconced in front of the TV for the night with crisps and Maltesers, laptops and drinks. They tell me that it looked like Remain was winning. 'Just edged it' was what everyone was saying. Farage is on the verge of conceding and I stand for a moment and watch. I have a huge sense of relief – happiness that the documentary isn't too awful, the show is now alive again and maybe the ghastly Brexit isn't going to happen. This vote has been in the background to the whole year, and to have a day when all this has come together is strange and powerful. I make myself a huge vodka and tonic, dump my bags and settle down to watch the commentary with the boys, Coco curled up on the sofa, images from the documentary and the exhibition dropping in and out of my mind as the results start trickling in.

Acknowledgements

My thanks go, first, to Nicholas Coleridge, managing director of Condé Nast Britain and president of Condé Nast International, who agreed to my writing this diary of a year in my job at *Vogue*, without any questions or conditions. Juliet Annan of Fig Tree was wonderfully enthusiastic from the word go, and the team at Penguin have been hugely supportive, especially Poppy North. Writing anything is always a leap in the dark and my agent, Eugenie Furniss, has been there right from the very beginning, before a word was put on the page, and has been an invaluable sounding board and encouraging presence throughout. And, last, many thanks must go to my team on the magazine for being so good at their jobs and such excellent subject matter.

Index

Cover and Picture Credits

He just wanted a decent book to read ...

Not too much to ask, is it? It was in 1935 when Allen Lane, Managing Director of Bodley Head Publishers, stood on a platform at Exeter railway station looking for something good to read on his journey back to London. His choice was limited to popular magazines and poor-quality paperbacks – the same choice faced every day by the vast majority of readers, few of whom could afford hardbacks. Lane's disappointment and subsequent anger at the range of books generally available led him to found a company – and change the world.

'We believed in the existence in this country of a vast reading public for intelligent books at a low price, and staked everything on it'
Sir Allen Lane, 1902–1970, founder of Penguin Books

The quality paperback had arrived – and not just in bookshops. Lane was adamant that his Penguins should appear in chain stores and tobacconists, and should cost no more than a packet of cigarettes.

Reading habits (and cigarette prices) have changed since 1935, but Penguin still believes in publishing the best books for everybody to enjoy. We still believe that good design costs no more than bad design, and we still believe that quality books published passionately and responsibly make the world a better place.

So wherever you see the little bird – whether it's on a piece of prize-winning literary fiction or a celebrity autobiography, political tour de force or historical masterpiece, a serial-killer thriller, reference book, world classic or a piece of pure escapism – you can bet that it represents the very best that the genre has to offer.

Whatever you like to read – trust Penguin.